828.8

LIKE SUN GONE DOWN

Like Sun Gone Down

Selections from the writings of John Canon O'Hanlon

PÁDRAIG Ó MACHÁIN

and

TONY DELANEY

Galmoy Press

Published by Galmoy Press, Ráth Oisín, Crosspatrick, Co. Kilkenny (056–8831347, galmoypress@eircom.net).

Dust jacket design based on sketch of Slieve Bloom Mountains, by John O'Hanlon 'in October 1890, from Pass House, a place in the Queen's County, endeared to him by early residence and associations' (*Lives of the Irish saints* VIII, 51).

Printed in the Republic of Ireland

Old scenes, old customs, olden time and tale
Like sun gone down, each instant fading pale,
Like music's notes suspended, still the strain
Wakes in the ear or mind, so sweet again,
We prize yet more the parting tones and light,
When harp-strings rest, and gloom leads on to night:
So ere the past be unregenerate, gone,
Seize on some traits that waft its features on,
And let the modern minstrel still rehearse,
Whate'er may grace, whate'er adorn his verse,

From John O'Hanlon, 'Legend of Dunamase' (*Poetical works of Lageniensis*, 206).

CONTENTS

ILLUSTRATIONS

PREFACE

THIS PUBLICATION OFFERS a selection of the writings of John Canon O'Hanlon (1821–1905), and seeks to mark, in a small way, the centenary of the death of one of the remarkable clerical historians and scholars of nineteenth-century Ireland. His career comprised his curacy in three parishes in Missouri, and one in Dublin, that of Saints Michael and John, after which he was promoted to Parish Priest of Sandymount, and based at Saint Mary's Church, Star of the Sea. During that career, he produced – under his own name and under his *nom de plume* Lageniensis ('Leinsterman') – numerous scholarly articles and twenty-five books, in addition to ten volumes of his monumental *Lives of the Irish saints*. Three further works were published after his death.

The title of this book, taken from a line in one of his poems, reflects John O'Hanlon's lifelong interest in preserving for future generations the memories of times past, be they the physical remains preserved in his sketches, the literary, hagiographical and historical traditions recorded in his major works, or the folk traditions remembered from his youth or gleaned from his research. The selections are therefore intended to give an insight into his range of interests, as well as being representative of his literary style. Footnotes occurring in that section of the book are to be taken as O'Hanlon's; all other annotation is our responsibility.

In Appendix 1 we attempt to bring together a chronology of John O'Hanlon's scholarly output and of his biographical details. Much work has been done heretofore on materials for O'Hanlon's biography, particularly by Seán O'Dooley and his daughter Johanna, and by Pádraig Mac Ionnraic; and this has been consolidated by Teddy Fennelly in his recent work. The papers left by Pádraig in his archive (referred to below as the Mac Ionnraic Archive) contain a wealth of genealogical information on O'Hanlon's forbears, and incorporate research on the descendants in America of O'Hanlon's brothers and sisters, much of it compiled by Terence O'Hanlon of Texas.

For permission to reproduce manuscript material in their possession we are grateful to the following: Most Rev. Diarmuid Martin D.D., Archbishop of Dublin; Agnes Nelligan, Librarian, NUI Maynooth; Séamus Helferty, Archives Department, UCD.

Táimíd fé chomaoin mhór ag Cáit Bean Mhic Ionnraic, Baile Átha Cliath, a chaomhnaigh iarsmaí de chuid an Chanónaigh ina cartlann, a chuir an t-ábhar sin ar fáil dúinn, agus a d'fháiltigh romhainn le croí mór. Is lena caoinchead a foilsítear na somplaí ar lgh 21, 30, 57, 93, 117, 127, 196, agus 199.

We are most grateful to Brian Siggins, an historian with expert knowledge of Irishtown, of Ringsend, and of John Canon O'Hanlon, who placed this knowledge at our disposal. The illustrations on pp. 144 and 185 are reproduced with his kind permission.

For much help and forbearance during our researches we are grateful to Penny Woods, Russell Library, Maynooth; David Sheehy, Dublin Diocesan Archives; Rev. Dr Fearghus Ó Fearghail, Mater Dei Institute of Education; Paddy Hawe, National Library of Ireland; and Siobhán Fitzpatrick, Librarian, Royal Irish Academy.

To others who have helped us in various ways, we are very grateful: Pádraig de Brún, Listowel; Philip Greene, Pass; Mary Lalor, The Heath; Gavin McCullagh, Dublin; Aoibheann Nic Dhonnchadha, Thurles; Anne Marie O'Brien, Dublin; Proinsias Ó Drisceoil, Kilkenny; Margaret and Seán Scully, Ballymaddock; Joan, Mary Ann and Harry Vaughan, Crosspatrick.

We wish, finally, to record our special gratitude to Paddy Mulhall of Abbeyleix. He was born in Pass House, and he gave us a guided tour of Ballyroan, Cullenagh and Stradbally. His father, James Mulhall, provided O'Hanlon with material for volume I of the *History of the Queen's County* (see Appendix 2 § 12b).

INTRODUCTION

IN THE ILLUMINATED address that they presented to John Canon O'Hanlon on the occasion of his Golden Jubilee, 29 May 1897, his parishioners and fellow priests laid emphasis on three aspects of his career in which he had distinguished himself. The first was his work as a priest: his care for the welfare of his parishioners, and his renovations to the two churches in his parish, St Mary's, Star of the Sea, in Irishtown, and St Patrick's in Ringsend. The second was his patriotism, as an advocate of 'the national interests of our long suffering country ... in endeavouring to realise the highest aspirations of our race'. The third was his work as an author, and in particular as a hagiologist or hagiographer, a chronicler of saints' lives.[1] While it is John O'Hanlon the writer who is in evidence in the following selections, it will be apparent that the three aspects of his life that were emphasised by his admirers in 1897 are interconnected, and form part of a continuity of learning and intellectual activity discernible throughout his life.

The experience of his emigration to the United States of America, at the age of 21, informs much of the work of John O'Hanlon. Not only was his scheme for the *Lives of the Irish saints* conceived during his time there, as his flair for writing began to emerge, but it was in Missouri that he became aware of the plight of Irish emigrants, and in particular that of the refugees from the Great Famine, during his ministry in St Louis. His own emigration, in the summer of 1842, though far more benign, had also the element of trauma attached to it, being occasioned, it would appear, by the death of his father about that time.[2] It also occurred at a time of great economic emigration from the Queen's County, as reported in the newspapers of the time:

[1] See Appendix 4.
[2] See Appendix 1, under the year 1842.

1

The rage for emigration during the present season far exceeds that of any former year, which argues how great and general must have been the depression under which this kingdom has suffered during the last few years. Agencies are established through all the inland towns, through whose means hundreds are leaving the rural districts. Men who have any substance are unwilling longer to risk it in a country where they expect no return; but are converting their goods into money, and are seeking in a distant land means of profitably investing it, and enriching themselves. Others, whose dependence for a livelihood consists in exertion of mind or body, are leaving a country where they are starving for want of employment, to seek for a means of subsistence, thus withdrawing from our shores what is no less valuable than capital, the sinews and energies of our countrymen.[3]

John O'Hanlon's twin vocations, to priesthood and to writing, were both nurtured in the trying circumstances in which he found himself in the American frontier. His own account of his years in Missouri shows that his literary work received early recognition in his appointment as editor of the short-lived Catholic newspaper, *The St. Louis News-Letter*, in 1847. The difficult circumstances under which the work on his lifelong project of the saints' lives was begun are hinted at by him in his introduction to his life of St Malachy:

Whilst the writer resided in the city of St. Louis, in the United States of America, that very imperfect biography [of Malachy] had been commenced, in the month of May, 1851, and completed during the summer of the same year. The circumstances, under which it had been composed, were not favourable for the successful completion of a work,

---

[3] *Leinster Express* 21 May 1842. In the edition of 30 April 1842, the *Express* stated: 'We witness the "bone and sinew" of the land – a bold and energetic race of men – leaving our shores in despair and disgust, and truly it is a melancholy – a degrading reflection.'

2

demanding a considerable amount of time and research, to render it accurate and elaborate. A fearful epidemic spread pestilence and death throughout the city of St. Louis, during that season; and, the consequent demands, on the time of an insufficient number of missionary clergymen, to minister to the wants of a large Catholic population, left few intervals of leisure, for extrinsic occupations.[4]

Against a background of personal experience as an emigrant and as a young priest, the coincidental developments of pastoral care and literary activity combined in a practical way in O'Hanlon's production, in 1851, of a handbook for the Irish emigrant to America. Even at a distance of over one hundred and fifty years, there is a freshness and immediacy in his account of the modalities and the pitfalls of travel to America from Ireland in the mid-nineteenth century that must have been all the more striking to contemporary readers. His concern for the Irish emigrant was to outlast the ten years he spent in Missouri. Forty years later, he produced a revised and updated edition of *The Irish emigrant's guide* in 1890; and this was followed in 1903 by his *Irish-American history of the United States*. The aim of the latter book was two-fold, historical and educational: to record the achievements of Irish-Americans from early colonial times to the time of writing; and to furnish for an Irish readership a general history of the United States.[5] Whatever its merits today, this book displays all the characteristics that distinguish O'Hanlon's scholarly work, in that it replicates in style and methodology the author's comprehensive mastery of an array of source material, and his ability to convey the essence of those sources while avoiding partisanship of any kind. In his account of the American Civil War, for example, he treats equally of the exploits of Clebourne and Meagher – Corkman and Waterfordman, Confederate and Federal respectively – and avoids exaggerating their part in the complex events of the time.

[4] *The life of Saint Malachy O'Morgair*, vi.
[5] *Irish-American history*, vi.

3

His American experience also seems to have cultivated in John O'Hanlon a taste and a remarkable energy for travel, and the spirit of enquiry that goes with it. In subsequent years, in the course of his hagiographical research, he would make many trips to continental Europe, undaunted by difficulties of travel or accommodation. At the age of seventy, on his return to America in the autumn and winter of 1891, he would cover thousands of miles as he travelled to numerous locations throughout the United States and Canada in less than three months.[6] To someone, who as a young priest had ridden on horseback to distant missionary outposts along the banks of the Missouri river, such travel may well have seemed relaxing and a luxury.

It is small wonder, then, that in recording some of his early journeys, O'Hanlon can be viewed not just as a scholar, but as a travel writer in his own right. His *Life and scenery in Missouri*, published in book format in 1890, is undoubtedly the best example of his talent in this regard, but the combination of historical writing and travel writing was one that had been long established in his work. It emerges particularly in the closing chapters of his *Life of St. Dympna* in 1863. His anxiety to give the reader practical information on how to travel to the destinations mentioned in this book is a feature of his narrative; so too is his delight in description and observation, and his scientific curiosity in anything connected with the care of the poor and the infirm. In his record of his trip to Gheel, for example, he pays particular attention to the hospital for the insane, erected in that city a year earlier, a record that we have reproduced below.

Writing and scholarship

John O'Hanlon was a bibliophile, and a minor littérateur of nineteenth-century Dublin.[7] His friends and correspondents

----

[6] Appendix 2 § 8.

[7] On 24 September 1902, O'Hanlon sent his friend Cardinal Moran 'a collection of Autograph Letters of celebrated Irish writers torn out of the books in which I had them bound, as material for your Museum' (Archives of the Catholic Archdiocese of Sydney: Cardinal Moran Archive, Box U 2419).

Introduction

included scholars such as Eugene O'Curry and R. R. Madden, and poets and writers such as Denis Florence MacCarthy,[8] John F. O'Donnell,[9] and John McCall and his son P. J.[10] In an age when expression in verse was not unusual, and where poetry in English was seen as important to the national cause,[11] O'Hanlon himself had more than a passing interest in making poems, both formal and occasional, including versified versions of legends that he had elsewhere expressed in prose.

He was also prominent in the Irish language movement. He joined the Ossianic Society shortly after his return from the United States, and his *The life of Saint Malachy O'Morgair* was published in 1859 by the Society's founder and secretary, John O'Daly, a parishioner of O'Hanlon's when he was a curate in Saints Michael and John.[12] While still a curate, he became a council member of the Society for the Preservation of the Irish Language, and remained on the council until his death in 1905, by which time he was also one of the vice-presidents.[13] Following the foundation

[8]'I had purposed on Monday evening next to attend the [Royal Irish] Academy for the purpose of electing him as a member of the Council. Alas! that instead of doing him this honour, I can only hope to manifest my deep regret and respect by attending his funeral on Tuesday' (NLI Denis Florence MacCarthy Papers, Accession 1550, Box 1, Folder 1: O'Hanlon to John MacCarthy, 8 April 1882). See Appendix 1, under the year 1882.

[9]'... my dear and delightful former friend John Francis O'Donnell' (UCD Department of Archives LA 15/1288).

[10]Shannon-Mangan, *James Clarence Mangan*, 72, 74. See O'Hanlon's letters of condolence to P. J. McCall (20 January, 18 February 1902) in NLI MS 13875.

[11]Cf. John Keegan Casey's 'Lecture on the influence of national poetry' in Roe, *Reliques of John K. Casey*, 221–8.

[12]O'Hanlon administered the Last Rights to O'Daly, 20 April 1878 (Colm, 'John O Daly'). O'Hanlon had the good fortune to be able to call on the scholarly and literary talents of his parishioners in the two Dublin parishes in which he served. In Irishtown, for instance, two of his parishioners were John Gerald McSweeny (editor of the *Weekly Freeman*, and signatory to the 1897 address), and the geologist Joseph P. O'Reilly (DDA Walsh Papers 1890, Secular Clergy: O'Hanlon to Walsh, 18 November 1890).

[13]See Appendix 1, under the year 1877. The council adjourned its meeting of 16 May 1905 as a mark of respect to O'Hanlon (*Society for the Preservation of the Irish Language report for 1905*, 69–70).

5

of the Star of the Sea branch of Conradh na Gaeilge, 29 November 1900, O'Hanlon, in his role as president of the branch, was recalled as maintaining a paternal presence at the Irish classes there:

> Scarcely a class-night passed at the Reult-na-Mara Branch, without a visit from the Canon, who went from desk to desk among the learners speaking words of encouragement.[14]

He was also very much part of the nineteenth-century culture of the antiquary-folklorist.[15] Mixing scholarly discipline with respect for the tradition-bearer, he connected both with the father of Irish folklore studies, Charles Vallancey (whom he quotes liberally in his writing), and with the literary tradition of writers such as Carleton and O'Hanlon's fellow Queen's County man, John Keegan, in whom he had a lifelong interest.

As the excerpt on the *seanchaí* given below (pp. 42–51) indicates, just as his classical education was to aid him in his career and in his scholarly writings, the less formal education and entertainment that was experienced by O'Hanlon in his youth in Stradbally was to remain as an influence on him for the rest of his life. To this, at least in part, is due the respect he had for the value of native tradition, and for what had come, by then, to be known as folklore. In his preface to *Irish folk lore* of 1870, O'Hanlon sets out his position regarding this subject, and his approach to it from a predominantly literary perspective:

> Few things are so evanescent in their nature as folk lore remembrances and theories; but their generic peculiarities have been fairly preserved in our ancient and modern literature. Of this source for information the writer has

---

[14] *United Irishman* 20 May 1905. See Appendix 1, under the year 1900. For more on his engagement with the Irish language, see Breatnach agus Ní Mhurchú, *Beathaisnéis*, 106–7.

[15] For the development of folklore studies in Ireland during this period see Ó Giolláin, *Locating Irish folklore*.

availed himself. Thousands of interesting legends have been totally forgotten, however, because unrecorded; and yet many of these were essentially important for a perfect solution to historic problems, while they characteristically illustrate a people's moral and intellectual organization or culture, and speculative opinions.

Continuing his preoccupation with the 'sun gone down' theme, he adds:

If unnoticed in some form, such as that now presented, it is probable those legends and traditions must have been consigned altogether to oblivion.

O'Hanlon was far from unique in his combination of scholarly and priestly vocations. He is instantly recognisable as a type of nineteenth-century clerical historian cum antiquarian represented by writers such as James O'Laverty, Anthony Cogan, Patrick Moran, John Francis Shearman, and, extending into the twentieth century, William Carrigan and Patrick Power. One of his fellow curates during his time in Saints Michael and John (1859–80) was the equally illustrious and prolific writer and historian, Fr Charles Patrick Meehan, and it was reported that 'many stories are told illustrative of their idiosyncrasies'.[16]

The inspiration for many of these writers was the work of John Lanigan,[17] and it is no coincidence that O'Hanlon's first involvement in monumental commemoration was his collaboration with

[16] 'Father Meehan met a woman who sought alms. He counted his treasury; it amounted to a shilling, and he gave her sixpence. He was rather sceptical about her *bona fides*, and after some consideration followed her round the corner to see if his doubts were justified. She went into a public house, and before Father Meehan could intervene, had demolished a glass of whiskey. As he came out he was caught by Father O'Hanlon; and the two regained the presbytery in silence, when the latter simply shook his comrade by the hand, more is sorrow than in anger' (*Irish Times* 16 May 1905).

[17] On Lanigan's influence on the study of Irish antiquity in the nineteenth century see Collins, *Catholic churchmen*, 64–7.

Petrie and O'Curry in the creation of a Celtic Cross for Lanigan's grave in Finglas.[18] In the writings of all these clerical scholars, there is a sense of purpose, as though the educational opportunities afforded them by their family backgrounds, and by Emancipation, placed upon them not just a duty of priestly ministry, but a duty also of scholarly publication of the history of their dioceses, counties and country, which had been concealed and proscribed *de facto* in the eighteenth century. This sense of purpose is most evident in O'Hanlon's core writings, where he pursues his project of chronicling the lives of the Irish saints, organised by feast-day, from 1 January to 31 December.

His *Life of St Malachy*, he tells us, was the first of the series commenced by him. He also had a life of St Patrick published in serial format in the *Boston Pilot* in 1853, the year he left America, and this, one supposes, formed the basis not just for the account that subsequently appeared in the *Lives of the Irish saints*, but also for the 'Life of Saint Patrick Apostle of Ireland by the Rev. John O'Hanlon' which was announced in 1859 as 'preparing for publication' in book format, but which never appeared.[19]

To a large extent, this method of repetition and re-cycling was to be his working template throughout his career. Saints' lives would appear initially in articles or monographs, and would again be published as part of the great work. The template held true also for other areas of his writings. His series on the 'Old churches of Leix', for example, published in the *Irish Builder* in the 1880s, had the dual function of preparing material to be included as background in the *Lives of the Irish saints*, and verbatim in his *History of the Queen's County*. Nor did he cavil at simultaneous publication in cases where, one deduces, he held that some of the matter published in book format could benefit from an independent existence as an article. For this purpose, the pages of the *Irish Ecclesiastical Record* were always at his disposal, it would appear, and a case in point was the parallel publication in that journal of

---

[18] See Appendix 1, under the year 1861.
[19] *The Life of Saint Malachy O'Morgair*, Prospectus [following p. 222], p. iii.

8

the historical portion of his introduction to Mason's *Essay on the antiquity and constitution of parliaments in Ireland* in February of 1891, at the very time that it was being published in his new edition of that book.

O'Hanlon's facility for the objective and unobtrusive presentation of historical and scholarly evidence has been recognised.[20] The same virtue is evident in his retrospective assessment of his own work, in a 'Prospectus' appended to some of the last published numbers of Volume X of *Lives of the Irish saints*:

> For many years past his [*sc.* O'Hanlon's] extensive collections have employed intervals of time that remained to the compiler after a discharge of more urgent occupations and duties. Early hours in the morning, and late hours at night have often been devoted to this long-continued and absorbing labour. The most critical supervision and anxious desire to attain accuracy have been exercised, both in the composition and correction of those volumes. The writer can safely assert that, as a matter of fact, few important or controvertible statements have been advanced throughout the work for which exact historical references are not presented to the reader. For individual deductions or opinions, wherever they occur, the author is responsible. He has examined and adopted the conclusions of many learned authorities consulted and cited in the pages of those volumes, whenever he conceived such accounts conformable to truth, or even in accordance with probability; nor has he ever ventured to dissent, except in cases where recent investigations or superior reasons afforded safe motives for a contrary judgement.[21]

In addition to his objectivity, the 'many learned authorities consulted and cited' are also a feature of his work that remains

---

[20]McCartney, 'Canon O'Hanlon: historian of the Queen's County', 594.

[21]*Lives of the Irish saints* X, numbers 100 and 101 (Dublin City Library and Archive).

9

relevant today. O'Hanlon can never be accused of fancy or fabrication in his writing. Every proposition, deduction and conclusion is painstakingly annotated and referenced, so that while one may at times demur at a style that verges on prolix – but that was, after all, very much of its time – one can still admire his scholarly methodology and his all-pervasive concern to be both precise and exhaustive. That desire for exhaustive annotation led O'Hanlon to the examination of sources that had been neglected or little used up to then, a case in point being the use made by him of the records of the Ordnance Survey.

Ordnance Survey records: O'Hanlon the artist

O'Hanlon's earliest publications on his return to Ireland were the two letters, written by him in 1856, and published in the *Journal of the Kilkenny and South-East of Ireland Archaeological Society*, on the value of the records of the Ordnance Survey in the Phoenix Park as a source for the study of the history of Co. Kilkenny and Queen's County respectively.[22] The first of these was in response to a request made to him by the Rev. James Graves, and it prompted O'Hanlon to produce a series of twenty similar communications, over the next ten years, covering the remaining counties of Ireland, in compliance with Graves's wish that he should complete his calendar of this archive. His early attachment to the South Dublin Union, 1853–7, with his addresses in James's Street and Parkgate Street, placed him in some proximity to the archive, prior to the transfer of some of the materials to the Royal Irish Academy. His oft-acknowledged friendship with and indebtedness to those giants of the Survey, and of Irish scholarship in the nineteenth century, John O'Donovan and Eugene O'Curry, were further elements in his awareness of this fruitful avenue of research.[23] O'Hanlon expresses the importance

---

[22] *Journal of the Kilkenny and South-East of Ireland Archaeological Society* New Series, 1 (1856–7) 153–4, 192–4.

[23] 'Owing to the kindness of his learned and lamented friend, the late John O'Donovan, LL.D., the writer was introduced to the chiefs of this department.... Many a solitary and studious hour has he passed in the Ordnance

of this source in his Prospectus for his *Lives of the Irish saints* that accompanied his first book on the topic of hagiography, his *Life of Saint Laurence O'Toole*:

> The full and free access which the writer has obtained to the MSS. and ancient maps, belonging to the Irish Ordnance Survey Office, Phoenix Park, has enabled him, in many instances, to identify the modern names and exact positions of places often mentioned in connection with the Lives of our national Saints.[24]

O'Hanlon's repeated advocacy of the publication of the records of the Ordnance Survey in the form of parish memoirs and county histories[25] amounted to more than just his usual predilection for the 'grand scheme' of his own devising. He saw in these records one of the foundations for the study of the history of local places, and he saw also their value as aids to preserving, for all time, information on structural antiquities then extant but which in future might well be destroyed. This perception confirmed him in his conviction of the importance of the role of the artist in antiquarian and historical studies.

> There are various topographical features of our Irish counties, neither described by the tourist, nor sketched by the artist; and yet they are illustrative of ancient manners, customs, and economy. An hundred years hence they will have disappeared from the face of the country, and not a single memorial of them will remain. A mere trifle, in the shape of a Government grant, would enable the Ordnance Department in Ireland to

---

Survey Library...' (*Lives of the Irish saints* I, lxvii n. 33). O'Donovan was the 'gentle *ollamh*' of O'Hanlon's verse in 'The Land of Leix' (*Poetical works of Lageniensis*, 92). For O'Hanlon's grief at the death of O'Curry, see Appendix 2 § 3.

[24] *The life of Saint Laurence O'Toole*, Prospectus [following p. 186], p. [iii].

[25] E.g. *Journal of the Kilkenny and South-East of Ireland Archaeological Society* New Series, 1 (1856–7) 297, 322, 324; 4 (1862–3) 238–40.

employ artists to preserve their outlines, for the enlightenment of succeeding generations. Would it be too much to
demand, in return, for the millions sent by Ireland, to the
Imperial Exchequer?[26]

Viewed in this context, the multitude of mostly contemporary
sketches included by O'Hanlon in *Lives of the Irish saints* has
more purpose than that of merely offering relief to the reader from
the highly detailed prose. They also serve to highlight a neglected
aspect of John O'Hanlon, that of the competent amateur artist.

O'Hanlon was scarcely returned from the United States in 1853
when he was engaged in making a sketch of Coolbanagher, in his
native Queen's County. This work of travelling throughout Ireland
and sketching antiquities was to continue for the next half-century,
with the dual purpose of illustrating his writings and of preserving
in art a fragile part of his country's heritage. Of the 596 drawings engraved in the ten volumes of *Lives of the Irish saints*, John
O'Hanlon is responsible for 128: just over one fifth. His drawings
range in date from December 1853[27] to June 1901,[28] three years
before his death. An original sketch by O'Hanlon is published for
the first time below, p. 173, and in Appendix 5 we catalogue the
engravings in *Lives of the Irish saints*.

His artistic talents translated themselves to an interest in church
architecture, an interest that is apparent early in his writings,
when, in *The life of Saint Laurence O'Toole*, he describes the
newly-built church of St Laurence, in Seville Place, and donates
the proceeds of that publication 'for the benefit of the new church
of St. Laurence O'Toole'.[29] This interest was put to practical
use in his pastoral work, where, as referred to in the illuminated
address of 1897, his talents were employed in the structural
alterations he instigated in the two churches that came under his
care after he became Parish Priest of Sandymount in 1880. His

[26]Ibid., New Series 2 (1858–9) 48.
[27]*Lives of the Irish saints* VIII, 329–30.
[28]Ibid. X, 206.
[29]*The life of Saint Laurence O'Toole*, vi.

improvements to St Mary's, Star of the Sea, are documented in his *History and description of St. Mary's Church, Star of the Sea, Irishtown*, while improvements to both Star of the Sea and St Patrick's, Ringsend, are referred to by him in a letter to the Archbishop of Dublin, William J. Walsh, in 1897:

> I set about the painting, decoration &c. of St. Patrick's Church Ringsend; flagging the Sanctuary with Portland stone and erecting a handsome marble altar with ascending steps of Sicilian marble, and a Porch in Portland stone is now being prepared for the front – all of this cost about £350. Iron railings are now being erected round the Star of the Sea Church at a cost of nearly an additional £100. This was very necessary to guard against damages to the church windows, and as containing flowering shrubs and flowers within, the railings must be ornamented.[30]

Politics

John O'Hanlon's childhood was a time of social and political unrest in the Queen's County. Emancipation apart, the agitation against tithes and other injustices engaged the efforts, on the side of 'moral force', of people such as Pat Lalor of Tinnakill, Peter Gale of Arless, and John Dunn of Ballinakill; while on the side of 'physical force' were a range of secret organisations such as the Rockites and the Whitefeet. O'Hanlon recorded the impression left on him by the Ballykilcavan evictions of 1828, and it is possible that the seeds of his advocacy of constitutional politics and of Home Rule may have been sown by his attendance in his fifteenth year at O'Connell's meeting on the Great Heath in January 1836.[31] It is likely that those early influences – in combination with his pastoral desire to better the lot of the

---

[30] DDA Walsh Papers 1897, Secular Clergy: O'Hanlon to Walsh, 17 May 1897.
[31] See notes to 'The Land of Leix', p. 278 below; and Appendix 1, under the year 1836. O'Hanlon's political outlook is analysed in McCartney, 'Canon O'Hanlon: historian of the Queen's County'.

despairing poor that he had encountered firstly in St Louis, then in the poorhouse in James's Street,[32] and subsequently throughout his career as a priest in central Dublin and in Sandymount – generated in him the vision that emerges in his writings in later life. By no means a radical priest, and always submissive to the authority of his archbishop,[33] he nevertheless had a political conscience, which surfaces in his attitude to the land question in 1881 (see pp. 126–30), and in two publications by him in 1891–2 in the context of the Home Rule debate of that time.

There seems no doubt that these works were produced as a deliberate contribution to that debate. Both were new editions by O'Hanlon of works by earlier authors: William Molyneux and Henry Joseph Monck Mason. In the edition of Molyneux, whose work on its first issue in 1698 had been publicly burned, O'Hanlon, writing in September 1891, says that he attempted 'to make it suitable for popular reading, at a period also when a study of Ireland's former struggles for parliamentary independence ought naturally aid in shaping and directing the future life of a nation, that demands the permanent establishment of Home Rule, and the inalienable rights of constitutional self-government'.[34] In his introduction to Mason's work – a book he dedicated to Gladstone – in March of the same year, he allowed himself a lengthy polemic on the subject, an extract from which we have reproduced below.

John O'Hanlon's interest in the Home Rule question extended beyond the polemical. He attended some of the Home Rule debates in the House of Commons in June 1893,[35] and, in September, in his dedication of his collected poems to the Countess of Aberdeen,

---

[32] Appendix 2 § 2.
[33] Appendix 2 § 4.
[34] *The case of Ireland's being bound by Acts of Parliament*, viii.
[35] 'I have to state that I am going to the House of Commons this evening, where I hope to meet my friend Mr. Alfred Webb, or some of the Irish members I happen to meet, to get me an order for admission to hear something about Home Rule and its prospects' (UCD Dept of Archives LA15/1297: O'Hanlon to D. J. O'Donoghue, 13 June 1893). Webb was MP for West Waterford, 1890–95.

Introduction

he allowed himself to compare the state of Canada, which he had visited less than two years before, with that of Ireland:

> The scope and powers for useful legislation contained in the Irish Home Rule Bill – which lately passed its third reading in the House of Commons – are, altogether, similar to those provisions, which confer on the Provinces of the Dominion their respective Charters of Freedom. The malign and sinister obstruction to which Irish Home Rule has been subjected through bigotry, unnatural party combination, class prejudice and selfishness, must finally give place to the establishment of a Constitution, which shall secure equal rights and liberties for all creeds and parties in Ireland, while promoting and consolidating still more the strength and resources of the British Empire.[36]

The bitterness with which he expresses himself in 1897 on 'this darkest hour of our degradation and disgrace',[37] following the Parnellite split, and the resignation of Gladstone, is heartfelt, but, having abandoned all hope of Home Rule, he still clung to his vision of O'Connell as the ideal Irish politician of the nineteenth century. But for his dedication and determination as its secretary, the various delays and setbacks encountered during the twenty years of the existence of the O'Connell Monument Committee might have proved fatal to that project. Even after the monument had been erected in Sackville Street, Dublin, O'Hanlon pursued for many years the Committee's plan, by then long abandoned, to produce a definitive and comprehensive biography of the Liberator, until eventually he too abandoned the work in favour of attempting to organise his long-planned project of the *History of the Queen's County*, in the years left to him before his death.[38]

[36] *The poetical works of Lageniensis*, viii.
[37] Notes to Appendix 2 § 9.
[38] O'Hanlon stated in 1902 that the *History* had 'engaged my time and researches for more than thirty past years of my life' (letter to *Leinster Express* 26 April 1902).

Introduction

It is tempting to view his efforts in the cause of the memory of Daniel O'Connell as another aspect of his hagiographical endeavours. To take this view, however, would be to deny O'Hanlon his right to be viewed as a conscientious historian. His 'Life of William Molyneux' is a fine piece of biographical writing,[39] and, from the evidence of proofs that survive of the abandoned work,[40] there is no reason to believe that his biography of Daniel O'Connell would have been anything other than that also.

The determination and single-mindedness that he brought to his work, and the wide reading and scholarship evident in his writing, do not detract from the reverence and affection in which he held the subjects he chronicled in the *Lives of the Irish saints*. Apart from his recognition of hagiography as a branch of history, O'Hanlon had a clear devotion to the subjects about whom he wrote. In that light, it has to be admitted that in his final assessment of the Liberator, there is a hint of O'Hanlon's regard for the otherness of the saints, statements of which we have reproduced in his writings below (pp. 172–5):

It would be difficult to estimate the qualifications of mind and body, this extraordinary moral force leader possessed. Comprehensive and clear in all its conceptions, gifted with rare prudence and caution, forecasting his own varied and far-reaching action by most rational safe and practical means to attain its ends through all the details of progress – keeping correct maxims and essentially self-evident moral principles steadily in view, whilst using temporary expedients and policy as occasions best served – his mind soared far above the selfish considerations and meaner ambition of many gifted men. An intense love of country and adhesion to the best interests of religion were the beacons that guided his honest and persistent career. Intrepid and daring when circumstances

[39] *The case of Ireland's being bound by Acts of Parliament*, xi–xlv.
[40] Appendix 3 § 2.

16

required, he knew the value and efficiency of selfrestraint and patient perseverance, under difficult and responsible trials. With a naturally warm, impulsive generous heart and disposition his judgement was ever sound and keenly penetrating. The powers of his amazing intellect were versatile, vigorous and sustained. His deep and exquisitely modulated tones of voice fell with magical effect on myriads of his humble countrymen; and even his startling and unpremeditated bursts of impassioned eloquence elicited the admiration of those most hostile to his measures and policy.[41]

****

The methodical and determined manner in which O'Hanlon pursued his literary and scholarly projects resulted in an extraordinary productivity in published work. With this came an equally extraordinary administrative burden. This was particularly the case with *Lives of the Irish saints*, which was issued in over one hundred separate parts, from 1873 onwards, as well as being bound in ten volumes. Despite the latter-day assertion that the subscriptions were administered by the publishers,[42] the hundreds of letters from subscribers bound in Russell Library MSS OH 15–37 show that much of the work was done by O'Hanlon himself, and that the administrative load must have been huge. By 1897 eight volumes of the work had been published, and the first two parts of Volume 9 were ready for issue in November of that year: 'but as over £400 had been owing to me,' wrote O'Hanlon, 'which I was obliged to collect through the Dublin Mercantile Association agency, what I could of that amount, and to get rid of defaulting subscribers, awaiting their report, I have deferred sending parts to *bona fide* subscribers.'[43] By 1899, with the desire to produce the

[41] Russell Library, Maynooth, MS OH 39/6, unnumbered page; cf. O'Hanlon, *Catechism of Irish history*, 494.
[42] Carey, 'O'Hanlon of "the Irish Saints" ', 159.
[43] DDA Walsh Papers 1897, Secular Clergy: O'Hanlon to Archbishop William J. Walsh, 1 November 1897.

History of the Queen's County still foremost in his mind, he had come to realize that the great project of the saints' lives would never be completed.[44] This was also to be the fate of the *History of the Queen's County*, though a death-bed plea from him in 1905 ensured that completion of sorts was brought to that publication in 1914.[45]

One hundred years after his death, hagiographical studies have moved on, as they must, and one's impression is that O'Hanlon is seldom cited as a source in modern, professional studies, though his work remains a treasury of local information and tradition. Looking back on that work now, on all of his interests and on the great energy that he devoted both to them and to his work as a priest, we can only wonder at and admire the list of accomplishments and achievements that are associated with his name. In the context of the *Lives of the Irish saints* alone, though a modest man, it is not difficult to imagine that John O'Hanlon might have had his own endeavours in mind when he described in the following words the work of the American Catholic historian, John Gilmary Shea:

> At last, a single individual was providentially found, who could appreciate at their true worth the great memories of men that had passed away, and who had a thorough capacity for historic investigation, as also an indefatigable industry to bring from their long hidden recesses those irrefragable evidences of achievements and heroic lives deserving to be registered and revered.[46]

---

[44] See Appendix 3 § 1.

[45] See Appendix 1, under the years 1907 and 1914. Despite the fact that he had been preparing the work since 1883 with his series 'Old churches of Leix', followed, in 1888, by his series 'Historic memorials of Leix', volume I of the *History*, which he had seen in proof, still bore the signs of hurried preparation, and, though generally well received, was not without its critics: 'We cannot commend the chapters dealing with the twelfth and thirteenth centuries, inasmuch as the numerous documents of the State Papers, the *Song of Dermot*, the Plea Rolls, etc., do not appear to have been consulted' (W. H. Grattan Flood in *New Ireland Review* 28 (1907–8) 317).

[46] O'Hanlon, 'The Catholic Church in the United States' (1892) 496–7.

1

Early Days

Early Days

Maternal Grandfather: Denis Downey

IN 1798, SOON after the general rising, a comfortable grazier named Denis Downey, who held a considerable tract of land, on which stood the Gray Abbey ruins, near the town of Kildare, had been induced by a relative to take up arms and join the insurgent ranks. Having been engaged in some of the desultory affairs previous to the Curragh massacre, and his helpless wife, with two small children, having been daily exposed to insults, and the rapacity of the military force, during his absence from home, it was at length found necessary to abandon the farm-stead. His wife and her infant charge sought a temporary place of refuge in Derryoughter, near the river Barrow. Here her aged father and mother resided. The insurgent husband found means for communicating to her his intentions of surrendering, with others, at the Gibbet Rath on the 3d of June.

It is a fact, well remembered and handed down by tradition amongst the townspeople of Kildare, that on the very day before, several of Lord Roden's foxhunters, in a riotous and drunken brawl, appeared in the streets, carrying articles of apparel on the top of their fixed bayonets, and swearing most vehemently, 'We are the boys who will slaughter the croppies to-morrow at the Curragh!' This announcement deterred many rebels from proceeding to the spot, and proved instrumental, no doubt, in saving their lives. Amongst the unnotified, however, Downey, in hopes of obtaining pardon, and mounted on a fine horse, went to the fatal trysting place.

Having surrendered his arms, and an indiscriminate slaughter of the rebels having commenced, he at once got on horseback, and was endeavouring to escape, when he observed a near relative running away on foot. The horseman stopped for a moment, but when stooping for the purpose of mounting his friend behind, a bullet brought Downey to the ground, when his horse galloped wildly forward towards Derryoughter, where it had been previously stabled.

Honor Hanlon (née Downey), John O'Hanlon's mother

Meantime, Mrs Downey, whose mind had been filled with alarm and anxiety to learn the state of her husband, remained up nearly the whole of that night, immediately preceding the 3d of June. Towards morning, wearied and careworn, she had been induced to take a brief rest. The most strange event of all then occurred, as afterwards frequently certified by herself and those with whom she at that time resided. About the very hour when the massacre took place on the Gibbet Rath, she started from a troubled sleep, during which she had a frightful dream or vision of her husband weltering in his blood. Her instant screams drew all the family to her bedside. In vain did the aged father represent to her that such a dream was only the result of her disordered fancies, and that better news might soon be expected. She wept bitterly and in utter despair of ever seeing her husband alive. The old man, taking his walking stick, turned down a retired road branching from his house towards the more public thoroughfare, leading from the Curragh. Almost the first object he encountered on the way was Downey's horse covered with foam and galloping furiously, without any rider, yet bridled and saddled. This unwonted sight furnished a sad presentiment of his son-in-law's fate.

Soon again he observed numbers of country people running along the high road in a state of wild excitement. The old man asked some of them what news from the Curragh. 'Bad news! bad news!' they exclaimed, 'our friends were all slaughtered on the Curragh to-day.' This heartrending intelligence was afterwards conveyed to his unhappy daughter. With all the energy of despair, Mrs Downey insisted on having one of the common farm cars prepared. In this she proceeded to the scene of the diabolical massacre. She afterwards stated that on the blood-stained plain she turned over at least two hundred dead bodies before she recognised that of her husband. This latter she deposited in the car, covering the corpse with straw and a quilt. Thus placing it beside her, the forlorn widow escaped without molestation to the house of a relative of her husband, living near the old burial-place, named Dunmurry, near the Red Hills of Kildare. Preparations were made for the interment. That very night, however, a rumour went abroad that the military were searching every house throughout the district. Wherever a rebel corpse was found, it was reported that the house containing it would be consigned to the flames. Hastily acting on such information, a grave was dug in an adjoining family burial-place of Dunmurrry, whilst the body of Denis Downey was wrapped in a shroud and covered with sheets, for time would not allow of a coffin being made. In this manner the remains were consigned to their last resting-place, and covered with earth.

The poor woman soon returned to find her former comfortable home a perfect wreck. For nights in succession, with a servant maid, she was obliged to rise from bed and allow the ruffian soldiery to despoil her of almost every remnant of property. Desponding and broken-hearted in her unprotected situation, and happily wishing a retirement from the scenes of former happiness, the farm was afterwards sold to a purchaser, and the desolate widow, with her small infant charge, removed to the neighbouring town of Monasterevan. Rarely could she be induced, in after years, to recur to this earlier period of her life, without tears moistening her eyes and stealing down her cheeks; nor could she ever regard a soldier without feelings of deep aversion.

Stradbally

IN THE EARLY part of this century, a Mrs. Mary St. John lived in Stradbally, Queen's County, and she was an industrious collector of stories, related by the townsfolk and country people. That lady and her companion, a Mrs. Bradshaw, occupied a handsome and convenient private home near the bridge, which spans the Beauteogue River running through the village. Both were favourites among the townspeople, and especially beloved by the poor old beggar women, who were always to be found assembled before their front door, during the hour for dinner; as soon afterwards the maid servant appeared, and distributed a portion of broken meat and of vegetables to each expectant of the compassionate ladies' charities. An afternoon walk usually preceded their dinner-hour, and their return home was the signal for the trooping after them of their poor *clientele*, who were always profuse in their praises, and with blessings on them, loudly and fervently expressed.

Each Sunday in the village there were different hours for service, both in the Protestant church, and in the old Catholic chapel, when their respective bells tolled the signal for the different congregations to enter. In a village community, observations are made that cannot well be avoided; and when the various families in town turned out to attend to their devotions, some were remarked as going forth at the first tap of the bell, and walking leisurely, since they were sure to be in good time. Others again were noticed leaving their homes only at the last moment, and sometimes after the last toll of the bell, then moving at a striding pace, or even running, and always in time to be late. In the little square outside the chapel gate, a crowd of country people was usually collected, at an early hour, but rather to engage in conversation or to discuss the current social and political subjects of the day. Sometimes these debates waxed warm, as voluble orators of differing opinions longed for the opportunity of engaging in contests, which were only adjourned as the bell ceased ringing, and a general rush was made for the gate, when Mass was about to commence. The square tower of the Protestant church had two bells, but these were of different tones; the first bell rung was pitched in a slow and deep measure, and it was called 'Solemn Bob'; while at its close, and for about five minutes before the service began, a much smaller bell sent forth a quick and jingling sound, supposed to express 'Come or Stay', and therefore so called by the townspeople. Then only were the numerous Protestant laggards on the run. Now Mrs. St. John and Mrs. Bradshaw were invariably out of their house, dressed in a most matronly and becoming fashion, the very moment 'Solemn Bob' gave the first note. With the Book of Common Prayer, Bible and Hymn Book, both ladies were to be seen moving towards the church, which was not far distant; while their dignified demeanour and praiseworthy punctuality in proceeding to commence their devout exercises gave edification to people of every rank, class and religious denomination. Hats were raised and courtesies were made as they passed along, and these salutes were courteously returned by the gentlewomen, who felt indeed, that they were greatly loved and respected by their neighbours, gentle and simple.

The external manner and bearing of both ladies were quite different: Mrs. Bradshaw, tall and lean, being distinguished by a reserved and distant mien in her intercourse with other persons, yet withal condescending and approachable enough, however puritanical she might seem; while Mrs. St. John, rather full and portly in figure, was ever cheery and good humoured, social and agreeable in conversation, knowing nearly all people in the village by name and occupation, having a kindly word for each in passing, and often stopping to inquire about themselves and families. She had ready wit, in a remarkable degree, and a knowledge of the world, for she had travelled to the East and lived for some time abroad. Yet, her exile altered not her truly Irish nature, and when she returned to her native country, the scenes of childhood had special attractions for her.

Being a student of village and peasant life, she loved to meet some eccentric character, and have a linguistic passage at arms in good humoured fashion with him or her, as the case might be. Such opportunities were often afforded, and several stories were current of the smart things said, and the repartees which were returned on either side.

With children she felt quite at home, and loved to converse with them, inquiring about their school proficiency, putting such questions as she thought interested them, and eliciting such replies as their information or intelligence permitted them to make. Oftentimes she drew from her reticule Shrewsbury cakes, which served to ingratiate her even more in their regards, while those marks of her favour were willingly received and thankfully acknowledged. She was an elderly lady in Stradbally, about the year 1834, and then in good health, but the writer has not been able to ascertain the year of her death.

Ballyroan

O N THE FORMER mail-coach road between Dublin and Cork is situated the village of Ballyroan, giving name also to a parish, having an area of 9,682 acres, in the barony of Cullinagh, Queen's County. That it is an ancient town, formerly under the jurisdiction of the O'Mores, chieftains of Leix, can scarcely be questioned; for a very remarkable high conical and artificial moat is still to be seen in the immediate vicinity, probably sustaining some sort of fortification on its summit in former times. A winding path-way affords gradual ascent from below, and trees have been planted along its sides. The earliest known Map of Leix we possess is that to be found in the Cottonian collection of the British Museum, supposed to have been made about 1563, in the reign of Queen Elizabeth. That it is misleading, both in topographical admeasurements and local denominations, must be admitted. Even a copy of that Map, with the names more clearly and correctly written, and now preserved in Trinity College Library, Dublin, labours under similar defects. Although Ballyroan is doubtless to be found marked by some one or other of the castellated figures, near to Coulinogh Mountain; yet, under the blundering designations supplied by the Saxon draftsman, it is quite impossible to define there with accuracy its exact position. However, after the subjugation of Leix, and when the Hetheringtons became possessors of Ballyroan, it began to grow into a considerable town; and, in 1686, Alderman Preston of Dublin founded there a Protestant Grammar School, endowed with lands in Cappaloughlan, which he bequeathed for its support, and assigned to trustees for its maintenance. In like manner, he founded a Protestant school at Navan, allowing £35, Irish money, as salary for the schoolmaster. Altogether 1,737 acres of land were granted to carry out the bequest of that testator.

Early Days

The principal of the school at Ballyroan was a graduate of Trinity College, Dublin, whose salary we may suppose to have varied at times, according to the revenue drawn from the estate, not always judiciously managed by the trustees. From Alderman Preston's foundation, the school was to be aided with £52, Irish money, *per annum*. A suit respecting his endowment was commenced in 1734, and for seventy-four years afterwards, the law costs amounted to £3,000. In the Irish Parliament, abuses connected with that endowment were fully set forth before the Committee of Inquiry into abused charities in the House of Lords of 1764; as also before the Education Commissioners of 1791, and before the Royal Commissioners of 1807–12. In consequence of those abuses, a special clause was introduced into the Act of 1813, 53 George III., chap. 107, sect. 14, vesting the estate in the Commissioners of Education established under that statute.

Small and remote as it was, still Ballyroan had its celebrities in days now past, and we have only to open the pages of Sir Jonah Barrington's amusing 'Personal Sketches and Recollections of his Own Times' to learn the facetious baronet's relations with its parish. The Rev. Mr. Barrett was rector there during the last century, and he was father to the celebrated and eccentric Rev. Dr. John Barrett, Vice-provost of Dublin University. On the occasion of a trial for libel in the King's Bench, happening to be counsel for Theophilus Swift defendant, Sir Jonah was engaged in a cross-examination of Dr. Barrett for more than an hour, without gaining a single point in law or logic from the learned witness he endeavoured to circumvent. At length, he thought to try cajolery and conciliation with the Vice-provost, by stating that his father had christened him Sir Jonah. 'Oh! indeed,' retorted Dr. Barrett, "I did not know you were a Christian.' This unexpected repartee raised such a laugh among his brother barristers, and in the court, that Sir Jonah could not further proceed with his cross-examination, and his client was sentenced to twelve months' imprisonment in the gaol of Newgate.

Early Days

In the year 1833, the law-suit connected with Ballyroan School concluded, having lasted for nearly 100 years; and in 1834, the writer of this notice – then a boy of thirteen – was first introduced to the principal Arthur Hutchins, an M.A. of Trinity College, Dublin, and examined by him for entrance to a Greek and Latin class. Having already received an elementary English and classical education, under a far more competent instructor, in his native town, the juvenile scholar was allowed to continue his Greek Testament and Lucian, with Virgil and Sallust as Latin authors, by a gracious permission of the head-master, as he then took care to remark. At that time, a Mr. Henderson was usher, conducting the English department in writing and arithmetic. About once a week, the Protestant curate of the parish attended to give catechetical instruction to the boys of his congregation.

At the period to which we allude, the large house in which Mr. Hutchins and his family lived was retired somewhat from the main street of the village; while on one side of it was an old-fashioned and dilapidated building, which as we conceive may have been erected about a century previous – the original casements of doors and windows having been removed. The masonry had even crumbled away from the openings. It seemed to have been the former foundation school-house, but then, the lower door and window spaces were built up with rough masonry, in front, while the interior was choked with mortar and slates, *debris* from the fallen roof. At the rear, all the doors and windows had been built on a level with the wall, and smoothly cemented, to serve for a ball-court, near which was the boys' play-ground. The modern school-house was a presentable and comfortable two-storied house, having many rooms above and below, while its extension towards the rear was considerable. The building was then centrally placed in the town of Ballyroan. About twenty boys were boarders in that house; while an equal number of day-boys frequented the school, from the town and neighbourhood.

The master was quite an original and eccentric character, yet not withstanding all his peculiarities, popular with his pupils and

the townspeople, to whom he was a familiar and respected person-
age. He was advanced in years, and the father of grown sons and
daughters, who lived with him. Their mother superintended the
household affairs very judiciously, and was assisted in the work
by some female servants. Mr. Hutchins was rather a tall man,
of lithesome shape, and having a good set of features, in which
seriousness and vivacity were at once blended. His motions were
restless, both within and without the house, and when walking
abroad his thumbs were placed in the armlets of his vest, while the
tips of his fingers were continually tattooing his breast on either
side. In dress he was a stylish gentleman of the olden time, wearing
a long-skirted black broad cloth frock-coat with lapels, a waistcoat
and pantaloons to match, a black silk stock, with shirt collars pro-
truding on either side of his cheeks. His shapely silk hat was worn
with a jaunty air, and his boots were highly polished; but probably the most noticeable appendage of his dress was a cambric frill,
snowy white, and elegantly crimped, which escaped in full dis-
play from the upper part of the vest. Altogether, he was a figure
to attract very particular notice, and he had a self-satisfied air of
superiority, when he appeared among his pupils or the villagers.

As became his profession, although well versed in the Greek
and Latin authors, Mr. Hutchins was a pedant, fond of interlarding
his vernacular conversation with classical phrases and quotations,
which to him were quite in use. Whenever he desired to asseverate
very strongly, or to express surprise at any statement, his usual
exclamation was 'By Hercules!' Hence it was the *soubriquet* by
which he was called among the pupils and townspeople, but not in
his own hearing; since he was too aristocratic and solemn looking,
not to repel familiarity or disrespect. His manner was formal and
condescendingly courteous to the humblest person who touched a
hat to him in the street, or who approached, either to seek a favour,
or to transact any ordinary business.

The school opened each morning about ten o'clock, and closed
at three in the afternoon. The pupils for the most part were well
grown lads, and many of them young men who aspired to the

Pass House, *c.* 1900

Catholic priesthood. Although excellent English and Classical Schools had been set up under competent instructors in the more considerable Irish towns, yet Catholic Colleges were then few, and only confined to some dioceses, nor had the National System of Lord Stanley made much progress to meet public requirements, or to arrest the higher educational enterprise of individual teachers. In our school of Ballyroan, a general laxity of discipline was allowed; except during the class-hours for individuals of the higher and lower grades, the other boys were mostly absent and amusing themselves in the playground, or in the fields adjoining the town, instead of preparing their coming lessons; frequently the principal was absent from the room in some other part of the house, or as often happened, sauntering about the street and gossiping with some person, as might be seen from the windows, and then all the wild spirits of the boys were in commotion to create as much confusion as possible, with all that love of mischief-making, so congenial to youths uncontrolled by the exercise of authority. Although a good classical scholar himself, still had Mr. Arthur Hutchins a defective manner for imparting instructions to tyros, being addicted to grandiloquent speech, and indulging in dissertations which his pupils could hardly comprehend, without those practical explanations suited to their age and intellectual capacity.

Withal such pomposity and high bearing, there was an undefinable simplicity of character in the man, and while he was approached with deference and respect, a latent sense of his amiable complacency and credulity caused many a practical joke to be played at his expense. Two or three small fields adjoining Ballyroan had been held by Mr. Hutchins; and these were in part under crops, and in part pasture for cows. One of his special foibles was to study farming, as if it had been a science of much importance to his establishment, and during the school hours he wished to seek advice from boys accustomed to agricultural pursuits, even at a time which should be devoted to class and teaching. Opinions were thus elicited of a very complex and even contradictory description; while discussions were prolonged, owing to the freedom of debate invited, and to the number of pupils who desired to spend the hours in a more agreeable round of relaxation than could be obtained from the prosecution of classical exercises. Thus many lessons were cut short, if not postponed to the day following, and the mental strain of a studious evening for the morrow was saved to the urchins for boyish sports and capricious idleness.

The boarders were all Protestants, with a single exception; and that boy had been very thoughtlessly placed by his parents or guardians under influences, not calculated to ground or direct him in Catholic doctrines and observances. Nearly all the other day-scholars were the sons of Catholic parents or friends living in the town or neighbourhood. Among the latter was the writer, who trudged each morning a distance of two miles from an old grand-uncle's house, Mr. John Lalor of Pass, and back again each evening, bearing a satchel rather heavily laden with books. In those days, it did not occur to publishers that the classics might be issued in any other form than in a complete collection of an author's works, usually enlarged with an editor's annotations; so that to carry a Delphin Virgil, M'Caul's Horace, and a Valpy's

Homer, with accessories of an Eton Latin Grammar and a student's Latin Dictionary or Greek Lexicon, besides other books, was rather much of a burden for young arms and shoulders. At present, the texts read by school-boys are cheaper, issued in smaller compass, and more to serve the practical work of special study. Moreover, in districts remote from Dublin – then a great centre for the publication of school classics and mostly edited by Trinity College men – it was difficult to procure the books in use, except at high prices – even when second-hand works – and through the book-pedlars, who travelled with cart-loads of a varied assortment through the provincial towns and villages. Many of our school-books were borrowed from friends that had used them, and not for the first time, as they had an antiquated imprint and a soiled appearance, while the texts or margins were interlined by comments, glosses, and *memoranda* of scholars belonging to a former generation. Through frequent use or want of care, the covers were worn or patched in most instances, and no uniform set of an author studied was ever to be seen in the hands of our class-mates. Our master's books were of a similar description, well thumbed and interlined, as we had frequent opportunities for observing, while he was engaged in hearing our lessons.

Some of the day scholars, more fully grown and knowing than the writer, joined him on the road to Ballyroan, and were always his companions on the way homewards, until they dropped off one by one at their several houses. For some time after my first acquaintance and arrival, they had a standing joke at my expense. A merry farmer's wife on the road-side used to accost us with some cheery remark; but taking advantage of unsuspecting inno-cence, and observing the load of books which the little fellow carried over his shoulders, she inquired in a seemingly serious manner if she might be permitted to place a dozen of eggs in my satchel, 'like a good boy,' and bring them to a huxter living in Ballyroan. The request was an exceedingly distressing one, at the time, as under the embarrassment of contending thoughts and emotions, it afflicted me to be disobliging towards a person so agreeable to myself and companions, while ashamed to be considered by them an egg-deliverer, and to one unknown to me, not to speak of the difficulty of preserving such a number unbroken, and my books from the danger of being besmeared with the contents. However, having passively assented to the proposal, but in no very cheerful humour, the eggs were collected, and the mouth of the satchel opened to the great amusement of all present; when to my great relief, the jovial housewife said she thought better of the project, and that she should send them in a basket by some one else who passed that way. For a long time afterwards, a cause for deep concern lest such a proposal might be renewed was excited, and my roguish comrades played on my fears very frequently, by calling out the farmer's wife, to ask if she had any more eggs for the shop in Ballyroan. At length it began to dawn on my comprehension, from the nods and winks interchanged, that all was intended merely as a hoax on a being so credulous and foolish as myself.

In those days, also, a teacher of far humbler pretensions than Mr. Hutchins kept a small boys' and girls' school, in one of the cabins which were placed at the entrance to Ballyroan, and those were taught the rudiments of spelling, reading, writing and arithmetic. The master's name was Charley Duffy, and besides these elementary branches, being a very correct man, he taught the little creatures under his charge polite behaviour towards all well dressed persons met by them in the village or on the road; so that, bareheaded and barefooted, for the most part, the boys made a low bow in passing with a pull of their front locks, as a mark of obeisance, while the girls gave a stiff jerk downwards, by way of curtsey. And as Ballyroan lay on the high road from Dublin to Cork, so Peter Purcell's mail-coach passed it twice daily, morning and evening, usually filled with well dressed passengers, inside and outside. These ladies and gentlemen were especially the objects of greatest respect and consideration, while the young urchins felt greatly delighted when their awkward salutes were politely returned.

The town of Ballyroan had a motley population, and in some of the thatched cabins that garnished its outlets were varlets, that led rather idle lives, doing job works occasionally, but for the most part living on their wits, or stealing from their more industrious neighbours. Poor Mr. Hutchins knew from experience, that after reaping his croft of wheat or oats, it was necessary to have a day and night watchman to guard it from the raiders. One Johnny Whelan had been engaged for that purpose; but notwithstanding, it was reported to the owner that the latter was often lured away by some village 'divarsion' which caused him to neglect his night vigils, and that in consequence, many of the wheaten stooks had been carried off. Before his kitchen-maids, Mr. Hutchins had declared by Hercules, that his determination was to go out that very night and see if the guardian to whom he paid regular wages had been at his post. Now it so happened that Johnny was a suitor for the hand of one among those girls, and he was duly informed by her of the master's purpose. Johnny Whelan took measures accordingly, and armed with a toughly knotted blackthorn stick, he contrived to keep himself concealed behind a high ditch well covered with brambles. When midnight was approaching, Mr. Hutchins sallied forth to inspect the field where the stooks of corn were ranged in rows, but no sign of a watchman could be discovered. By way of test, he advanced stealthily to one of the stooks, and inserting his shoulders beneath the sheaves began to bear it away; but almost immediately afterwards Johnny Whelan was on his track, and soon his vociferous shout was heard, with a hard thwack of the blackthorn on the moving stook. 'You bloody vagabone! Is that the way you come to steal the honest gintleman's corn? But I'll beat your brains out, you scamp of perdition, before ye lave the field. Take that' – whack – 'and that' – whack 'and that' – whack. For a time, the blows rained incessantly on the pyramid of wheat; while from underneath his frail armour of straw a voice ejaculated in frighted and piteous tones: 'Johnny, Johnny Whelan, it's I, Arthur Hutchins, it's I, Arthur Hutchins; stop, stop, for God's sake!' Still more vigorously fell the strokes of the blackthorn, and still more menacingly rose the voice: 'I'll tache ye, my good fellow, to keep better hours nor this, and brake every bone in yer body, afore I give you up to the polis!' Having well thrashed the sheaves of wheat, and staggered the bearer, whom he affected not to know, at last, Johnny Whelan allowed him to protrude the head from its covering, and there by the misty light stood Mr. Hutchins fully revealed. 'Oh, Sir', cried Johnny, 'I beg, a thousand pardons, but I never expected that you could have come here to steal away your own sheaves!' The employer felt humiliated beyond measure, when he was enabled to fully extricate himself; yet, as he could not find the watchman neglectful of his trust, he in turn was obliged to beg the servant's pardon for entertaining unworthy suspicions of his fidelity. Mr. Hutchins reasoned as a philosopher and logician. With aching arms and shoulders, he returned home, leaving Johnny Whelan to continue his vigil on the field, and triumphant in that worthy's own estimation. Thenceforward, he rose in the master's confidence, and on all occasions he was highly praised for his honest and faithful discharge of duties entrusted to him. The story got abroad, however, and to all others in the town of Ballyroan, Whelan was regarded as 'a lad' – the expression intimating that he was ever ready to indulge in a practical joke, and that no great reliance could be placed on his earnestness or sincerity.

Another anecdote of a nearly similar character must here be related. Those same fields were more a source of annoyance than of profit to Mr. Arthur Hutchins. Among the wild boys of Ballyroan was a tinker, who rambled in a wide circuit from the village with an ass and cart filled with tinware, as also with implements and materials to mend pots, kettles and pans at the farmers' houses. When at home, the ass was brought out to graze on the road-side, wherever the grass appeared growing plentifully in the ditches or under the hedge-rows; but occasionally, the wily owner, who was on the look out, opened a gate and introduced the poor animal to more luxuriant pasturage, or mayhap watched his opportunity to take an armful of hay or oats from the field to regale him. Now Mr. Hutchins' field was convenient as any other to turn the donkey loose in, as so frequent were the trespasses reported, that after repeated warnings and without any satisfactory result, the principal of our school, taking one of his sons along with him, sallied forth and surprised the ass, *flagrante delicto.* He expressed a firm resolution to have the offending animal put into pound – the gaol then destined for the detention of all such delinquents. Accordingly, the donkey was driven out of the field by the master and his well grown son, while the former, in his usual pompous manner, and with his thumbs in the armlets of his vest, nodded his head very ominously. Full of wrath against the vagrant owner and his beast, Mr. Hutchins exclaimed: 'By Hercules, my good ass, you have fallen into severe hands!' However, the tinker was on the alert. Jumping over the road-side fence and flourishing a stout *kippeen*, he faced the principal and his attendant in a threatening manner, crying out, 'No, but by Hercules, you have fallen into severe hands, Mr. Hutchins, if you put the poor creathur into pound. It would be the manest action of your life, Sir, because she took a little mouthful of grass from your field, when she saw the gate open. The creathur meanin' no harm in life would have come out of her own accord in a few minutes, and now to deprive a poor man of his baste and his manes of livin' would make you the laughin' stock of the whole town and neighbourhood. So you had better think well of it and let her alone!' As he spoke in angry tones, and thus pleaded for the poor innocent donkey, the son's resentment was sufficiently manifested; but never distinguished for personal bravery, Mr. Hutchins began to tremble violently, affrighted at the menacing aspect of that tinker, who played alternately on his fears and his reason. He hastily capitulated, and surrendered the ass to the importunate and impudent rascal to whom it belonged. Returning to town, abashed in the presence of his plucky son, who was ready for a rude encounter, Mr. Hutchins never afterwards attempted to restrain the ass, although a continuous trespasser, lest he might again arouse the resentment of its wicked owner.

One of the singular characters that still survived in Ballyroan was Jemmy Doxey, already celebrated as having figured in Sir Jonah Barrington's original pages. It must be remarked, that in some later editions the anecdote has been omitted. On a certain occasion, when the Queen's County gentry were engaged in the chase of Reynard, one of the number got a fall from his horse, and was so stunned thereby, that he lay senseless and motionless for a considerable time. Among the sons of Hubert was a doctor from Mountrath, who in the general confusion dismounted with other members of the hunt, whose sympathies and assistance were excited on behalf of their prostrate companion. The doctor approached, and having felt his pulse and otherwise hastily examined the gentleman's body, shook his head with emotion, and at once professionally pronounced him dead. In turn, however, Jemmy Doxey approached, and felt his pulse. Turning to the crowd of hunters around, he declared there was still life in the prostrate form, and by way of proof – drawing a flask of brandy which he uncorked from his side pocket – applied it in the first instance to the gentleman's nose. This had such an effect, that his eyes opened to the delight of all present – the doctor alone excepted; and a second application to the patient's mouth, into which some of the liquor was poured, proved so effective, that his consciousness gradually returned. Soon was he enabled to rise and thank his benefactor for the timely service rendered. The result of all was, that the gentleman, thus quite restored and to the great delight of his friends, the doctor was discredited before most of his influential patrons present, and especially when the story became generally known; while Jemmy Doxey's fame spread abroad, distinguished alike by his forethought and skill in the application of a remedy, equally gratifying to the taste and conducive to the restoration of a fellow-creature in *extremis*.

Early Days

This humorist lived with his son Hector Doxey of Ballyroan, and he had a grandson, a day scholar in our school, which circumstance furnished a pretext of frequent visits to us, during the hour set apart for luncheon and recreation. He was evidently fond of the boys' society, and having no settled occupation, as a gentleman at large he amused us exceedingly with his antics and funny stories, as also with a number of hunting and comic songs, which were current in his prime of life; nor were these all of the most delicate sentiment, as sung by the sporting gentry of his early days. The townspeople used to designate him 'a divartin' vagabond', and of course such a character always enjoyed a great measure of popularity. Whenever he appeared in the ball-court, all play was suspended, and a group of the boys was immediately formed around the old man, whose powers of mimicry and grimace were really surprising, while these were sure to elicit shouts of laughter and approbation from his youthful auditors.

Among the denizens of Ballyroan then living, and commemorated by Sir Jonah Barrington, was Moll Harding, a woman possessing in a remarkable degree a fund of genuine humour and a readiness of repartee, not sufficiently illustrated in the single anecdote related of her by that rollicking writer. As frequently seen and heard by ourselves, although much advanced beyond middle life at the time, she presented a full and portly figure, a florid and clear complexion, with masculine bearing and gestures, features characteristic of resolution and self-assertion, eyes sparkling with intelligence and expressive of shrewdness, her whole countenance and manner indicating business capacity, and a long experience through life with people of all grades in the social ladder. During earlier years and while her husband lived, she managed the public hostelry of Ballyroan, at which the mail-coach from Dublin to Cork there changed horses, and with which a considerable car and posting establishment was then connected. Besides, Mr. and Mrs. Harding held a large farm adjoining the town. Both were in very comfortable circumstances, before and after retiring from the hotel business. At that period of active life, Dame Quickley herself evinced not greater aptitude, in the management of her hostelry, and in humouring the varied characters she was obliged to entertain, than did the hostess of Ballyroan with the motley gang that served within her inn, or without in the stables. Indeed, Sir John Falstaff should have met his match better in the wordy contest, had he to deal with Mistress Harding, rather than with the landlady of the Eastcheap tavern. One resolute word spoken by the termagant was quite enough to awe the maid-servants and to force ready obedience; while the ostlers were quick as lightning in getting horses ready and harnessed for a journey, nor were the field labourers allowed one moment of idleness, for all were quite aware that she would stand no nonsense, as their wages were justly and punctually paid.

The hostess was an especial favourite with the Queen's County gentry, and especially with the sporting characters who patronised her establishment. They delighted in her sallies of wit and humour, and whenever choosing to challenge either to a contest, they invariably received tit-for-tat in exchange. As such friendly familiarities invited return, in compliment to their rank and influence, no reply was given, but what was sure to evoke enjoyment and peals of hearty laughter. Far different was it when pretentious and low-bred persons attempted to assume airs unbecoming their position, or when they fell into awkward mistakes and escapades in the conduct of their affairs. Then, indeed, ludicrous and sarcastic enough were the winged words of caustic application in reproof and condemnation that fell from the lips of Mistress Harding. By the townspeople those sayings were well remembered, and by our school-fellows repeated with special zest; but, how lively were the sallies of wit or how racy the humour, we cannot here record, as the occasions and persons to whom they had reference are at present well nigh forgotten.

A talented and handsome young priest of the diocese, as likewise an accomplished classical scholar, was a son of Mrs. Harding, and having been a pupil of Mr. Hutchins, whenever he came on a family visit to Ballyroan, he was sure to see his former teacher and the boys during school-hours – thus keeping up a standing intimacy, and renewing old or forming new acquaintances. He was complimented, likewise, in being asked to teach one or other of our classes, which task he readily undertook and executed with distinguished ability. We all desired much to have the benefit of his instructions. Moreover, the Rev. Nicholas Harding had other qualifications, which rendered him not less popular among the school-boys; for we knew him to be fond of athletic sports, and able to beat the best of our ballplayers in the alley during hours of recreation. But, what we enjoyed of all other performances was to see him mounted on a magnificent hunter, which he constantly rode, and brought out for exercise into the fields, at the rear of Mr. Hutchins' garden. Having thence a commanding view, we witnessed the grace and agility with which his hunter and himself took the leaps and cleared the fences, until both were sufficiently heated with the exertion. In after life, we knew Rev. Nicholas Harding socially, as a most agreeable and well informed gentleman; but he lived not to middle age, for his health became impaired, and he fell into a premature decline. When last we met him, the appearances of approaching dissolution had far advanced; he was breathing with difficulty, and on inquiring about his state, he replied sadly with the classical phrase, 'haeret lateri lethalis arundo'. He did not long survive.

One of our teacher's illustrations regarding the manner in which our classic studies were to proceed was peculiar. He would first place the Latin Grammar on the table, clap it with his open palm, then lay the Latin Dictionary over that corner-stone; afterwards, he piled in succession Swain's Sentences, Hoole's Terminations, Cordery's Colloquies, Caesar's Commentaries, Ovid's Metamorphoses, Sallust, Virgil, Livy, Horace, and lastly Tacitus, which latter author usually crowned the serial edifice. This enumeration formed the school *curriculum*, and when the structure was completed, an energetic stroke was bestowed on the upper *stratum*. It is doubtful if the pupils derived much practical instruction from the object-lesson. But, on a certain occasion, when the master had furnished as he conceived a sufficient exposition of his system, and had left the school-room for a moment: a tall and active boy, lithe and agile as a grey hound, placing both his hands on the table, to the great amusement of his comrades, vaulted completely over Mr. Hutchins' classic pyramid.

In those days, political feeling ran high between Tories and Liberals, while polemical controversies between Catholics and Protestants were also rife; and as a matter of course, in our school were exciting debates and discussions among the boys, on the men and measures there occupying public attention. While O'Connell and Repeal of the Union were subjects for the approval of one party, they were as vigorously denounced by the other; since both were equally earnest and vociferous in their pronouncements, while their views clouded with family and school-boy prejudices were tempered with heat and passion, as also with occasional offensive expressions. As an exemplification of a mixed system of training, the results did not lead to kindly or conciliatory feeling, nor tend to promote private or personal friendship in after life. Indeed, by a sort of mutual aversion then contracted by the Catholic and Protestant boys at school, they did not afterwards when grown to manhood seek to renew and cultivate the acquaintance then formed. Our master – to his credit be it spoken – was not the promoter of those boyish disputes, which even took place without his knowledge; and to the last, he preserved the esteem and respect of all his pupils.

The Endowed Schools Commission of 1858 reported most unfavourably regarding both the schools, founded by Alderman Preston, viz., Navan and Ballyroan, and censured the Commissioners of Education for their neglect of the benevolent and material interests involved. The latter school had not been inspected by them for ten years previously. Relating to Ballyroan school, the annual value of premises was then estimated at £23 17s. 5d., the master of which had £92 6s. 2d a-year, and a house worth £12, with an assistant having £55 7s. 8d. a-year, and a cottage worth £5, or a total income of £164 13s. 10d. It was then reported as being in a disgraceful condition, attended by only two day pupils, out of three on the roll, and it stated, moreover, that their education was very much neglected.

In subsequent years, that former building we have already described was deserted, when the school was removed to a mansion outside of Ballyroan, and known as Rockbrook. There a Rev. Mr. Lyons conducted it for some years; and of late, under more favourable auspices, the testamentary conditions being changed by Act of Parliament, that endowment of Alderman Preston has been re-modelled, and the establishment itself transferred to the more prosperous and populous town of Abbeyleix. Every trace of the Ballyroan endowed school has been effaced, but, on its former site, a Police Barrack and a Dispensary have been erected, all other features of the town remaining little changed since the days of its classical celebrity. However, more than a generation has elapsed since the events occurred, as we have here related them; a few of those actors on the stage of life now survive, as we have known them in earlier times. Moreover, to seize the passing features as they were presented, in point of fact and fancy, may instruct or amuse our readers, who desire to learn some particulars of manners and customs as they then transpired, while only faint traces now remain partially to revive their recollection and note their record.

The Seanchaí

THE DAYS AND nights of the old rustic Shanachie and his stories by the cottage fire-side are now numbered among the customs and traditions of by-gone times; but we well remember the delight it afforded ourselves as juveniles, to have seen and heard such a historiographer, and to have learned much curious lore from his narratives to those audiences so frequently assembled in the evenings, as additions to his domestic circle. The lapse of years has driven the name of that chronicler from our recollection, although having vividly impressed on our memory the scenes presented on such occasions. These were unfolded in the chief apartment of a small farmer's thatched dwelling, entered through an open door, with a half-door usually closed, to exclude the sow and her litter of *boniveens* in the bawn from the interior. Much less imposing than a cathedral vaulted roof, yet was the apex of the pointed gables and ridge-pole of the cabin highly pitched, the rafters were rude and wide apart, connected with cross braces and stout spans of deal to support the dark heather scraw-roof, which served as a ceiling beneath the superincumbent thick outer covering of straw. The mud-walls were plastered on the inside, while both within and without, they were periodically refreshed with a coating of whitewash, and everything was kept scrupulously clean about the aged couple's household. A great ornament of the interior was the kitchen dresser, with rows of plates, dishes and mugs of Chinese design and gaudy colours displayed, and again these were flanked by a pan and gridiron, with bright tin porringers, hanging from pegs driven into the walls. A kitchen table and a settle were on either side. The latter served its double purpose, 'a bed by night, a couch for seats by day,' – we much correct the absurd reading in Oliver Goldsmith's text – a few deal chairs and a few four-legged elm-stools, with the cosy bench in the ingle-nook, and facing the hearth within the partition, accommodated the group of uninvited neighbours and friends that dropped in during the gloaming of evening to pay visits in a homely way. A cheerful welcome always awaited them from the kindly old master and matron of the homestead; they were invariably provided with seats; conversation soon became general, and it was often prolonged to late hours in the night before the company separated.

Never did Dryden preside with a greater sense of importance in Will's Coffee House, when the wits and worthies of London flocked thither to enjoy the conversation of 'glorious John', than did their Shanachie over the rustics of Cullenagh, who came far and near to learn wisdom from the lips of their venerable and sociable host. When gossip and banter, song and repartee had passed good-humouredly around, it was generally the veteran's turn to pour forth the stores of his varied experience, reflections, and learning, for the information and delight of the men and women, boys and girls assembled. Among these latter, the writer was privileged to take his place, and to learn his first lesson of American history; for the Shanachie's uncle Mick had served, we were told, as a full private under General Burgoyne, and had been necessitated to live upon horse-flesh for some days, before the surrender of his chief at Saratoga to General Gates and the Yankees. The subsequent career of that warrior we have now quite forgotten.

It need scarcely be added, that the master of the cottage was a man of great natural intelligence, and greatly respected by his neighbours and acquaintances. He was a keen politician, moreover, and although not a subscriber for any newspaper of the period – the stamp and paper duty was then prohibitive from allowing such regular and wide circulation as at present in the people's homes – still was a journal of rather old date occasionally procured and read out for the assembled guests, followed by comments and discussions on the stirring events of the time. From the curate of the parish – with whom the Shanachie was an especial favourite – the paper of his choice was generally obtained, after Father Perkinson of Ballyroan had pored over it, and satisfied his own thirst for information, and perhaps had lent it previously to other villagers. About that time, likewise, two rival newspapers, *The Leinster Express* and *The Leinster Independent*, had been started in Maryborough, chiefly for county and provincial circulation, and containing news of political, local and agricultural interest for their respective patrons. A kindly disposed gentleman, named Cooney, proprietor of a large cotton-mill and an extensive employer of many young boys and girls in the neighbourhood, was a subscriber to the former, then issued weekly, and he invariably lent it to the Shanachie, for his own and the delectation of his fire-side club.

Above and before all other topics for discussion, the political state of the country at that time was matter which afforded exciting subjects for comment, and frequently for divided opinion, among the rustic patriots; for all were sincere in their love of country, but in speculation on her future, none could with certainty forecast what measures were likely to be devised or adopted, in order to ameliorate her condition. Party feeling then ran high, and the newspapers were acrimonious and personal in their attacks; while the Queen's County was especially in a disturbed state, owing to the factions of Whitefeet and Blackfeet, and the existence of Orange Lodges – all secret organisations – that gave great unrest to the more sensible and well disposed portion of the population. The Tithe-war was at its most acute stage, and Daniel O'Connell had unfurled the flag of Repeal of the Legislative Union between England and Ireland. The latter great national leader and orator was then in the zenith of his fame and power; he was the people's idol, and by none was he more enthusiastically admired than by our Shanachie, who read his speeches aloud for the attentive listeners around him, and afterwards expounded what he believed to be the various political intentions and motions of the celebrated Agitator. To give the reader an idea of the rustic lecturer's opinions and mode of expressing them, on one occasion of the sort, we heard him declare in a tone of energy and earnestness: 'This O'Connell is such a great man, you see, that he is impelled by foreign powers, you see, and if they don't grant his requests for Ireland, you see, he'll knock them from east to west, you see, and Patt Lalor of Tinakill, and Dr. Jacob of Maryborough, and John Dunne of Ballynakill, and Richard Ledbetter and Burrowes Kelly of Stradbally, you see, will stand to him shoulder to shoulder, you see, to put in Peter Gale for the Queen's County, and turn out the Tory Sir Charles Coote, you see, to brain the bloody Tithes, you see.' This habitual interpolation was often introduced to impress his audience the more effectively; and seldom, indeed, was a dissenting objection raised to any conclusion the master of the house arrived at, for on the whole, he was regarded as a thoroughly well informed and knowledgeable man.

What greatly interested that select gathering in the cottage was their host's reading 'The Tales and Legends of the Queen's County

45

Peasantry,' contributed by John Keegan, a national schoolmaster and a man of genius as a poet and romancist. Those contributions were well worthy insertion in the best Magazines of that day, and were admired by readers of literary taste and judgment; but they were especially relished by the peasants, familiar with the scenes and customs depicted, with the *patois* of their class he introduced, and sometimes with the topics and characters of their native county. They were most eagerly read for their fun, their fancy, style and descriptive power; while at once, those stories established the reputation and circulation of *The Leinster Express*. Had they issued in any other country than our own, such accessions to a truly national literature should not have remained unculled from the columns of a country newspaper, and they must have found their preservation in book-form, to amuse and instruct succeeding generations. Sixty years have elapsed since they appeared, and still are they hidden away in the earlier volumes and files of a paper, which only gave them an ephemeral and a restricted celebrity. At the time to which we allude, the fame of John Keegan as a story-teller was widely diffused among the people, and his name was a household word throughout the Queen's County. Subsequently, he wrote tales of Irish life and poetry of exquisite pathos for the *Dublin University Magazine*, *Dolman's Magazine*, and other high-class periodicals; but, when his reputation as a writer had been fairly established, while engaged at his humble and useful calling, he died in 1849, having only completed his fortieth year. What is not generally known must here be recorded: he was a most amiable and loveable character; a man strictly moral and religious; devoted to the duties of his profession, and greatly respected by his family relations and acquaintances. The afternoons of Sundays he usually spent in the rural chapel of Clough – about three miles from Abbeyleix – and then he taught catechism to the children of the parishioners. Some few years have passed over since the late Rev. Denis Murphy, S.J. – so great a lover and promoter of Irish and national literature – made a pilgrimage with the writer to that place, where lived the niece of John Keegan;

but we were informed by her that she was too young at the time of his death to have any personal recollection of her uncle and that nearly all of their surviving relations were then living in the United States of America. She possessed none of his letters or manuscripts, nor could she say if any had been preserved. One prized document, in his elegant handwriting, and framed, contains the Rules of the Christian Confraternity. It is hung against the wall within the chapel of Clough, and probably in the adjoining graveyard the remains of John Keegan were deposited.

No more sincere admirer had that *litterateur* of *The Leinster Express* than the Cullenagh Shanachie; but whether any personal acquaintance or correspondence existed between them or not is a problem that cannot be solved by the writer. However, in those days, the themes for narrative were not confined to any particular locality; each peasant could relate his own tale of wonder, and tradition had left him in possession of many coming down from his grandsires, and still well remembered. But, in every townland or parish a specially accomplished raconteur was pre-eminent; and for miles around his modest dwelling, none was to be found better versed in such lore than our venerable sage.

One of the Shanachie's stories we still recollect – yet only in general outline – was the following. We were informed the time reached back over a hundred years, and when that picturesque and triple range, the Black, Middle and White Mountains of Cullenagh were covered with a thick growth of primeval timber, the forest was infested with wild black cats, which were known to be malicious, and were dreaded by the country-people, as if they were demons. In a deep gorge, through which a small rapid stream descends in a succession of tiny waterfalls between the Black and Middle Mountains, there lived all alone an old hag, who practised charms, and healed various diseases and affections, by gathering herbs and simples. She gave it to be understood that these were mixed with the blood of a black cat, which she caught occasionally, and then sacrificed, with some incantations calculated to effect a cure. How she lived there was a mystery to many, and few of the Cullenagh people cared to cultivate the acquaintance of that sorceress, whose reputation for magic, nevertheless, was widely extended. From distant places, people were known to visit her, and having been guided through the by-ways which led to her shieling, they returned with philtres and ointments and drugs to be applied as she directed. A fee was exacted and cheerfully paid in each case. A natural enmity sprung up between herself and the wild cats, so that whenever she ventured abroad, these animals beset her way in troops, and grinned vengefully and screamed loudly on her approach. The hag carried a stout blackthorn stick, which she was able to wield with vigour, and if any came too near its stroke, they were sure to pay the forfeit with their lives. The resentment of the survivors resembled that of the peasant's wild justice of revenge, and it was treasured up for an opportunity of wreaking dire vengeance on the oppressor of their breed and race.

The fine castellated mansion of the Cullenagh Barringtons then arose on the northern slope of the Black Mountain, and there at the present day, its ruined and roofless walls are still to be seen. It was sheltered towards the rear by the spreading forests, then a great covert for game, while an extensive view opened in front over pasture and corn fields, and this was closed in the distance by the circling range of Fossey and Timahoe Mountains. There the celebrated Sir Jonah Barrington spent much of his youthful life in the last century with his aged grandfather, whose peculiarities are so humorously described in his Personal Memoirs. At all times, the Barringtons were addicted to hunting and field sports. They kept packs of harriers, while pointers and setters and greyhounds accompanied their rambles over the fields and through the woods. Frequently their fowling pieces rang through the latter, and being excellent shots, after a day's sport, they returned home, their game-bags usually filled with woodcock, grouse and pheasants.

Now they had a wood-ranger, called Watt, who had charge of preserving the game, and of rambling among the brakes, to warn poachers against trespass on the hares and rabbits that preyed in numbers on their tenants' growing corn. Watt was a frolicsome and foolhardy character, never brought up to any other occupation, and who preferred entirely the wood-man's independent and rather solitary life, to any regular course of manual industry. He often passed through that glen, where the old hag's cabin stood, and in his rounds sometimes stopped awhile to make observations; for, in common with all living on the estate, he was curious to glean some definite knowledge of her habits and mode of living. Sometimes she opened the door very cautiously, to learn who was coming, and then to bid him the time of day; but all the professions of friendship and blandishments he used could not induce her to invite him into her cabin.

It so happened, nevertheless, that while on his range one day, with greyhound and gun, and peering through the woods, a hare suddenly appeared across his path-way, and from all sides he heard a growling of wild cats, as if approaching towards himself. He soon found, however, that the object of their pursuit was the poor frightened hare, and in whatever quarter she turned, one or other of the cats seemed to head her off, as the circle narrowed around her. At last, after several doublings, she turned towards Watt, and making one desperate spring, the hare jumped full onto his breast, and she clung to him with paws extended on his shoulders, her heart violently palpitating with fear. At first he was startled, but moved to compassion for the poor animal's terror, he resolved to save her. The dog by his side was even impatient to pounce on the poor creature; yet was he restrained by the looks and motions of his master. Still the growlers around him seemed to be increasing in number, while the trees seemed to be alive with the wild cats, and their shrill screams were piercing to the ear. Meanwhile, to the astonishment of her protector, the hare cried out in a plaintive voice: 'For your life, Watt, for your life, Watt, don't let them near me!' Terrified out of his wits at the idea of holding a bewitched creature in his arms, the wood-ranger lost all presence of mind, and at once vigorously wrenched the hare from his embrace, and threw her far away from him. Immediately the dog gave chase, and she bounded up the glen towards the old hag's cabin with the speed of lightning, the greyhound gaining on her at every stretch, but frequently balked of his prey by her occasioned doublings. At last she reached the cabin, the window of which lay open, while the woods around echoed the vengeful screams of the wild cats. However, just as the terrified hare had jumped on the window-sill, the greyhound was so close on her trail, that with open jaws he seized her hindmost leg, and his sharp teeth severed it completely from the body. Having thus narrowly escaped capture, the hare reached the interior, when the window casement suddenly closed down and excluded her pursuer.

Following up the chase with the keen interest of a sportsman, Watt was soon on the scene, and he heard piteous wailings from within the hag's cabin. Raising the latch, he entered, and found only the occupant of his acquaintance in a bed, but with the stump of her amputated limb extended from the covering, and blood streaming from it in great profusion. He now well knew that she was a sorceress, who had assumed the form of a hare for some unaccountable purpose he could not divine; and therefore he thought it best to get away with all haste from the cottage, unheeding her screams and entreaties to remain and bandage her limb, as otherwise she must bleed to death. In the flurry of the moment, he left the door open, and calling away the greyhound, both followed the bridle-road down the wooded glen. No sooner had the hag been left alone, than the troop of wild cats entered the cabin, and finding its former occupant maimed and helpless, they fell upon her, scratched and gnawed her to that degree that she perished miserably. Only her mangled remains were found the next day, when such a ghastly discovery was made.

Every vestige of the cabin tenanted by the sorceress has long since disappeared; even the grand forest trees have been cut down, with the exception of a stripe of wood-land, which winds down the rugged glen, on either side of the gurgling stream, that separates the over-topping Slieve Dubh from the Middle Mountain of lesser elevation. In our school-boy days, it was a famous haunt for

thrushes and blackbirds; while their melodious throats sent war-
bling thrills to betoken Summer's approach in the leafy screens,
and other feathered minstrels were emulous to rival in vocal efforts
those more admired songsters of the grove. We know not if the
Shanachie's cosy tenement is yet in possession of any member of
his family, for long since he has been gathered to the graves of his
kindred. The sports and rambles of childhood soon pass away to
engage us in more serious and responsible pursuits; seldom do we
revisit the scenes of infancy, when duty calls to a distant sphere of
labour. While a brief interval sometimes affords time and leisure
to renew an acquaintance with well remembered localities, how
seldom do we find all our former playmates and companions of
olden times there living. Then do unwelcome regrets overshadow
the remembrances of by-gone days, and we feel how swiftly the
annual revolutions have passed, and are passing, with a train of
reflections sobered and subdued, while gazing on the varied beauties of places so lovingly associated with the friends and resorts of
our early youth.

Fr Mathew visits Carlow College

ON THE DAY following, the students who had resolved on
taking the pledge ranged themselves on the steps of the
platform before the high altar, whilst a vast multitude assembled
in the nave and transepts of the cathedral. With a feeling of proud
gratulation, Father Mathew pointed to the band of students who
were prepared to set an example to the people, and after an
animated address to the congregation, the candidates knelt down
and repeated the words of the Total Abstinence pledge after the
great representative of the temperance movement. Immediately
afterwards, the good Father, full of emotion and bending over
each student in succession, embraced him warmly, and kissed
him on the cheek, whilst he repeated words of the following
import on passing before the line of kneeling ecclesiastics: 'God
bless you, my dear sir! God bless you! God bless you, my dear
young gentlemen!' Before leaving Carlow, he requested a list of

51

the names of all those students to be left with his secretary, and no long interval elapsed until each one received from him the gift of a silver medal as a *souvenir* of the occasion, and as a token of the Very Rev. Father's grateful appreciation of this accession to the ranks of his teetotallers.

Whilst successive congregations filled the cathedral at intervals during each day, the late Most Rev. Dr. Healy, Bishop of the Dioceses of Kildare and Leighlin, was in almost constant attendance, as a spectator, whilst he seemed truly anxious in every way to promote the success of the good Father's mission. Although the pious missionary frequently disclaimed all pretensions to the possession of supernatural or miraculous powers, yet such was the faith and fervour of the peasantry, that many afflicted with various diseases felt desirous of receiving the pledge at his hands, and of obtaining his benediction, in confident expectation that they would experience instant relief and a permanent cure. In very many instances, by a sort of preternatural effort, cripples were seen casting away their staves and crutches, as no longer needful, whilst they walked erect, or nearly so, to the great astonishment of all present, Protestants as well as Catholics. In those instances, pious ejaculations resounded through the cathedral, both from the afflicted patients themselves and from the crowds that flocked around them, within and without the sacred building. For any restoration of this kind, Father Mathew invariably requested the people to give all praise and glory to God, under whom he was an unworthy instrument, permitted to exercise the duties of a holy ministry, and to effect only what he believed to be a great social reformation.

All day on Tuesday, the crowds pouring into the cathedral were in no manner diminished, and the sun went down without the slightest interruption to the immense mental and physical exertions of Father Mathew. At an early hour on Wednesday he was similarly employed; but his engagements elsewhere obliged him to leave by the midday coach, which awaited his arrival on the Dublin road. The good Father sent his luggage forward, and remained himself in the cathedral to the last possible moment, when he told

Carlow College and Cathedral (from Comerford, *Kildare and
Leighlin* I, facing p. 165)

the people he must absolutely leave, but he promised that he would
take the first available opportunity to return again and resume the
labours of his abundant harvest in Carlow. The coach had been
already delayed beyond its time, and Father Mathew, with a hurried grasp of the hand to a few of the numerous friends about him,
and a courteous adieu waved to others, ran through the College
Park by the nearest route to his destination. Groups of men had
contrived to scale the College walls, and these threw themselves
on their knees before him, asking to take the pledge before he
should leave. In breathless haste, it was administered in a number of instances, and whilst he was in rapid motion across the
park. Others, again, had passed round the road to the coach, where
a great multitude of men, women, and children were collected.
It was utterly impossible to comply with their urgent requests to
be enrolled, as the coach-driver was obliged to ply his whip with
vigour, to make good his time between the intermediate stages to
his ultimate destination.

2

America

America

The Irish Emigrant

Preparations

IT SELDOM HAPPENS indeed that a vessel starting from any of the British ports, to Boston or New York, will not make the passage in six weeks; but this would not always be a safe calculation. The voyage to Quebec and New Orleans usually occupies a longer time. This matter depends on the winds, the trim and swiftness of the vessel, experience of the master, &c. Ten weeks is the longest time specified as deemed necessary for accomplishing the voyage to North America, and the appointment of vessels for this length of time is attended to in the provisions of the Act of Parliament. The Emigrant must, therefore, use his own discretion in the matter of sea store and the quantity of supply. The number of those emigrating in company will have a bearing on this consideration. As to the quality of food, this will furthermore depend on the preference, habit, taste, means, &c, of the consumer; however, in all instances it should be procured of a wholesome kind, and such as will not be liable to spoil on the voyage. The stores most generally preferred on ship board are potatoes, oatmeal, wheat, flour, fine or shorts, bacon, eggs, butter, &c, in good preservation. The inferior kind of Navy Bread served out on board is considered as hard fare, especially to those not accustomed to it; an excellent kind can be procured at an advanced price. It must be added also, that in a general manner, the pork furnished is not of a good quality. A supply of biscuit is in some degree requisite; since the accommodations necessary for kneading and baking bread are indifferent, or rather not furnished, unless by the ingenuity of the emigrant, who must use, for instance, the lid of one of his travelling chests for a kneading board. The same must serve for his table, sitting bench, and other purposes, in what is ostentatiously called second cabin, as well as in the steerage. Knives, spoons, cups, plates, cooking utensils, must be furnished by the emigrants, unless he take passage in the First Cabin, where he has comfortable berths, and all other requisites are procured by the owners of the vessel.

Young Fr O'Hanlon

Bedding is also required, as the berths are unprovided with mattresses, or covering, and usually of such dimensions as will only allow two persons to each, but in some instances three are inconveniently crowded together. Washing buckets can be procured on board; soap must be furnished by the emigrant.

Cautionary words

THE UNSOPHISTICATED HABITS of most emigrants will render them peculiarly liable to imposition in most sea-ports, and especially in Liverpool. From the moment of arrival there the emigrant is surrounded by bullying draymen, who, if out of the sight of the city police, will often endeavour to extort for services more than their legal demand; sometimes confederates will be called to their assistance, and the luggage of the emigrant divided on two drays, although it would not be an overload for one, and double charge is then insisted on; sometimes a blustering fellow will attempt to enforce payment for a few moment's time, which will be lost through his own delay. The whipster, and the emigrant or boarding-house runner, are ever on the watch to entrap their victims. Numbers of runners may be in the employment of one house and company, and, moreover, may be the compatriots of the emigrant; their movements are combined in the most dextrous manner imaginable; they dodge the movements of the emigrant they design to entrap, recommend him as disinterested persons to a certain house or office, appeal to one another for confirmation of false statements, and study the very lineaments of his countenance; if he be accompanied by a companion, they will be so stationed as to overhear their conversation and be governed by it – this is especially the case when issuing from a passenger office. Boatmen, when removing the passengers' luggage on board a vessel lying out from the docks, demand exorbitant fares, particularly if the emigrant be of a mild and yielding nature; if he attempts to remonstrate with them, a volley of oaths and blasphemies ensues, a threat is made of pitching himself and baggage overboard if the demand be not complied with; of course this threat is never put in execution, but forms only part of the system of harassing the mind, playing on the fears, and extorting the money of the owner. The object of these characters is to extract as much money as the emigrant can afford to lose – to obtain by swindling, advantages that could not be obtained in fair business transactions.

Public works

AMONGST THE MANY employments in which the Irish have been engaged on this continent, we turn with less satisfaction and national pride to the consideration of public works. Unfortunately for the credit of Ireland, the worst and most objectionable characteristic failings of her sons are found displayed on these public stages, and in no enviable light. The disorderly conduct, absurd prejudices, half-civilised and intemperate mode of life of too many of our countrymen in times past – (happily a visible improvement has taken place within late years), has been the occasion of fomenting a dislike towards our country and her people, amongst many Americans. But alas! that it must be said – the intelligent, patriotic and respectable Irishmen of the United States have often blushed deeply, whilst reprobating the conduct of their degenerate brothers; and almost hopelessly sighed for the regeneration of their native land, in witnessing the demon of discord continue to rage amongst those misguided persons in the land of their adoption.

The mode of carrying on public works in the United States is attended with many grievous injustices to the labourer. When an estimate for the construction of a canal or railroad has been received, sections of the work are let out to different contractors under a superintendent – the lowest proposal with security for its fulfilment is usually taken by the company. No sooner have the contractors (many of whom are Irishmen) obtained the section proposed for, than a number of labourers and mechanics necessary to carry out the work must be engaged. The object will be to procure them at the lowest wages possible, and for this purpose emissaries will be despatched to the places most likely to furnish workmen, and representations of a higher rate of wages than can be obtained are given. Sometimes an advertisement appears in the public papers of the large cities, where numbers of Irish are known to congregate, requiring two or three thousand hands, and promising the highest rates for labor, at a particular point. The consequences are, numbers leave remunerative employments behind them, and after incurring expense in travelling, find when they arrive, that but few hands are wanted, whilst numbers are on the spot to supply the demand, and the rates of wages are thus reduced to a very low standard. These must be accepted or no employment can be obtained. Those disappointed in obtaining work, or unwilling to work for the remuneration given, form themselves into factions, driving off, and using violence towards such as are willing to take the wages offered. In many instances, the public authorities are called in to restore peace, and this is not always effected without bloodshed. Payment in many cases has to be taken in part from a public store belonging to the contractor, and furnished by him with such necessaries as are required for the board and maintenance of his workmen. This store is nothing better than a temporary shed. Like the miserable wooden shanties in which the labourers lodge, it is movable at pleasure, along the work. One of these shanties will perhaps lodge some four or six men, who mess together; the wife of one of these, or some female relative perhaps, attends to the cookery and washing. A more demoralising kind of life, in every sense of the word, can scarcely be imagined.

The public works of the country, in a great majority of instances, have been constructed by Irishmen. In general, American labourers and mechanics are not accustomed to the hard mode of living they necessarily require, and German labourers mostly prefer the lower, but more profitable wages of agricultural employment; so that, unfortunately for their own wellbeing, in many instances, the Irish are allowed the exclusive monopoly of such works. As many of these engaged are addicted to the use of spirituous liquors, those are furnished according to previous agreement by the contractor, or at least, a groggery is always close at hand. By an indulgence in the use of liquor, the worst passions are fomented, and the most pernicious habits formed. Casual disputes arise, and from individual quarrels faction fights ensue. The shibboleths of 'Far-Down', and 'Corkonian', 'East' and 'West', 'North' and 'South', arise from the private bickerings of some of the most worthless and ignorant wretches; numbers are summoned to the conflict on either side, who if asked to assign a reason for their partisanship could give none, these differences arising rather from miserable provincial and local prejudices, than from personal insults or injuries. Many who would willingly decline participation in those disgraceful affrays if left to their own good sense, are forced, by threat and compulsion, to join one party or the other. A want of moral courage – the courage often most wanting, and most necessary for many Irishmen – leaves no other choice, but compliance or expulsion from amongst their companions.

Citizenship

A S A PEOPLE, the inhabitants of the United States are intelligent, enterprising, industrious and brave. The sort of education most generally prevailing is what has been acquired in the common schools, and of course does not exceed a good knowledge of reading, writing, arithmetic, grammar, geography and the history of the country. Professional men, in addition, acquire a knowledge of ancient and modern languages, or, oftentimes a college or university education in the older States; but, in the West, this advantage is not always obtained. The enterprise of the people often leads them into ruinous speculation; and industry is assisted by every ingenious contrivance and mechanism that can be devised. The history of the country, and the brilliant triumphs of the land and naval forces of the United States have established that bravery of character now acknowledged by rival nations. In civil life it must be indeed regretted that so many tragic occurrences, arising from the vindication of real or imaginary insults and injuries, should be recorded. In most instances, we believe, that a sturdy and strict administration of the law would be effectual in suppressing these outrages and diminishing their evil influence on the morals of the community. The practice of duelling, reprehensible as it undoubtedly is, has, notwithstanding, some false notions of honor connected with it in the minds of many; but we are utterly at a loss to conceive how the ends of justice or worldly honor can be attained by the actors in so many deadly and disgraceful personal rencontres. These being the most objectionable features, and of too frequent occurrence in this country, we trust that the sound judgment and patriotism of our people will bring them into utter disrepute. All the generous and amiable qualities of character will be found to influence strongly the American people. Civility of deportment, frankness of manner, hospitality, individual self-respect, want of servility, and an obliging disposition stand forth pre-eminent. An appreciation of the natural and acquired advantages of the great country in which we live, renders them justly proud of their Republic and its institutions; and their patriotism is of that practical and devoted cast which makes the individual conceive himself an incorporated part of the nation, and, as such, bound to fulfil the duties and obligations of patriot and citizen.

It will be obvious, therefore, that the Irish emigrant in order to discharge well the duties of an adopted citizen, must endeavour to assimilate himself, in a great measure, to those traits of national habits, manners, and character that are really worthy of praise and admiration. Besides conciliating the esteem and approbation of the people amongst whom he is called upon to reside, it becomes a principle of duty or politeness to adopt those practices, which are in no manner reprehensible, and which, however different from our own, may be adjudged preferable, when weighed calmly and dispassionately. There are certain habits, however, peculiar to each country, which it would neither be expedient nor reasonable to adopt; nor is it expected by the inhabitants of this or any other country that strangers should conform to them. The versatile powers of many of our countrymen render them peculiarly fitted to become citizens of the world; and it has been especially remarked, that of all other strangers, the educated

Irishman finds himself most at home in the United States, – he seems to have been destined by nature for a participation in the active and business pursuits of the country, and in the benefits and advantages derived from its laws and institutions. His innate feelings and disposition, moreover, seem to be almost congenial to the habits and general character of the people amongst whom he is called upon to reside; and no man takes a deeper and more abiding interest in the honor, prosperity and institutions of the country of his adoption. Even the uneducated classes of Irishmen are actuated by like motives and impulses; and it is amusing to observe how often, in many respects, their zeal outruns discretion. We have known instances in which the voice, accent, gesture, air, and even the most minute practices of Americans have been assumed, but nevertheless, to all eyes save their own, they appeared, unmistakably, Irish. Although, 'to hold, as 't were, the mirror up to nature' had been the object of the actors, yet, from some strange distortions in the objects or reflectors, the 'modesty of nature' had been o'erstepped, and the effect on the whole appeared indescribably ludicrous. But, we pass over these amusing exhibitions, and shall direct a few remarks against the most noted and objectionable traits of Celtic character, and on the means to be employed for their reformation.

Irresolution or want of determination with regard to the future, defeats the active projects of too many of our countrymen. Many distracting schemes for a future livelihood will be indulged in, and many pursued, without a direct reference to the ultimate end to be accomplished. A want of sober reflection and steady perseverance has been deeply injurious to the prospects of many Irishmen. In these respects they would do well to remark the conduct of our German fellow-citizens, who, in general, with greater disadvantages, proceed by slow, steady and sure steps to the acquisition of a competence. In progressing through life, the mind should be directed, in a general way, to the attainment of one leading object, and all appliances should be mainly directed to secure its acquisition. We are now understood to leave religion out of the question, whilst admitting its paramount excellence; – but we must bear in mind, that it should ever actuate the motives, and guide the conduct of individuals intent upon extraneous objects.

The tendency of the Irish to crowd into cities or be engaged together in large bodies on public works has already been remarked; and we believe it will be generally acknowledged, that the country must be the proper sphere for the exertions of the agricultural emigrant. Solitude or want of his accustomed society may at first appear irksome, but habit will soon reconcile him to it, and even render it agreeable; for he must recollect that the kindly offices of his new neighbours can be easily secured by his own deserts, and that no portion even of the most newly-settled country will present the gloom and desolation his imagination represents. Besides, he should reflect, that if higher wages can be obtained elsewhere the outlay for his maintenance and that of his family will be proportionately great; and he must also find how little can be saved for a future day, even after years of unremitting toil and careful economy. A time must undoubtedly arrive when he will be broken down by age, sickness, or want of strength to labour; he cannot depend on the aid of his children, in consideration of the habits of the country, which teach them at an early age to attempt something on their own account. If he possesses not a home, or the means of securing the requisites of life, what other asylum can be afforded him in old age, but the cold charity of a public hospital or alms-house? On the other hand, once his homestead has been secured in the country, he will live contented and respected, and have the satisfaction of seeing his family grow up around him prosperous and industrious, and removed from the pestilential examples and practices of city life.

We are happy to be enabled to congratulate our countrymen, on the great reformation that has been wrought on the national character of late years, by the exertions of the world renowned Father Mathew. Intemperance has in a great measure, disappeared, and if in some instances it be yet indulged, the shame which justly attaches its seal to the drunkard's character, prevents those open and offensive violations of public decency, that were once so common. Yet, we must say, public taverns, and still worse, low groggeries, absorb too much of the hard earnings of many Irishmen. These, when conducted by unscrupulous characters, are the besetting nuisances of large cities and public works. A most absurd belief once pervaded too many of our countrymen, that if a man were not liberal, nay profuse in spending his money to treat others to ardent spirits, he could not be considered in any other light than as a niggardly person, and undeserving the regards of his companions. This false notion of honor and spirit led persons to indulge in excesses that were distasteful to themselves in more than one respect. We have likewise known some, who although they have abandoned the use of liquor, yet delight to recount the sums they have spent in treating others, the carousing that ensued, and the wild freaks of passion, and violence afterwards excited. Irishmen sometimes imagine they give a very high impression of the national spirit and courage of their compatriots, by relating those disgraceful brawls and contemptible quarrels that have occurred at home and abroad; whereas in reality these lawless outrages disgust all sensible men, and are as far removed from true manly spirit and courage, and national reputation, as disparaging actions can well be. To apply the sentiment of Lord Chesterfield to boasters of a like stamp, we would desire for their own, and the national honor, to account them liars, since we would not wish to compare them to beasts.

We are not amongst the number of those who would wish to extinguish all feelings of national sentiment, pride and affection in the breast of the Irishman. On the contrary, the dictates of nature, strong in the minds of all men, and especially in the sons of the Green Isle, must ever bring strongly to recollection and heart, the memories, hopes, and interests of the land of our birth. Without a deep feeling of this kind, we would conceive it scarcely poss-ible to entertain a just attachment to the land of our adoption. Love of country, however, must not be rendered exclusive; it is the part of a good citizen to discharge his practical duties, and give an undivided and willing allegiance to that country, whose protection and advantages have been afforded him. No man will suffer in the estimation of native American citizens, for a love of the country of his birth; but it would be highly objectionable, as well as imprudent to obtrude offensive comparisons between the country of his nativity and adoption, to the prejudice of the latter, and especially when uncalled for, they would be indelicate and ungenerous. On this head we have an apposite remark to make. It has been frequently our lot, to hear very loose assertions made by Irishmen, regarding the extreme wretchedness and misery of our country and its inhabitants, and the whole attributed to the system of government therein exercised, without taking other causes into account, and this in the presence of Americans. The object no doubt very often is, to exaggerate the highly wrought pictures of political discontent at home, or to flatter the national pride of free born Americans. This is often attained, not only by unfavourable and frequently unjust impressions made on their minds regarding Ireland and Irishmen, but most commonly at the expense of truth. Whilst we deprecate the whole system of governmental and social wrong inflicted upon our country, we are not at liberty to exculpate our countrymen from being instrumental to some extent in the continuance of these evils. Neither can we admit the fidelity of those broad caricatures of Ireland and Irishmen, that pass current in the fictions of tale writers and travellers; it has never been our misfortune to witness the joint occupancy of the poorest cabin, by the owner, and his pig or cow, or to be offended by any other unseemly practice, but such as much result from the struggle of honest poverty. True it is, cleanliness and health might oftentimes be more attended to, and with advantage, in some instances, in Ireland, as well as in all other countries.

Missouri

Arrival

MANY YEARS AGO – in the Autumn of 1843 – the broad waters of the deep and full-flowing Mississippi were first revealed to my view, when white morning mists began to fade away before the rising sun. Our steamer had been moored for a night previous, near that depressed point of land where the town of Cairo is situated, at the mouth of Ohio, 'La belle riviere,' or the 'beautiful river,' as first called by the early French voyagers. Familiar as I had been with the varied attractions of magnificent scenery, while descending the latter noble stream, I had yet to receive impressions of land and water lines, on a yet more majestic scale. Our passengers were early on the alert, and carefully wrapt in warm clothing, to guard against chill and ague-bearing exhalations, rising from the Illinois and Missouri marshes or low-lands, and which served to vitiate the surrounding atmosphere. By degrees, vapours were wreathing upwards and clearing off in fantastic shapes, from the wide expanse of water; bright and warm solar rays soon covered a burnished surface, over 'the Father of Waters;' and, so shining out with great brilliancy over the green masses of foliage on distant shores, contemplative emotion and pleasurable excitement had their own resources, in a novelty of situation, presented to our minds. Eager eyes strained in every direction, to fill the memory and imagination with impressions of beautiful wild natural scenery, stretching away to mysterious distances.

Yet its banks were not very elevated, on either shore of the Mississippi, near its junction with the Ohio river. Stately and tall cotton trees threw out their gigantic oscillating branches and large light-green feathery leaves, waving with every breath of air. Tangled underwood and forest wild vines filled intermediate spaces around their roots, or, as in some instances, drifts of sand covered those rich and alluvial bottoms. Sloping upwards, at intervals, the eye rested on more distant heights, covered with forest timber. While the swiftly-moving steamer tracked her course through the middle channel, where the current's ripple and our pilot's experienced guidance directed, wood-covered islands and head-lands occasionally diversified the prospect, seeming to bound before and behind our range of vision. But, as the measured and monotonous heavings of the engines and the foaming waves which surged in arrowy trail behind our vessel rolled their echoes through the adjoining shores, other objects came successively in view. Delightful changes of nearer scenes and of distant natural features, sometimes hazily defined, yet always leaving mingled combinations of light and shadow, blent almost imperceptibly with overhanging clouds.

Having left the old French town of Kaskaskia – pleasantly and for river traffic conveniently – situated on the Illinois shore, a long stretch of bottom lands on that side first tires upon the gaze of a traveller, and directs his attention towards more interesting eastern boundaries along the State of Missouri. Clearings of woodland and farmsteads are occasionally seen, with woodcutters' loghouses dotting the river margin. Soon we reach Cape Girardeau, an early and a flourishing French settlement in Missouri, and which has an elevated site on the edge of a plateau. This plain gradually slopes westward and southward, to those great swamps, which cover interior bottom lands with ooze and malaria. Our course bearing northwards up the magnificent and giant river, we must leave for subsequent notice this interesting locality. Soon as we had parted from Cape Girardeau landing, our captain proposed, as the 'stage of water' was sufficiently high for his vessel, to take his passengers round a long wooded island, which lay between the deep water channel and a rather shallow sound towards the main shore, so that we might have a good view of Cornice Rock. For nearly a mile this wonderfully regular stratified embankment overhung at some height the waters beneath; it ran in lines perfectly parallel, and in beautifully fluted groves or projections, regular as the most artistic entablature of some grand architectural structure, but on a scale not deemed possible of erection by any race save that of the fabled Titans. No break or fissure in those mouldings was visible. Here nature more than rivalled art, in the graduated and gracefully recessed curves, which receded in cornice fashion to the undermost ledge, where the rock fell sheer and perpendicular as a wall, far beneath the water surface. Slowly and cautiously our steamer glided onwards, amid the intricacies of a narrow channel, having on one side sand-banks covered with decayed drift-wood, or thick branches and foliage skirting the island, whilst on the other shore, Cornice Rock ran like some vast terrace-surmounted rampart along the river's edge.

Once more our vessel rode outwards, and turning the head of that island towards the middle channel. Soon again was the gaze arrested by castellated crags and natural bastions, which rounded nearly every promontory on the Missouri side. Fancy could almost trace Cyclopean courses of masonry in these gigantic turrets, which sometimes assumed fantastic shapes, giving us the idea of vast field or city fortifications, systematically constructed by the provident engineering genius of a Vauban, and with the resources of some mighty earthly potentate. Occasionally a dwarfed tree or stunted bush struck root in the interstices of a rock, tufts of grass and wild plants were draped here and there over the grey parapets; and, although groups of crowning trees arose from their summits in many instances, yet for the most part, craggy tops loomed bare and stern against the sky. A brilliant sunshine then brought all their wild rugged features into prominence and bright relief; but I have seen them afterwards, when the dun shades of evening and still darker night clothed them with a look of depressing loneliness and of solemn grandeur, calculated to fill the soul with some undefinable and mysterious awe. The most remarkable of those romantic objects is known as 'the Devil's Rock,' while another columnar and isolated limestone projection, perched on the summit of a beetling cliff is called 'the Devil's Candlestick.' His Satanic Majesty is supposed to have peculiar claims on the scenic features of this romantic region; for his name is taken in one combination or other with many of them. But over those chaotic masses of hoary ramparts, we do not discern bright uniforms, polished plume-waving helmets, nor the glittering steel of serried ranks, the glaring bomb-shells, the cannon's flash and powder smoke; nor do we hear the measured tread or challenge of sentinels pacing their rounds, nor the crash or repeated vollies, waking war-echoes from those river valleys. Flocks of dark turkey-buzzards are seen floating in the sky above them, and discordant harsh cries are alone heard from the throats of those birds, hovering around to seize their peculiar garbage amid the secluded rocks.

Near the outlet of a beautiful and rapid stream, known as the Merrimac, and which enters the Mississippi, stands Herculaneum – not the ancient lava-covered city, but its modern and less celebrated namesake, as yet having little claim to be shrined in history. Here the rocks recede for some distance, and the locality should afford a town site sufficiently eligible, but unfortunately a sand-bar obstructs the near approach of steamers to bear off the mineral products of lead and iron mines from the interior country. That town, in consequence, had a decaying look. As we approach St. Louis, the rocky shores of Missouri are less bold and magnificent, although they are steep and picturesque, even to the city of Carondelet, which nestles within a semi-circular bay. The streets of this growing city rise abruptly from a fine river landing. A few miles northward, we sight St. Louis, the metropolis of Missouri, on its fine natural elevation over the Mississippi, and resting on a firm substratum limestone rock. When first seen by the writer, it was small indeed compared with its present proportions. Then it scarcely contained 10,000 inhabitants. That number has since rapidly increased to considerably over 500,000, and in all probability its population must yet greatly exceed this latter figure. In trade, wealth and importance, it has wonderfully progressed, with its annual extension of houses, and its constant accession of inhabitants.

As we neared the levee, and found ourselves moored fast among many steamers heading towards this city, our passengers began to disembark. Many, like myself, adventured to cast their lots for domicile in the state of Missouri. Others were bound for states and territories yet more distant. Some had already found a home in this Queen-city of the West. People of different nationalities were around and before us. In the bustle consequent on landing, the romantic scenes we had so lately witnessed, if not altogether forgotten, were for a time unheeded. Although it may be impossible adequately to describe the varied features we had passed on 'the Father of Waters,' but few would be disposed to question a prosaic and matter-of-fact observation, emanating from an honest philosophic German, familiar with the scenery of the Rhine and Maine. Being asked his opinion regarding the noble waters we had sailed upon, this man declared with a grave shake of the head, 'Mynheer, I conshidher de Mishshishschippi ish a ver goot und pig riffer vor a new coundhry.' In the estimation of most persons – and even for an old country – the Mississippi should deserve such a character; but more felicitous terms might easily be found to express a tourist's appreciation of its scenic beauties and wild magnificence.

St Louis

THE SUNDAY AFTER the writer's arrival in that city, he attended a late Mass in the Bishop's cathedral. There, for the first time, he had the happiness and pleasure of both seeing and hearing Dr. Kenrick. He preached from the pulpit a most instructive and impressive sermon on a suitable observance of the Sabbath, which rivetted the attention of his whole audience. The handsome, animated, and regular features of the comparatively young prelate were accompanied as he proceeded by graceful yet subdued gestures; his rather tall and fine figure lent dignity and effect to his every sentence; while his statement and reasonings, his accent and tone of voice, were thrilling to a degree, which carried conviction and sensibility to the soul of every member in a crowded congregation. How different was not this style of preaching from the florid and verbose discourses of those pulpit rhetoricians, who leave no solid and earnest impression on the mind or heart. I then well understood – for both eye and ear assured me – that I was under the spell of an apostolic as of a highly-gifted man, which my subsequent experience and opportunities for observation more than confirmed.

Before I had well resolved on my future course and destination, I was accustomed to assist at an early and a daily Mass in the Cathedral of St. Louis. It so happened, that I occupied a pew which adjoined that of a gentleman, very remarkable for his fine personal appearance and gracious demeanour. I noticed, that he assisted at Mass with very profound recollection and evident devotion. One morning, we happened to leave the cathedral together, and he accosted me in a kindly way, to learn if I were a stranger in or a resident of the rising city. When he learned I was an Irishman and an aspirant to the sacred ministry, he asked me to accompany him to his law office, giving me his name as Judge Bryan Mullanphy, of the St. Louis Criminal Court. I felt quite delighted with his courtesy and affability of manner; nor shall I ever forget the fortunate circumstance, that contributed so much to my happiness and enjoyment in after life. He most kindly proposed to accompany me to the cathedral and to introduce me personally to his dear friend, Bishop Kenrick. I at once very gratefully accepted his warm-hearted proposal. I was greatly astonished, to find such a reception and such zeal to serve me a perfect stranger, and from a gentleman in his high station. Even then, I had no very distinct idea regarding the place he held in the estimation of his fellow-citizens. When we arrived at the residence of the good bishop and of his clergy adjoining the cathedral, we learned that he had already parted that very morning for a visitation of his extensive diocese, nor was he expected soon to return. Our next drive in the carriage, which the judge had ordered, was to the Ecclesiastical Seminary, where I was introduced to Father Paquin, and where arrangements were made for my immediate entrance.

Judge Mullanphy's father was an Irish refugee of 1798, who had been accompanied to St. Louis by another revolutionary Irishman. Both settled in that city. The former immigrant, satisfied that its favourable situation for commerce and manufactures should soon enhance the value of property there, made a judicious purchase of land, afterwards known as the Mullanphy estate. On this tract, several fine streets were now built. The latter immigrant followed the legal profession, and became known as Judge Lawless of the Criminal Court, being also in that capacity a colleague and friend of the worthy Judge Mullanphy. A brother, 'Honest Jack Lawless,' was a distinguished agitator in O' Connell's celebrated historical Catholic Association. Both Judges were eminently popular, and deservedly so, among the St. Louisians. With the Irish citizens their influence was unbounded, and it was strenuously used to serve the interests of the old Democrative Party – then all-powerful in the State of Missouri.

Western Missouri

D URING THE TIME I remained in north-western Missouri, it was my good fortune to make the acquaintance of an old Irish settler and a widower, Mr. James O'Toole, who had purchased a fine farm, on which lived his son – also named James – and his wife, both natives of Missouri. The latter had several young children. On more than one occasion, I visited this excellent and agreeable family, and as old Mr. O'Toole had arranged a journey to Independence on the southern side of the Missouri River, he proposed that I should accompany him. Besides being a man of uncommon intelligence and abounding in native wit, he had traversed the State of Missouri in all directions during his earlier life, and following his avocations as a travelling pedlar, he had realized a competency, which enabled him to settle down in comfort for the remainder of his days. He was a zealous Catholic, and extremely well read in books on religious controversy; so that wherever he stayed, even for a single night, he was almost sure to dilate on topics, which presented newer lights respecting the Catholic Church, than most of his Protestant hosts had previously entertained. In fact, he had established for himself the character of a lay missionary, and his instructions were for many the first seeds of faith, which afterwards effected their entire conversion.

I was sure to have a few days of enjoyment and not a few fatiguing rides before our return. It was winter time, and the cold was pretty severe, while the roads were hard with frost. Before setting out, I accompanied Mr. James O'Toole, jun., to a neighbouring forge, so that our horses might be newly shod, and have frost-nails well fastened to their shoes. I well recollect the forge was kept by a highly intelligent Yankee, who had settled on a farm there, only a few years before, while he plied a good trade at the anvil, assisted by two stout young sons. This blacksmith and farmer had the moral courage to avow himself an abolitionist in a slave state, such as Missouri then was; and I felt greatly interested and delighted with the progress of a discussion between himself and my companion on the subject. 'Mr. O'Toole,' said the blacksmith, 'this State of Missouri should be a fine one to live in, but that it is ruined in its resources owing to the misfortune of having slaves to work instead of free labour to develop it; and all the more, while there is an insufficient number of negroes to aid farmers and manufacturers in their operations, there are quite too many to allow white labourers to settle among us, and so it shall always be kept in a backward condition.' Knowing well the pro-slave feelings and prepossessions of my friend, I was amused beyond measure to hear his incoherent and heated defence of the institution, which was sure to fail before the Yankee's unanswerable arguments. 'But,' interjected the slave owner, Mr. O'Toole, 'it is for us a necessary evil.' 'Unless we desire to make it so,' retorted the Yankee, 'it need not be; and I hold, that there can be no such thing in reason as a necessary evil if we are willing and able to abolish it.' 'Why,' replied my friend, 'slavery was introduced by the English and Dutch colonists, before the War of Independence, and as the Constitution of Missouri has been framed by southern men and influences, we must take things as we now find them.' 'Do you not know, Mr. O'Toole,' returned the Yankee, 'that we had little regard for English rule and laws when the War of Independence was over; since one by one the Eastern and Middle States got rid of slavery, in accordance with the original declaration, "that all men were created equal; that they are endowed by their Creator with certain inalienable rights; that among these are life, liberty and the pursuit of happiness." Now could not Missouri undo the evil she has done, and thus benefit the entire state by drawing energetic white settlers here as immigrants?'

As I had been a cordial hater of slavery under every shape and guise, I quite enjoyed my friend's discomfiture, and professed my convictions to be guided by the force of his opponent's arguments. I parted from the liberty-loving blacksmith with a warm shake of the hand, hoping that his sentiments and principles should one day prevail. Fortunately, similar opinions are now all prevalent, not alone in the State of Missouri, but in all the former slave states of the Union.

****

One of the leading merchants and property holders of Independence was an elderly gentleman from Kentucky, Mr. Davy, and who had settled there soon after the town had been laid out in 1824. With him Mr. O'Toole had some business arrangements to make, and for two or three days we were his guests. Mr. Davy was a fervent Catholic, and universally esteemed for his integrity and capacity in all his mercantile pursuits; he was also a generous benefactor of the Catholic Church, which he had been mainly instrumental in building there, and it was under the pastoral care of Reverend Bernard Donnelly. Being a widower, his household arrangements were in charge of a coloured woman, a faithful servant of a respectable character; and who, from having been a born slave in his family, obtained her freedom through the bounty of her master. As was usual in Missouri, the religion of masters or mistresses mostly indicated that followed by the slaves; or when the heads of families belonged to no particular religious denomination, the negroes were generally Methodists, the singing of hymns and the excitement of camp meetings having a special attraction for them. Most usually, however, their moral training was altogether neglected.

The worthy merchant, Mr. Davy, lived in style of ease and comfort, which the appointments of his fine business house sufficiently indicated. He had a family of sons and daughters, some of whom were at home, while others had been placed in Catholic colleges and convent-schools for the benefit of their education. While there, nothing could exceed the kindness and courtesy of our host and of his agreeable family. For myself, it was a holiday-time, nor did I care to hasten my friend Mr. O'Toole's arrangements for departure. The son of Mr. Davy, named Allan, soon introduced me to many of the townspeople; while, being a high-spirited and an adventurous youth, his thoughts were bent on raising a local volunteer company for the Mexican War then progressing. This meant sacrificing his commercial – or as I believe his legal professional – prospects and studies for a long time. I endeavoured to dissuade him from a course to which his father and family were opposed, but he seemed bent on following the troops already engaged, and under the command of General Fremont. I had some pleasant rides and conversations with that very agreeable and intelligent young gentleman, through the fine district of country around Independence; yet I know not if his military project miscarried, after my taking leave of him and starting homeward on our return journey.

The last day's ride was a fatiguing one, as the frost was intense, and it hardened into ice the rudely-constructed unmacadamised roads, cut up into uneven surfaces by the traces of waggons and horses. There was danger every moment of our animals stumbling, if we did not proceed slowly and with caution. It was near midnight when we arrived, very weary and benumbed with cold. On rising at a late hour next morning, while the veteran Mr. O'Toole seemed nothing the worse after his journey, I found myself stiffened all over with rheumatism; while that first attack left its impress on my recollections, and an undesirable inheritance, which no after time or treatment was able wholly to eradicate.

So wore on the winter and the spring of 1847, while I had opportunities for hearing many strange adventures of the early settlers in

the Platte district, during the evenings often devoted to social converse. One incident as I recollect, was the defence of a log-house
near St. Joseph against the Indians, by a brave Creole squatter and
his sons, whom I well knew. The marauders had attempted to burn
the cabin over their heads, and some of the Indians were shot during the attack, which was prolonged until succour arrived, and the
Red Men were beaten out of the settlement. While winter lasted,
the Missouri River was frozen over at one time, so that numbers
of wolves crossed it from the Indian territory, and destroyed several sheep on the farms around St. Joseph. The hunting to death
of those wild animals afforded employment and pleasure to all the
young men, who were eager with dogs and rifles to exterminate
the intruders.

Lawlessness and deeds of rapine were rife in that district during
the early times. Our friend, Jules Roubidoux, related one evening,
and with evident glee, a narrative in which he was concerned with
many other men. It appears a gang of horse-stealers had penetrated
into the thinly-settled country of Platte, and had commenced operations on an extensive scale by capturing horses belonging to the
farmers, and by forwarding these animals to remote towns, where
they were sold and converted into ready cash by the thieves. A
plan was laid for the capture of about half a dozen of the gang,
and it succeeded. They were subjected to a rough and ready trial
by a jury, empannelled on the system of Lynch law. The proofs of
guilt were held to be sufficient, but when it came to the question
of punishment, for a long time their lives were in jeopardy, and
the robbers were in agony of terror. Some of the crowd assembled voted for hanging them outright from the nearest trees; but,
at length, it was agreed to put ropes around their necks, and only
just move their feet from the ground by a gentle pull of the ropes,
letting them down half hung and almost choked, with their faces
black and contorted. Afterwards, I believe, they were handed over
to the more regularly constituted authorities, and condemned to
penal servitude by due process of law.

The ice on the river, breaking up towards the close of spring, was an interesting sight to witness, as great floes were constantly tilting up along the middle course with crackling noise, and masses were still descending the middle stream from the Rocky Mountains. During this time, the young and active Indians appeared in considerable numbers, and with shouts of joy and excitement, their amusement was to jump from one floe of ice on to another, fearless of the danger to be incurred by sliding off them into the deep and rapid current below. I was amazed at their dexterity and agility, while I feared every moment such an accident must have occurred, without a possibility of rendering a drowning man any assistance. However, nothing of the kind occurred.

Meantime, Mr. Corby had obtained a charter from the Missouri State Legislature for establishing a ferry at St. Joseph, and a most serviceable boat was built, on which I was one of the first to cross over into the Indian territory, when the river was completely freed from ice. At this point I would judge the Missouri to be fully half a mile in width; but, the boat, furnished with great swinging oars, took an oblique course of very nearly twice that distance, to stem the force of its mighty current. I witnessed also the departure of the first Mormon contingent from St. Joseph, on their migration over the plains to the Rocky Mountains, and I bid farewell to many of them at the levee when parting. Almost daily, other families and groups of emigrants with their horses and canvas-covered waggons went on board – the men well armed with rifles and supplied with ammunition, to guard against Indian depredations. Nothing of more particular interest remains to be recorded; but, before the month of May came round, I received an intimation from St. Louis, that it was desirable I should return and prepare for the reception of Holy Orders. Father Scanlan timed his annual visit to St. Louis, so that both of us should start together, and we re-embarked on the Amaranth once more, as we had been invited by our good friend the captain, whom we invariably called to visit whenever his steamer touched at St. Joseph. I took an affectionate leave of Mr. John Corby and of other friends, who came on board

to see us off, when I bid a last adieu to St. Joseph, on the 8th of
May. We had a most enjoyable passage of some days, sailing down
the river.

****

Ordination

WE ARRIVED IN St. Louis, on the 14th of May – a passage
of six days from St. Joseph – and soon we disembarked.
After returning to the seminary, an early visit was made by three
candidates for Holy Orders to the Cathedral Residence. In 1847,
the city of St. Louis had been erected into an Archiepiscopal See,
while His Grace the Most Reverend Peter Richard Kenrick became
its first Archbishop. We were now to be examined by him, prepara-
tory to our reception of Orders, and having passed this ordeal
successfully, we were directed to prepare by a spiritual retreat,
which was conducted for us by one of the Vincentian Fathers.
Accordingly, we received Subdeaconship on May 27th, deacon-
ship 28th, and priesthood on the 29th, in the Cathedral, and at the
hands of His Grace the Archbishop. My companions were also
class-fellows in Theology, Reverend James Duggan, afterwards
Bishop of Chicago, and Reverend Patrick Ward, pastor of Liberty, Clay County, in the north-western part of Missouri. I well
recollect the oldest ordained priest in the United States, Very Reverend Stephen Theodore Badin – then extremely old and retired
from missionary duty – was on a visit with the Archbishop, and
he assisted at our Ordination. After the ceremony we were introduced to him, and that venerable French ecclesiastic said he took
the privilege as being the first priest ordained in the United States,
and as we had been the latest at that time, to give us advice of
a practical character, which was truly most valuable; while we
received it with expressions of thankfulness, as we were over-
joyed to meet and converse with such an apostolic man, for even
then we were well acquainted with the particulars of his arduous
missionary career, through an interesting work, which had been

previously published by the Very Reverend Martin John Spauld-
ing, D.D., afterwards Archbishop of Baltimore. This was intituled
'Sketches of Kentucky,' and several pages were devoted to record
the adventures of Reverend Stephen Theodore Badin.

That very year, my good friend, Judge Mullanphy had been
elected Mayor of St. Louis, and one of my first visits the day
of my Ordination was to thank him for his many kindnesses to
me. He received me with hearty congratulations, and expressed a
desire that I should often see him. This I promised to do, and then I
returned to the seminary to wait my future missionary destination.
I celebrated my first Mass on the feast of Corpus Christi, June 3, in
the Church of St. Vincent de Paul, and on the Altar of the Blessed
Virgin, in one of the transepts.

Before receiving my appointment as assistant priest to
St. Patrick's Church in the city of St. Louis, I had an interview
with the Archbishop; and he, too, gave a most paternal and
friendly advice, which made a deep impression on me at the time,
and which ever since has remained in my memory. He knew that
I was fond of study, and that I had a great turn for reading and
general literature; but, he wisely observed, when we embrace a
profession, it should be our first duty to acquire all the knowledge
necessary to discharge it fully and conscientiously, so that we
ought avoid, as far as possible, all extraneous duty, until we had
become well versed in what was most essential. Therefore, he
said, lose no day, that you shall not apply some part of it to the
learning of dogmatic and moral theology, as also, to the reading
of commentaries on the sacred Scripture. The History of the
Church and the Lives of the Saints he recommended, also, as
full of interest and edification, while he deemed it all important
to have a favourite book of devotion to nourish piety within the
soul. Then careful preparation for preaching was recommended.
So far as a busy course of missionary duty allowed, I tried for
some years afterwards, to follow these instructions; and, as I was
obliged to rise each morning at an early hour, and spent most of

my hours after dark at study and reading, I found how useful was the practice, however defective the performance.

At this time, Reverend William Wheeler was pastor of St. Patrick's Church, and the district under his charge extended a considerable distance through the northern suburbs of St. Louis, so that we had a large number of Catholics to serve. That district now comprises at least more than a dozen churches and congregations. Although the Church of St. Patrick was of plain style, and built of brick, for the most part, yet we were then obliged to live in the upper part of a large frame house adjoining it, the lower portions being set apart for a parochial Catholic male school. There my clerical duties commenced, about the middle of June, and I well recollect the very first person I was called upon to anoint on his sick bed happened to be a young man, nearly of my own age, not only a native of my own town in Ireland, but actually a schoolfellow in our earlier years. This I only learned, after the Sacraments of the Church had been administered.

Each morning I celebrated Mass for the Community of American Sisters of Charity – Sister Benedicta, Superioress; and on the corner of Tenth and Biddle Streets they had erected a Female Orphanage for the accommodation of nearly one hundred children, mainly owing to the munificent aid given by Mrs. Anne Biddle, owner of a fine property in that part of the city. The remainder of the day was fully occupied with the various active duties of my sacred calling.

Famine-ships

THE PAINFUL NEWS of Irish famine, ship-fever consequent on its effects, and the crowded state of emigrant sailing vessels, awakened loudly-expressed complaints at all the sea-ports of the United States that year; for a pestilent and deadly plague broke out on board various ships, while hundreds died at sea without even the consolations of religion, and the vessels were found to be pest-houses when they arrived at their destination, discharging numbers of their passengers attacked with malignant typhus. Hospitals to receive the unfortunate victims had to be erected at every

St Patrick's Church, St Louis (*Lives* III, 819)

sea-port, and quarantine regulations were rigorously enforced at a vast expense. Although St. Louis was at least twelve hundred miles from New Orleans, yet daily were steamers coming up the river, and crowded with sick persons in a state of utter prostration. Many men, women and children died on the upward passage, and their corpses were either buried in sand-drifts along the banks, or heaved overboard, to seek un-noted graves beneath deep and broad waters of the Mississippi. As the survivors landed, generally at first on the levee near St. Patrick's Church, messengers or deck-hands, mostly Irish, came from each vessel, and we were obliged to hasten on board, sometimes to find groups of infected persons on deck, and lying in what we believed to be a moribund state. Extreme Unction had to be administered in haste, before the patients could be landed or be removed to the City Hospital maintained by the City Rates, and consigned to the care of the Sisters of Charity.

Early in the stage of suffering and panic, I waited on the noble-hearted mayor, and on representing to him the actual state of things, he accompanied me to one of the newly-arrived river steamers, and, with tears in his eyes, he witnessed one of those harrowing spectacles. He thereupon gave me a *carte blanche* to order cabs for transportation of the patients to the City Hospitals, not only then, but on every future similar occasion; and he directed me to send any charges incurred to the City Accountant, who was instructed to pay the bills. His Honour the Mayor had ample provision made for their reception in the City Hospitals. With that prompt benevolence characteristic of Judge Mullanphy, he hastened at once to convene a meeting of the City Council, and measures were instantly taken to erect hospital-sheds on an island below St. Louis, where sick emigrants were to be landed, and where a staff of doctors and of nurses was soon engaged to attend on them. This was done regardless of expense, and the arrangements not only gave universal satisfaction, but they were attended with considerable success.

Not only was the mayor an active member of the St. Vincent de Paul Society, then lately established in the city, but he took a leading part in the formation of a local Irish Emigrant Society, which was founded by himself and many of the respectable citizens of St. Louis. In one of the newspapers having a large circulation, I recollect writing an article to promote its establishment, and while in the city and disengaged from duty, I pretty regularly attended the meetings of its council. I believe the mayor was seldom, if ever, absent.

That Irish Emigrant Society endeavoured with great zeal and charity to meet the exigencies of the stranger's wretched condition, to provide shelter for widows and orphan children, as also work for those capable of being employed. Frequently had I been aboard the steamers after landing, and the scenes I witnessed were heartrending beyond description. Sometimes whole families, with perhaps one or two individual exceptions, were found in the last stage of typhus, and scarcely able to bear removal in covered vehicles provided for their transit to hospital. Grateful indeed were many poor creatures for the attention bestowed on them, when His Honour the mayor walked among beds, in which lay those struck down by ship fever. Often would he address words of comfort and promise, which greatly cheered forlorn and breaking hearts. Besides his own active and frequent personal supervision, the good mayor frequently supplied me with liberal donations, for the benefit of surviving members of those unfortunate families. To others of the city priests, he was equally accessible, and at all times most liberal and thoughtful, in supplying whatever might be required for necessitous persons.

****

A priest's life

THE VARIED ENGAGEMENTS of a missionary priest's life required unremitting attention and activity among the people intrusted to his care, in such a sphere of duty, and in a state of society, such as then prevailed in our district of St. Louis. As may well be surmised, those exercises were far from being monotonous, since the population was rapidly increasing each day; and while houses were springing up around us as if by magic, our Church of St. Patrick soon became crowded to its utmost capacity on Sundays and holydays of obligation at our different Masses. The rule then followed in all our city churches was to have a *Missa Cantata* with a sermon at the last Mass; and, as two priests were, at least, attached to each secular church, we usually alternated every Sunday in the discharge of one or other office. The vastly greater number of our people were Irish; however, many were native Americans and Germans, with representatives of other nationalities. These were employed in every sort of occupation during the week-days, and yet it was customary with a great many to assist at the early seven o'clock Mass, before engaging at their respective callings and daily work. Nothing could be finer than the genuine spirit of Catholicity manifested by nearly all the residents in our quasi-parochial district; and, judging by the number that frequented our confessionals, and who presented themselves for Holy Communion on the Sundays and greater festivals, no congregation could give truer satisfaction and edification to their priests, than that which had been afforded by our own people at St. Patrick's. It is true, indeed, that many – especially among the men – were frequently absentees from the discharge of those religious duties; but, they generally alleged, as excuses, the nature of their calling, the incessant demands on their time, or the inconvenience arising from their migratory habits. However, these difficulties were often overcome by a little arrangement and influence exercised through members of their families, so that they soon began to experience how groundless were the causes assigned for postponement.

To this agreeable condition of affairs there was a serious drawback at that time, for the chief drinking saloons and low groggeries were thickly grouped along the levee in our part of the city; the chief mercantile warehouses and stores lying more to the south, and along the right bank of the Mississippi. The great majority of the hard workers on board the river steamers, known as deck hands, were Irishmen, who led very wild and reckless lives, who lived much together in a vicious circle of demoralizing companionship, and who spent too frequently and thoughtlessly their hard earnings in drink, while the vessels lay to preparing for their next trip. As bravos, nearly all wore sheathed dirks or bowie knives in their belts, and, under the influence of drink, these were sometimes drawn in broils and used with murderous effect. The city police declared that they had more trouble in quelling disturbance and in seizing delinquents there, than in all other parts of St. Louis put together; and, as nothing but disorder reigned in those public-houses, whose keepers were mainly Irish, we – their priests – felt greatly shocked and scandalized at those scenes which were so frequently witnessed on their premises.

In vain did we endeavour, by remonstrance and exhortation, to prevent this evil; in vain did we administer the pledge of total abstinence to whole groups of our people, destined to keep it only for a short time; in vain did we urge them to seek other quarters, and to abandon their hard mode of living for more steady city work, or better still, to take advantages of facilities always afforded to every industrious and steady man in the United States, to become the owner, in fee-simple, of a farm in the interior: nothing could be done to change their habits of living, and while high wages on public works, or acting as deck hands or as firemen on board steamers, tempted them to follow the courses to which they were accustomed; it, unfortunately, too often happened that waste and extravagance, bad companionship and intemperance, brought many to an untimely grave. The cases of *delirium tremens* were numerous and frightful enough to behold; and, it was sad indeed to know that many a hale constitution was utterly wrecked, and many a stalwart man was carried off by a sudden death, unannealed and unanointed. Yet, strange to relate, nearly all of those wretched creatures had the greatest possible reverence for their priests and for that Church, of which they proclaimed themselves unworthy members.

I recollect on a particular night having retired to rest, a sudden and violent knocking was heard below; and almost immediately afterwards, the door not being fastened for the night, several men ran upstairs to my very bedroom with loud cries that a man had been shot on the streets, and they knew not if he were then alive. They told me, moreover, that he was an Irishman and a Catholic. I arose and hurriedly put on my clothes; then I hastened to the place where that river-man lay, and in a house to which he had been brought. On the way, I learned from the messengers accompanying me, on the morning of that same day he had been declared the victor in a prizefight, which had been arranged to come off near the city. As usual in such cases, his backers and admirers must needs treat him and have a carouse, in one of the public-houses near the levee. They prolonged such a meeting until late at night, and when issuing forth to seek their respective lodgings, excited as they were by drink, their yells and outcries attracted the attention of the city officers, who were gathered in force to quell the disturbance. A riot ensued, and soon the police, who were armed with loaded pistols, were assaulted by the rioters in a body. Many of these were arrested and brought off as prisoners. The prize fighter was the recognized leader of the band, and having seized a bar of iron which he found on the levee, with terrible force he was about to attack one of the peace guardians, when the latter drew his pistol and fired, the shot passing quite through the man's stomach. He fell at once, and an immense effusion of blood ensued.

When I arrived at the house to which he had been removed, I found the City Marshal and a strong body of police in possession, with a crowd clamouring outside the door to procure admission. Way was made for me, when at a running pace I reached the spot, and I was soon ushered into the wounded man's presence. The surgeon had succeeded in bandaging the wound in some measure, but a basin that was near had been nearly filled with blood, which the wretched man was vomiting forth almost incessantly. However, he recognized me as a priest, and weakened as he was, I thought him to be mortally wounded, when his hands were thrown upwards, and he was able barely to ejaculate: 'Father, Father, I am dying fast!'

The surgeon and police officers then left us alone, and I proceeded to hear the unfortunate man's confession as best I could; and to prepare him for Extreme Unction – the administration of Holy Viaticum being impossible under the circumstances. I had actually to stand in blood beside him, and at long intervals to wait, until he was able to cough away the heavy clots of gore that came from his throat. The danger in which he was now placed completely sobered this remarkably fine looking young man; so that, with great fortitude and true penitence, he prepared for death and he was anointed before I left. I never saw a figure of nobler symmetry; and, being of almost gigantic height, it was evident he had been endowed with almost prodigious strength and muscular power in proportion. He was well known to have been a desperado; and yet this man, addicted to such a stormy course of life, wept like a child when he wrung my hand on taking leave. I then thought he had not long to live.

Soon afterwards, however, he was removed to the City Hospital, and I was quite surprised next morning on receiving a message that he there desired to see me. On my arrival, I learned that the bullet, which the surgeon could not find in the first instance, had been extracted from his body, that his wound had been bandaged anew, and that even hopes of his recovery were then entertained. I spent some time in conference with the penitent. His restoration appeared to progress slowly, but his fine vigorous constitution and youth were greatly in his favour. The police were constantly on the watch within and without the hospital; for that moment, when he might safely be brought to answer a criminal charge to be preferred against him before the City Recorder, was expected soon to arrive.

Notwithstanding their vigilance, and in a manner unknown to the Sisters of Charity and to their hospital attendants, the delinquent found means to select his opportunity, to leave the room in which he had been so long confined, and to get on board a vessel under way and then leaving St. Louis. The authorities were completely hoodwinked and baffled; for the river-man succeeded in escaping to parts unknown, and nothing appeared afterwards to give any expectation of his capture.

Departure

THE TERM HAD now arrived when my connexion with St. Louis must be severed. Exposed one night of sick-call duty to very severe cold, I had an acute attack of bronchitis in the spring of 1853. It was succeeded by an almost total loss of voice and a great debility, which completely prostrated me. Notwithstanding careful medical treatment, and the kind offices of friends, my strength was constantly on the decline, and inflammation of the lungs supervened. This attack totally incapacitated me from attending to duty, and for several days I was confined to my sick room. The Doctor now advised my retirement from all missionary labour. For a long period I remained seriously unwell. Although weakened and prostrate, yet a time of convalescence had set in at last, and I availed of it to visit my mother and brothers in Milwood. I left St. Louis, on the 6th of June, and I again felt cheered when joining my near relations, as also my other kind friends in that settlement. During the time, I was hardly able to walk without experiencing great faintness; but I took several drives over the prairie, to return thanks for the kind attentions of many good members belonging to my former flock.

On the 10th of August, I returned once more to St. Louis, but only partially restored. Then I was told by my medical attendant that I should not resume duty, while he hoped that a good long sea-voyage to Europe might prove effectual in renovating my health. For myself, I had little anticipation at that time of living very long, as even breathing was painful. When the matter was represented to his Grace the Archbishop, and that a change of climate and scene should possibly be of benefit to me, he kindly gave his consent that I might return to my native country. I was also furnished with letters of recommendation and a testimonial intended for those Irish prelates he had best known. I took an affectionate leave of my dear relatives in Milwood, of his Grace the Archbishop, of the priests, and of other attached friends in St. Louis. Having arranged matters for departure as best I could, towards the latter end of August 1853, I took passage on one of the river steamers bound for Alton, intending to reach New York by way of the great Northern Lakes. At that time, rail-way communication between the latter city and St. Louis had not been continuously extended.

Having then formed an assured presentiment that I was taking a last farewell of an adopted country, endeared to me by so many agreeable associations, and of relatives and friends I did not expect to meet with in this life, a variety of contending emotions arose while standing on the steamer's deck, there, beholding the levee with its crowded wharfs, and St. Louis itself glide rapidly away from the lines of vision. I recurred in thought to its rapid growth during the decade of years that had elapsed since I first entered it as a stranger, and had afterwards learned to regard it as a cherished home. The scene itself and the circumstances in which I was placed brought a melancholy train of reflection for a time, until the tall towers, steeples, and flues of the city had faded from view.

Then did I begin to recall those earlier scenes and still surviving relatives and friends in the land of my birth, when a mysterious reaction of feeling gave me a fresh and pleasurable sensation, as I yet hoped to reach the shores of old Ireland, were it only there to greet them in the first instance, even if destined soon afterwards to close my earthly career.

3

Folklore and Tradition

Folklore and Tradition

Irish Marriage Customs

INNOCENT MERRIMENT IS practised at Irish weddings, but nothing indecorous is ever allowed. The bride's and bridegroom's stockings were sometimes removed, and thrown amongst young unmarried people. It was prognosticated, that the persons on whose heads those articles fell should be married before that day twelvemonths.

So late as the seventeenth century, before an Irish marriage took place – especially in districts where cattle abounded – the parents and friends of the parties about to contract were accustomed to meet on a hill-side, or, if the weather were cold, at some sheltered place, midway between the dwellings of those parties concerned. If satisfactory arrangements ensued, the people there assembled drank what was called the bottle of agreement, which was filled with strong *usquebagh*, or whiskey. The marriage portion was usually a determinate number of kine. It was borrowed by the bride's father, or next kinsman, and from friends or neighbours in many cases. Each one of the latter lent a cow or heifer, security being taken from the bridegroom on the day of delivery, that the cattle he received should be restored, if his bride died childless within a certain time, limited by this agreement. Thus, care was taken that, by frequent marriages, no man should grow over-rich. On the day of bringing home his bride, the bridegroom and his friends rode out and met herself and friends at the place of treaty. It was customary, in approaching each other, to cast darts at the bride's company; yet at such a distance, that no hurt equally ensued. Still, it was known to people living in 1682, that Lord Howth lost an eye on a similar occasion.

In Sampson's *Statistical Survey of Londonderry*, published A.D. 1802, we are told how at Scotch descendants' weddings in that county, the groom and his party vie with other youngsters, as to the man who shall gallop first to the bride's house. Nor is this feat of gallantry always accomplished without danger; for in every village through which they are expected, pistol and gun shots salute them.

Drawing of Fr John O'Hanlon

These discharges are intended to honour the parties, yet often promote their disgrace, if a tumble in the dirt may be so considered. At the bride's house a bowl of broth is prepared. This was intended to be a reward for the victor in the race. Hence it was called running for the *brose*.

In the mountainous districts especially, Irish wedding customs were somewhat different. There the groom must first affect to run away with the bride. After a few days' carousal among the groom's friends, the *weddingers* moved towards the bride's country. On this occasion, not only every relative, but every well-wisher of either party brought with him a bottle of whiskey, or the price of a bottle, to the place of rendezvous. After this hilarious matrimonial escapade, the bride and groom proceeded quietly to their designed home. Then, forgetting frolic, they settled down to their ordinary occupations.

On coming home to her new dwelling, the bride must not step over the bridegroom's threshold, but her nearest relations were required to lift her over it, by locking their hands together, when she sat over their arms and leant upon their shoulders. This practise of carrying is known as the play of *shough-sollaghawn*, so merrily enjoyed by little Irish boys and girls, who thus coach one another about, until tired with the performance.

Lavish expenditure and unlimited hospitality characterized marriage feasts in the olden time, especially within the houses of respectable farmers. Family pride and a natural generosity of disposition urged them to indulge in outlay for creature comforts and other objects, admittedly in excess of what the occasion and their social position naturally warranted. Not alone near and distant relations of the contracting parties, but even all neighbours and acquaintances, considered suitable as guests, had invitations to a real Irish country wedding. The humblest labourers or cottiers, and also strolling mendicants, who assembled there, were bountifully regaled; while to each comer was vouchsafed, not only the word, but also the look and feeling of welcome.

Folklore and Tradition

Popular Notions Concerning Good And Ill Luck

THE OBSERVANCE OF lucky and unlucky months, or days and nights, of omens and prognostications, of meteoric and elementary changes, of colours, dreams, and bodily sensations, the practice of sorcery and adjurations, form an almost endless concatenation of superstitions. It would be quite impossible to recollect or enumerate any very considerable portion of those various empiricisms, which have not wholly lost their influences over the opinions and acts of many foolish persons.

From the heathens are derived those vain and idle observations, which especially characterise the ignorant and superstitious. St. Paul cautions the Galatians against noticing in an unchristian sense 'days, months, times, and years,'[1] while he specially inveighs against idolatry and witchcrafts, with other associated and degrading passions, which exclude from the kingdom of God.[2]

The ancients seem to have regarded some days as peculiarly lucky, and these were marked with a white stone or character in their calendars, to denote a day of good fortune; while other days are considered unlucky; and these were noted with a black stone or mark, to signify their being destined for misfortune or mourning. Traffic, journeys, expeditions, plantings, field labours, enterprises, sailings, marriages, surgical operations, physicians' practices, were followed or suspended, according as the ancient diviners or astrologers laid down such old wives' decrees for a special day of the week or month, or for the moon's change or season.

The Irish, like the ancient Greeks and Romans, paid especial attention to lucky and unlucky days. Augustus, the pious, never went abroad on that day succeeding the *Nundinoe*, nor did he undertake any serious business on the *Nonoe*, in order to avoid an unlucky omen.[3] It was considered unlucky by the Irish to get

[1] Gal. iv.10.
[2] Gal. v.19, 20, 21.
[3] See Suetonius, *Vita Augusti*, c. 92.

95

married during the month of May. The ancient Romans had a like superstition against entering this matrimonial state at this period, as Ovid testifies.[4]

In the Highlands of Scotland, the 3rd of May was called *La Sheachanna na bleanagh*, or 'the dismal day.' It was considered unlucky to begin any affair of consequence on that particular day.

A superstition prevailed that there were two days in the change of every moon, and which were peculiarly unlucky. These days were considered perilous for many issues, and they were regarded as being unpropitious for any undertaking then commenced. Although it would be possible to give the months and days of each month so designated, we prefer to leave many of our readers uninformed on this matter; for not only, as the poet Gray says:

Where ignorance is bliss, 'tis folly to be wise

but we consider it, moreover, as a very useless exercise of memory for either the learned or illiterate when it cannot add to the stock of practical information.

Mariners feared to sail on Friday from their port of departure; but they always thought Sunday a lucky day for the commencement of a voyage. Whistling on board a vessel, they think, will raise or increase the violence of a gale. The Irish boatmen around our coasts show their religious faith and feeling by desiring a priest to bless every new boat or ship launched or about to sail out on the deep sea. They also ask their pastor's prayers for a safe return. They consider it a circumstance happy beyond their hopes, should a priest or religious person sail with them in their barks. This is very different in some other countries, where seamen think, if a clergyman of any persuasion embark with them, they are sure to encounter a storm or calamity.

In some places, Monday is thought to be an unlucky day, and Wednesday is not held much in popular esteem. January and May are not favourite months for the solemnization of marriage.

[4] *Fastorum*, lib. v. vv, 489, 490.

Tuesdays and Thursdays, but especially the Sundays, are usually preferred or selected for the performance of this ceremony; and Shrove Tuesday was often remarkable, especially in the country districts, for the number of marriages taking place on that day. This may be accounted for because of Lent commencing on Ash Wednesday, which followed; as, according to the Church's discipline, a solemn celebration of marriage had been forbidden during the seasons of Lent and Advent.

Some field-works or other occupations are supposed to be best done before the full moon; while others are regarded as only suitable for performance after its wane. Respecting this planet, the following lines are considered referable to the unlucky event of

> Friday's moon,
> Come when it will, it comes too soon.

A growing moon and a flowing tide are considered lucky at the time of any marriage.

There are various social customs in Ireland, which are especially practised in country parts, and which are observed as a matter of courtesy and kindness. When a stranger comes into a farm-house, while churning takes place, if a hand be not given to the well-plied dash by this visitant, it is supposed the butter must be abstracted in some mysterious manner. Even the upper classes will not refuse a share in this labour, through a motive of kindliness and consideration towards the residents' feelings, and to prevent ill luck.

To pluck a fairy hawthorn tree is supposed to be extremely dangerous and rash, as it provokes elfin resentment, and bodes ill luck. Cairns and raths are respected for the very same reason; and probably to a fear of removing them, many now remain. Instances are often cited of evil consequences incurred by the leveller or desecrator of such objects.

Among the strange habits and observations of our peasantry, the following deserve to be noticed: a horse shoe is nailed on the threshold of an Irish peasant's cabin, and cloves of wild garlick are planted on the thatch over the door, for good luck. House-leek is also thought a preservative against the destruction of a person or a cottage by fire. The throwing of an old shoe after a person going out of doors, or about to undertake a journey, will insure a fortunate issue. The following couplet is often quoted, and much importance is attached to it by the country people:

Happy is the bride that the sun shines on,
Happy is the corpse that the rain rains on.

It is regarded as unlucky to find a pin with the point turned towards you; but it is considered a lucky circumstance to find a crooked pin. A red-haired woman, if met first in the morning, betokens some unlucky accident happening during the day. It is considered lucky to see magpies in even numbers; but it is regarded as unlucky to find them in odd numbers. It is deemed unlucky to build a house on the usually travelled path, where *sheeoges* or fairies pass. The occupant of such a dwelling is said to merit their vengeance. It is thought he will suffer evil consequences, by the wreck of his property, or by the premature death of his stock. Disasters often happen to members of his family as a supposed result; and sometimes by his own maiming, or sudden decease, his children, or relatives, are deprived of necessary means wanting for their support.

Whoever breaks a looking-glass is supposed to incur some future calamity. On this superstition, an appropriate ballad, called 'The Doom of the Mirror,' has been written by B. Simmons. And our greatest national poet, Thomas Moore, makes a playful allusion to the mirror, in his Irish melody on 'ill omens,' when the enraged beauty brushes away an insect from its surface, and moralizes on the result. Again, many remark that the upsetting of a salt-cellar, or of salt, indicates ill-luck to the person who has done it, even through accident. Many other such notices might be included; but as they are not of any real importance in extending the range of useful knowledge, our readers must be satisfied with the instances already produced.

Irish Fortune-Tellers And Predictions

FORTUNE-TELLING IS too generally in vogue among young and credulous persons. Sometimes the future is predicted for them by ignorant and cunning deceivers, and by means of cup-tossing, card-cutting, or other similar absurd devices. Many fragments of prophecies, in prose and verse, attributed to Irish saints, are to be found written in our native tongue. These are yet recited, and they have attained wide-spread popular approval, The composition of several, however, may fairly he assigned to periods subsequent to special events, described with apparent historic accuracy. Numbers of these prophecies contain intrinsic evidences of having been prepared to serve some local, clan or political purpose.

Pretended prophetic deductions from spells and divinations prevail among the humbler classes of our peasantry. However, they are fast waning into almost utter oblivion and contempt. In Vallancey's time, he tells us, that the Wise or Knowledgeable Men in Ireland were called *Tamans*, and that he knew a farmer's wife, of Waterford county, who had lost a parcel of linen. She travelled three days' journey to one of those persons, who lived in the county of Tipperary. He consulted a black book, and assured his visitor that she should recover her linen. The robbery was proclaimed, and a reward was offered for the recovery of this stolen property. It returned into the owner's possession, not because of the reward offered, it was thought, but owing to the *taman's* efforts.

Englishmen and Scotchmen, as well as Irishmen, were entertained and duped by the issuing and publication of many strange predictions. In Queen Elizabeth's day, Ezekiel Grebner wrote a *Book of Visions and Prophecies concerning England, Scotland, and Ireland*. These are very curious, and they have been published in a small volume, so late as 1861. These prophecies, it is said, had been presented to the Queen. At a later period still, Elias Ashmole wrote the *Life, Times, and History of William Lilly, from the year 1602 to 1681*. It contains a portrait. Lilly wrote a work which was published in the latter year, and it is intituled, *Strange and Wonderful Prophecy; being a Relation of many Universal Accidents that will come to pass in this year, 1681 according to the Prognostication of the Celestial Bodies.* This formed a quarto tract, and it has a rude woodcut on the title-page. Various other similar productions were largely circulated; while at the present time, the gipsies, and even more fashionable pretenders to the gift of prophecy, have cheated credulous people in all the different ranks of social life.

Islain Ceallmhuin, the fortune-teller, or, literally, 'the humble oracle', was a person to whose predictions much importance has been attached by the young and unmarried. This pretender to a foreknowledge of future events was generally a female, who led a sort of wandering life. She made occasional rounds, through a pretty considerable district, over which her reputation prevailed. Such, especially, was the case in the southern parts of Ireland. But in the northern province, men followed this vocation. We find in Charles Gavan Duffy's spirited ballad, entitled, 'Innis-Eoghain', allusion made to these seers, supposed to have been gifted by the Highlander's prophetic 'second sight'. They are there designated 'spaemen', tantamount to 'diviners'. The women fortune-tellers of the north are called 'spaewives'; and these were usually consulted by foolish young people, on the probabilities or future contingencies of a married life. They were supposed to have had supernatural knowledge respecting family secrets, which they often acquired by very ordinary means; and thus they were able to direct or predict, as occasion served, for those credulous dupes that sought their counsel. To such practices, we find reference made by James Orr, in a little volume of poems, published at Belfast, in 1804. One of these compositions is entitled the 'Spaewife', and set to a popular northern air. It is written in the Ulster or Scottish dialect. The concluding verse gives us the prevailing notion of a spaewoman's peculiar profession. The author of these *Poems on various occasions* dates his dedication from Ballycarry, and intimates that he is an unschooled mechanic.

Towards the close of last century, and also in the beginning of the present, a certain roving character, called the prophecy-man, was often hospitably entertained in Irish cottagers' and farmers' houses. He was supposed to be well versed in all ancient traditions of the country, and especially able to explain or unravel many of those prophecies referred to Saints Patrick, Brigid, and Columbkille, or to other Irish saints. Such effusions were generally versified in the native tongue, and evidently had their origin in times long subsequent to the English invasion. Many of these were also fabricated during the dark period of our penal days, when discontent and disaffection were deeply and widely spread among Irish Catholics. At this period of depression, although the liberation of Ireland from English domination was anxiously expected, yet the hero destined to achieve this result was thought to be some foreign general or potentate, then engaged at war with the ruling power. The revival of the Jacobite or Stuart cause was often the subject. Under some dark allegory or figure of speech, the late Emperor of France, Napoleon Bonaparte, was frequently regarded as Ireland's future deliverer, until the great defeat at Waterloo, and his subsequent captivity in St. Helena, completely destroyed such illusions.

The prophecy-man's usual predictions regarding Ireland were, that although her night of sorrow may have been long and dreary, a time of happiness and of liberty should come, before the last day. The stones shall cry out on the road side first; and, according to a gloss of the commentator, this has happened already, as our milestones speak of distance to the traveller. Fishes will be frightened from the strand and sea shore. Would the unproductiveness of our coast fisheries, and the arriving or departing steamers, account for the supposed fulfilment of this latter prophecy? A woman shall stand on the highest hill in Ireland, for three days, and shall not see a man. The cows will not be milked. The harvest shall not find reapers. The ghosts of murdered persons shall walk through the country by noonday. The last battle will be fought on the banks of Loughail, or the Lake of Sorrow, in Westmeath. For three long days, a mill in the neighbourhood shall be turned by a stream running with human gore. Then the Irish must drive their enemies into this lake, where all shall be drowned. Such a prophecy, however general in the main features, is referred for accomplishment to different localities in Ireland.

During late political ferments in this country, predictions of a nearly similar nature were industriously circulated among the people. Well-known names and localities were introduced, and circumstantial particulars were related; but so clumsily had these matters been concocted, that they were too ridiculous to obtain acceptance, even by the most credulous. The progress of education is already so far advanced, that popular taste and intelligence in Ireland require more rational, interesting, and creditable efforts, on the part of the writers and publishers, to satisfy the growing demand for amusing themes and solid information.

The Solitary Fairies

B Y MANY WRITERS on Irish superstitions, the following individuals of our elfin tribes have been confounded. All of them, indeed, belong to the *solitaire* species of sprites, but they have distinct peculiarities and callings. In the traditions and ideas of our peasantry, they are likewise constantly distinguished. How nearly or distantly they claim relationship with the social denizens of the raths may admit of various explanations.

The Luricaune, Lurigadawne, or Leprechawn, is an elf essentially to be discriminated from the wandering *sighes*, or trooping fairies. His lonely habits and love of solitude are remarkable characteristics; for he is always found alone, and never in any company. He is regarded also as being more material and less richly clad than the ordinary *sighe*. During day-time, the Leprechawn appears as a little wrinkled old fellow, usually dressed in a three-cornered cocked hat, with a leathern apron over a green coat of antique cut, having large buttons. He wears shorts and white stockings, with great silver buckles upon his old-fashioned shoes. His countenance is grotesquely deformed, and his features very irregular. He has piercing black eyes, always twinkling with mischief or dry humour; his nose is hooked; his mouth grins from ear to ear; his jagged teeth are of a yellowish-white colour; and his face altogether covered with wrinkles. In Ulster he is known as the Logheryman.

The Leprechawn knows where all hidden treasures lie; but he will not reveal them unless compelled by some resolute person who captures him, while engaged at the shoemaking trade. This he pursues under some shady hedgerow, or within a clump of hazels. As Mab is the fairies' midwife, so the Leprechawn appears to be the fairies's shoemaker. The odds-and-ends of his work are sometimes gathered after he decamps from the *gite*, where his open-air workshop had been placed. These are supposed to furnish an indication of where he may again be found; and Leprechawn-hunters keep on the watch for his reappearance, especially towards the close of a warm summer's day.

His love for evil-doing makes him an object of suspicion; and he is feared by all the peasantry. He is often seen tapping his little hammer, and working away at a pair of shoes, while whistling some tune or other. A lapstone is on his knee. Thus, it is possible to catch him when you steal upon him, his attention being otherwise engaged; but it is necessary to keep your eye steadily on him, for he is a great rogue, and a skilful deceiver. He ever possesses a power of becoming invisible; and he can easily escape from the hands of those whose glance he succeeds in diverting from him for a single instant. To effect this object, when captured, he uses every possible artifice. No matter how quick-witted or persevering the mortal may prove, the Leprechawn has so many devices, that he generally throws a captor off his guard, diverts attention by some alarm, and then disappears, to the great annoyance, mortification, and disappointment of the treasure-seeker. Hoarse, cackling laughter is generally heard from the Leprechawn, when he has safely escaped from a person's grasp.

By premeditation or design, mortals have been known to surprise him. This opportunity being afforded, they must pounce on him with a sudden spring, and grasp him firmly with both hands. Then it is thought requisite to threaten him with death, unless he will deliver the money of which he is guardian. He first endeavours to treat the matter as a joke; he next urges various excuses to create delay. When pressed to deliver, he points out some spot where the treasure lies concealed, if only a pick or spade were to be had for digging. Sometimes the captor will consent to have this place marked, by putting up a stake, or the branch of a tree, over it; but on returning with the instrument required, he will find several similar objects multiplied and scattered all around the former sign. Meanwhile, the Leprechawn may be laughing in his sleeve at the simplicity of the disappointed man. He seems to be in great terror while under arrest. Women have alighted on him betimes; but he fears them less than men, – for he knows how to put the oil of flattery on his tongue, and turn the poor creatures' heads with pleasant allusions to, and delusive promises regarding, some happy matrimonial engagement nearly affecting them. Sometimes he affects to espy their husbands or sweethearts approaching at a distance, and then he calls the supposed comers by name. This word, pronounced by him, usually diverts attention to some quarter indicated by the wily Leprechawn; the female takes her eye off him for a moment, and the next he has escaped from her hands.

He carries two purses, for the sake of deceiving a person by whom he may happen to be surprised. In one there is a magical shilling. This coin invisibly returns to his purse after having been expended, to that the Leprechawn can pay out large sums without growing the poorer on this account. In the other purse, he puts a common shilling, or a copper coin, which he gives to any one who has attempted to make him surrender his magic treasures. If the latter be not accepted as a legal tender, the Leprechawn presents the former to his captor; and while the mortal thinks he has secured a prize, yet, on searching a pocket-book, or purse, he finds that the coin has most unaccountably vanished.

The Cluricaune is an idly-inclined, a mischievous, and a busy little sprite. His pleasures are smoking and tippling. He sometimes attaches himself to certain families; and he is found to prove rather partial towards their wine-cellars. He dwells with his favourites, so long as any of the family members exist, – indeed, they cannot fairly get rid of him. He is usually dressed in a red coat, and he wears a red cap; so that, owing to these circumstances, he gets the name of Fir Darrig. Some, however, distinguish this latter fairy from the Cluricaune. He plays all sorts of tricks and practical jokes; but, if not thwarted, he is hardly ever malevolent. However, the Cluricaune is a great disturber of order and quietness in a household. He makes every sort of noise by day and night. Whenever seen, he is usually engaged in vaulting, tumbling, or playing at hop-step-and-leap. He is thought to take special care of his selected family's house, property, or life, and to ward off coming dangers or accidents, – provided he be left to the bent of his own sportive humours, and not molested.

Another sort of sprite, distinct from either of the former, must here be noticed. Notwithstanding his bad or sullen dispositions, the house fairy respects the head of a family, and renders him many a service, when he becomes attached; yet, he is very choleric, and he gets huffed if neglected, or his food be forgotten, or not placed in the spot he has indicated by some peculiar token. He is industriously inclined, and will do handy turns about that house he frequents. His visits are always made during the night, and when all members of the family are presumed to be in bed. The house fairy is lubberly and uncouth in his motions, – his figure is less accurately defined than that of other *sighes*, and all his labour is silently performed. Sometimes, however, he is heard stumping about the room he enters, or his approach and exit may be discovered by a slamming of doors or windows. All our information leads us to state, that the old castles, or mansions, and their generous occupants, were alone favoured with his visits. The farmhouses and peasants' cabins were not frequented by the house fairy.

Divinations, Enchantments, Astrology, and Nostrums

D IVINERS FORMERLY LOOKED through the bare blade-bone of a sheep; and if they saw a spot in it darker than ordinary, they foretold that somebody would be buried out of that particular house. The howling of dogs, or the croaking of ravens, at night, is supposed to indicate the near approach of some person's death in a dwelling, where it may happen to be heard.

When the Irishman of that day happened to fall, he sprang up again, turning round three times to the right. He then took a sword or knife, and dug the soil, taking up some turf, because it was through the earth his shadow was reflected to him. This strange action was owing to the belief of a spirit dwelling in the earth. If the man fell sick within two or three days afterwards, a woman skilled in those matters was sent to the spot, when she said: 'I call thee P. from the east, west, south, and north; from the groves, woods, rivers, marshes, fairies white, red, black,' &c. After uttering certain short prayers, she returned home to the sick person to discover if he were afflicted with a sickness called the *esane*, which was supposed to be inflicted on him by the fairies. She whispered in his ear a short prayer, with the *Pater noster*, and put some burning coals into a cup of clear water. We are told, that she then formed a better judgment regarding the cause of this disorder than most physicians.[5]

When speaking of our people, in his work called *The Glory of England*, Gainsford tells us that, in 1619, the Irish used incantations and spells, wearing girdles of women's hair, and locks of their lovers. They were also curious about their horses tending to witchcraft. This information he seems to have drawn from Good's account. But while decrying these practices, in giving a description of the many excellent prerogatives and remarkable blessings whereby England triumphed over all nations of the world, the writer already quoted seems altogether to overlook several much

---

[5] See Gough's *Camden*, vol. iii., page 668, &c. Edition, 1789.

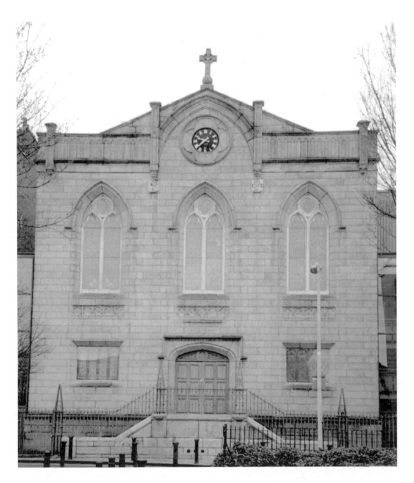

Church of Saints Michael and John, Lower Exchange St, Dublin

more offensive forms of superstition, and which prevailed in the country he so much glorified.

The Irish game of Shec Shona, or Jack Stones, played by the youth of both sexes, comes from an old custom of divination at the time of marriage, if we are to credit Vallancey. Then the sorcerers sought to learn the fortunes of a married couple from the success or failure of the cast. The five small round stones were taken up, one by one, tossed in the air, and then caught in succession, on the back of the hand. Sleeping on bride-cake, it was thought, would call up in a dream the apparition of a future wife or husband.

During the continuance of a well-known astronomical phenomenon, known as the harvest moon, it was customary with young women to place a prayer-book, a pack of cards, and many other emblematic objects, under their pillows. Then lying down to rest, and before falling asleep, they recited some invocation verses to the moon. Afterwards, if dreams succeeded, and had reference to those special objects placed under the pillow, it was thought their future fortunes might be derived from its connection with those articles beneath their heads.

****

A singular and very revolting event occurred in the northern part of Normandy, towards the close of 1864. The *Courrier du Havre* related the following extraordinary affair, which caused great excitement in that town and neighbourhood: 'As a sportsman named Lemonnier was out shooting in a small wood not far from the cemetery of St. Adresse, he found the dead body of an old woman wrapped up in a shroud. He immediately informed the authorities; and the body was recognised as that of a Mme. Allain, aged eighty-two, buried at St. Adresse on the 24th of October. It was at first supposed the corpse had been disinterred, for the purpose of stealing any jewellery that might have been buried with it; but a closer examination having shown that the corpse had been in part deprived of the skin, and that the chest and abdomen had been cut open, it was concluded some believer in witchcraft had taken the skin and fat to use as charms in his incantations. It appears, that a belief in the magical virtues of human remains is prevalent in that neighbourhood; for only a few months previously, a young mason dug up a body in the same cemetery, cut off one hand, and burned it to ashes, which he mixed with gunpowder, in the belief that he should then be able to shoot game, without his gun making any report to attract the notice of the *garde champêtre.*' Such ideas and practices occurring are almost incredible at the present time; but superstition has extraordinary demoralizing influences over its votaries.

As in certain parts of northern France, at the present day, it was supposed the possession of a dead hand, in Ireland, when burned and reduced to ashes, would produce certain effects. Such charms or witchcrafts appear to have had some superstitious power over the imaginations of our peasantry. This dead hand was usually kept for the practice of peculiar incantations, grossly repugnant as well to reason as to religion.

At Rathdangan, in the County of Wicklow, there is a well called Tubber Rowan, or 'Well of the Ash Tree', formerly visited by mothers who suspected fairies for having made to them an unsatisfactory exchange of children. The mode of operation employed was to dip a supposed changeling three times in the well. If their own child was there, it would at once thrive and flourish after this dipping; if not, it was thought death must immediately ensue. The water of this well used to be brought away to distant parts of the country in order to cure fairy-stricken cattle, such animals being rather large and unwieldy for the plunge bath.

In the fine ballad of Samuel Ferguson, 'The Fairy Well of Lagnanay', the following superstitious opinion, with other magic arts, is found, and thus rendered into verse:

Úna, I've heard wise women say –
(Hearken to my tale of woe) –
That if before the dews arise,
True maiden in its icy flow

With pure hand bathe her bosom thrice,
Three lady-brackens pluck likewise,
And three times round the fountain go,
She straight forgets her tears and sighs.

The Yarrow, or *Achillea millefolium*, is supposed to represent Fame. Its botanic name was conferred in honour of Achilles, who is said to have discovered its virtues. With such a little herb, that warrior's earthly greatness is strangely consorted. This renowned hero of antiquity, although celebrated in the poets' songs and fables, should hardly be recognizable in the emblematic name or properties of this humble divining weed. A Wicklow woman gave us another version of the Kildare woman's lines, in reference to the full moon, as a form used at Hallow Eve by girls, when pulling the mystic yarrow. The only change introduced is found in the first line, where 'Good-morrow, good yarrow', &c, has been substituted for 'Good-morrow, full moon', &c. On pulling the yarrow, and repeating these lines, a person using the invocation was obliged to retire for the night, without speaking. Should a single word be said, this invocation was pronounced in vain; and a great deal of the evening's fun arose from parties trying to engage in talk those they suspected of making the invocation.

In her beautiful poem of 'The Indian Bride', where Zaide sets her flower-decked lantern afloat upon the river Ganges, to divine by its course if her love will have a prosperous termination, L.E.L. thus gracefully and leniently speaks concerning such youthful follies:

Oh, it is not for those whose feelings are cold,
Wither'd by care, or blunted by gold,
Whose brows have darken'd with many years,
To feel again youth's hopes and fears;
What they now might blush to confess,
Yet what made their spring-day's happiness.

Among the MSS. of the Royal Irish Academy are some tracts, which embody a good many recipes in furtherance of the fairy doctor's art. One of these is a herb preparation against the evil eye or fairy cast; another contains a remedy for cows overlooked or otherwise injured by necromantic agency; another nostrum is intended for a fairy stroke; while we find one for the recovery of a child, who has received a fairy touch or start during sleep. It would prove an endless task to enumerate all those prescriptions, which are administered by adepts in the use of simples, throughout the country parts of Ireland.

After Clontarf

Forget not our wounded companions who stood
    In the day of distress by our side,
While the moss of the valley grew red with their blood,
    They stirred not but conquered and died.
The sun that now blesses our arms with his light,
    Saw them fall upon Ossory's plain:
Oh! let him not blush, when he leaves us to-night,
    To find that they fell there in vain.

– Moore's *Irish Melodies*

AFTER THE CELEBRATED Battle of Clontarf, Donogh, son to Giallapatrick, King of Ossory, in conjunction with the men of Leix, formed an encampment on the plain known as Magh Chloinne Ceallaigh – probably around the present Cloney Castle, east of the Barrow River – to oppose the Dalcassian troops then returning victorious to Munster. The exact site of that encampment we have now no means for ascertaining. The plain in question is known to have been within the territory of the O'Kellys. Their district also bore the name of Magh Dructain, and it formed one of the dependencies of Leix.

The position of this armed force barred the passage of the Munster army on their homeward-bound march. Faint and wearied, the Dalcassians rested at Athy, where they washed their wounds in the River Barrow. Intimation of opposition to be encountered had been conveyed to Donough O'Brien, who commanded the Munster forces. A very short time before this event, and soon after the decisive Battle of Clontarf had been gained, dissentions had broken out among the surviving leaders of the Munstermen. The chiefs of Desmond, taking advantage of the broken state of the Dalcassians, who had lost great numbers in the late battle, put forward a claim to sovereignty in Munster.

Full of provincial jealousy and rivalry, the dissentient bands had separately marched from Dublin to Mullaghmast, about six miles to the eastward of Athy. Here a very remarkable fort had been erected on a rising ground, while it was enclosed with a high circular rampart, and surrounded by a deep ditch, as if intended for a place of defence and security from invaders. It affords a far-reaching field of vision over all the surrounding country; and even at present, it forms an attractive object, as hawthorns and other bushes have mantled over its sides, and they serve to shade the beautiful green sward within, to which access is attainable through an opening in the mound.

Evening had now approached, and the troops wearied with their march resolved on halting for the night. They lighted fires, on which were boiled or roasted the joints of beeves and sheep intended for their meals. However, the Desmondians selected a field for their tents apart from that occupied by the Dalcassians. They formed into hostile camps – Donough O'Brien as chief of the Dalcassians, and Cian the son of Molloy commanding the Desmondians. This latter chieftain sent messengers to Donough demanding hostages, and stating that as the people of Desmond had submitted to Brien Boroimhe and to his brother Mathgamhain, the turn of Munster sovereignty then justly reverted to Cian. But Donough replied that the Desmondians had submitted to his uncle and father by right of conquest, and not in recognition of any alternate right to the throne. Brien had bravely wrested Munster from Danish power, at a time when the chiefs of Desmond submitted to foreign domination and tyranny. He had also established his claim to the throne of Ireland, and owing to his prowess, had proclaimed himself as supreme Monarch.

Wherefore, refusing to give hostages, Donough declared his determination of defending with the sword his right to the title of his renowned father. This was regarded as a defiant answer to Cian, who resolved to lead his men forward, and attack the diminished ranks of the Dalcassians.

Preparations for battle were not neglected on the side of Donough O'Brien. He had ordered the sick and wounded to be placed within the fort of Mullaghmast for protection. But these heroic men refused the inglorious position assigned to them. Filling their wounds with moss, and snatching up arms, they insisted on taking their place among the ranks of warriors.

Clannishness, more than a sense of enlarged national sentiment, arrayed these combatants in battle line. But their determination caused the Desmondian troops to hesitate; especially as a subordinate chief, disappointed in his own petty scheme of ambition, refused co-operation in supporting the pretensions of Cian. The Desmondians, thus divided among themselves, again separated into distinct bodies, and then they marched homewards to their respective tribe lands.

The rumour of this dissention probably reached Donogh MacGiallapatrick, and he must have thought it a favourable opportunity to avenge a private feud and hereditary enmity. The warrior King of Munster had asserted his right to rule over Ossory, which he claimed as a dependency of his kingdom. This claim however was resisted by the dynast of Ossory, but he was unable to defend himself in an independent position by force of arms. As an enemy of Brien Boroimhe, this latter powerful monarch had kept the father of the Ossorian king in captivity for a whole year.

Having rested for some time, the men of Thomond under Donough O'Brien set out on their march, and crossing the Barrow, their most direct course lay through the plains of northern Ossory. The camp of Donogh MacGiallapatrick was broken up to intercept their homeward-bound course, and according to local tradition, he resolved to bar the Thomondian right of passage

113

near Gortnaclea on the banks of the River Nore, which there bounded the Ossorian territory on the western frontier of Leix. Having collected a large army under his immediate command, MacGiallapatrick then thought himself in a position to assume the offensive, and to assert his supremacy. Accordingly with great insolence, he sent ambassadors to demand hostages from Donough O'Brien, or, in other words, to claim the sovereignty of Munster. These proposals were indignantly rejected, and there the wounded Thomondians again insisted on being led to battle with their comrades. Stakes were driven into the ground, against which the scarred veterans were to lean for support during the time of action. The unwounded soldiers were expected not to abandon them with life, while in this exposed condition. Such determined heroism produced once more its moral effect, and the Ossorians became intimidated by this amazing valour of the Thomondian battalions. The men of Ossory and of Leix were withdrawn by their leader, and the Eugenians pursued their march. Yet, when all danger had passed over, one hundred and fifty of the war-worn veterans fainted away on that spot, and these soon expired. There likewise they were buried, with few exceptions; the bodies of some of the most distinguished warriors being borne to their native territories. Thus the remains of the chiefs were interred in the family burial-grounds of their ancestors.

The march of this valiant body of troops homewards seems to have been right through the level plains of Leix territory, and over the southern slopes of the Sliabh Bloom Mountains, by the old Ballaghmore road, which was the former chief highway between Ossory and Thomond.

4

Five Poems

Five Poems

The Land of Leix (excerpt)

Long curves the wall, inlaced with many a wreath
  Of matted ivy o'er the travelled road;
But higher still than canopy beneath
  Gigantic branches bear their verdant load
  Of fluttering leaves, in festoons thick and broad;
While hedge-rows opposite adorned with art
  Restrain the blatant flocks and herds that lowed
O'er fields from which displaced poor rustics part,
No more to gaze on scenes that brightened eye and heart.

Say, would you deem it just, ye lords of men,
  To doom your race for days of black despair,
To mar all happiness and peace within
  A generous soul and sensitive? Why sear
  The peasant's pale-worn cheek, with burning tear?
Why send him and his loved ones forth in pain
  To beg that pittance now, he once could share,
Ere yet an outcast, he did toilsome gain
His bread 'mid summer heats and winter's chilly rain?

Ah! call you this improvement? Sweep the thatch
  With moss and weeds begrimed from his roof-tree,
Wreck the rude cabin – if you will – but watch
  Man's still unaliened rights: men should be free
  From tyrant power, oppression's weight, and dree.
Should lords despoil the hedge-rows trim and twined
  Around the peasant's croft, where hummed the bee
From field to garden-flower, where cots woodbined
Once stood, and golden corn, the cultured furrows lined?

Clear from his bawn, ye lords, th'unsavoury ooze
  Engendering disease and speedy death;
Spread neatly gravelled walks within the mews
  And let poor inmates draw a purer breath;
  Nor love them less that keep their ancient Faith;

116

Fr John O'Hanlon, *c.* 1875

Refine their tastes; their ties to home increase;
   Root to the soil its tillers who had rathe
A natural title; nor should failing lease
Infringe the rule to live, nor joys of life efface.

How burned his soul indignant, when the strife
   Was raised by bigotry within that vale;
Its homeless ones upon the waves of life
   Were cast abroad to drift before the gale,
   Which surged around them: nor could aught avail
To save from ruin son and aged sire,
   Evicted maid and matron – sad the tale
Drawn from the patriot's memory to inspire
Deep sympathy for those – for outrage lasting ire.

To the memory of Fr Joseph M. Paquin

Ah! what is life, when all that makes life dear
    is found on earth, but momently to last;
and scarce our promised joys their blossoms bear,
    when spring is o'er, and all their sweetness past.
Oh! thus it was, my friend! thy virtues bloom'd
    their ripened fruits for us too early riven;
yet, in our hearts, thy memory be entombed,
    those virtues lost to earth were gained to Heaven.
To weep were not to love thee – tears are vain –
    man should not mourn when Angel choirs rejoice;
and heavenly joys reward thee for the pain
    by earth imparted to the noble choice,
that leaves without regret false pleasures here,
for those eternal ones, that gild a brighter sphere.

There is a balm in the air of old Ireland

There is a balm in the air of our Island,
    with incense the breath of each breeze
sweeps freshly o'er valley and highland
    through her green meadows, pastures, and trees.
What joy feels the exile returning
    to the land that hath haunted his dreams,
his full heart with love ever burning
    to meet with dear friends and old scenes.

When her shores looming high o'er the ocean
    first break on his sight from the wave
his soul swells with earnest emotion
    to find there a home and a grave.
Loved land of the saints and the sages,
    thy heroes of shadowy years
even yet live in History's pages,
    to lighten thy gloom and thy tears.

The sons of old Ireland, though lowly
    and long in the land of their love,
had bowed to a bondage unholy
    by tyrants and conquerors wove,
still soft when the tocsin of danger
    for country and liberty pealed,
right nobly avenged on the stranger
    those wrongs which his action revealed.

Yet, frail was their bond of alliance,
    as bootless their contest and might,
foul discord dissolved that reliance
    for freemen the safeguard of right.
But, trust in a God watching o'er us,
    and courage to fight for our home,
the present and future before us
    give promise of triumphs to come.

Like Erin's own crystalline waters
   revealing the pearls below,
are the eyes of her true-hearted daughters
   not fairer than purer they glow.
Health-hues mantling over each feature
   so beauteous and changeful and bright
proclaim the best moulding of nature
   hath mirrored their charms in light.

Their cheeks, freshly tinted and blooming
   with blush like the young rose's blow,
contrast with a whiteness assuming
   its virginal type from the snow.
Yet frail and to fade are all traces
   of sense; but, when pure is the mind
every feeling of soul moves and graces
   woman true to her kindred and kind.

Fair land, most beloved and endearing
   above every region or clime,
where friendships revived are so cheering
   and wake the lost joys of our prime.
Though we fail even here to recover
   many social delights of the past,
we can prize what remain, and discover
   affections still destined to last.

John Shearman of the Hill
Air. – The Lass of Richmond Hill

On Howth's brown Hill, from Winter's chill,
A curate's house is entered,
Oft in the year, guests find good cheer,
And social glee there centered.
The master's one folks look upon
Right fair through good or ill
And, free from pain, long may he reign,
John Shearman of the Hill.

He blesses boats, babes, praties, oats
Near each Fingalian arbour,
Then spring the blades, braw men and maids,
Red herrings fill the harbour:
He rubs old stones, turns dead men's bones,
Beside each cairn and rill;
He traces graves, and ogham caves,
John Shearman of the Hill.

He's fresh and fair, the mountain air
Doth freely breathe around him,
Ben Edair kist, by ocean mist,
Crags, cliffs and waves surround him;
But while he lives and sherry gives,
Our glasses we must fill,
Our joy and boast shall be to toast
John Shearman of the Hill.

On Death

Though fair those shadowy forms which meet our gaze,
    all living things must fade with lapse of years;
even inanimate nature through the maze
    of cycles gone and passing changed appears;
one uncreated Being sole survives
    the flight and wreck of time – His fixed decree
    calls man to share that immortality;
happy when freed from sin his term arrives,
no fear the grave presents, but bless'd repose:
    and in Thy presence, Lord, oh guide my ways
to serve and love Thee faithful to the close
    of life's uncertainties that end our days;
then let me humbly crave with parting breath
Thy mercies great to save, that solemn hour in Death.

5

'Home Ruler as I am'

'Home Ruler as I am'

The Land Question

A Letter

Dublin, SS. Michael and John,
Nov. 21st, 1879.

My Dear Mr. Gray — Like many of our Irish priests, owing to various important duties I cannot always take a very active part in Irish politics, yet you will credit me with never wanting earnestness in affording all the sympathy and aid in my power to the cause of Ireland and of freedom. For many reasons I should desire specially to be present at your meeting in the Rotunda; but it so happens that this day's parochial work, the Vincent de Paul's Society here at that exact hour, eight o'clock p.m, and our usual Friday evening's confessions afterwards, altogether preclude me from being present. The lately manifested desire and action of the Tory Government to suppress, under false pretences, the liberties of the subject, are only an abortive and a mock imitation of the old Algerine Acts, whereby attempts were vainly made to put down O'Connell's agitation for the redress of Irish grievances. I have studied with great interest late public proceedings, and I have read most of the leading speeches of the priests and lay gentlemen who have so ably and argumentatively shown the demerits and evils of our Irish land system; nor can I find a single reported sentence, which, fairly interpreted, could be deemed untrue, or more filled with exaggerations, than are incident to public speeches in general. I fail to see any fair reason for the arbitrary arrest of those patriotic gentlemen now incarcerated, and I must therefore assume them to be innocent until Government can prove their guilt. I suppose a Defence Fund to procure a fair trial will be a main object of this evening's proceedings, and you will kindly take charge of the enclosed £1 towards it. Home Ruler as I am, I hereby wish to declare my individual opinion that no Home Rule Conservative in the future should receive a single Irish vote, nor be allowed to misrepresent any Irish constituency at the coming elections. Since the evil days of William Pitt no Premier has acquired a less enviable niche in Irish and English history

John Canon O'Hanlon, *c.* 1900

than the present Earl of Beaconsfield. He has repressed English Constitutional rights and legitimate Irish aspirations, diverting the public funds from social, economic, and reproductive works to maintain wasteful, aggressive, and cruel wars, he being an irresponsible disturber of the public peace at home and abroad. How eagerly do I look to the future for a change in the principles and policy of Government. — I remain, my dear Mr. Gray, very faithfully yours,

John O'Hanlon

Notes on Land Tenure

WE READ OF A CHAIRMAN – the administrator of the land laws, who has to decide whether the tenants are entitled to compensation or not, with other questions of justice between landlord and tenant – recently addressing a grand jury. He alluded to the prevailing distress in 1879 and 1880, and he said it was a sort of claptrap, and a delusion. He gave, as an instance, the state of his own tenantry. He spoke of himself as a model landlord and of the great advantages his tenantry enjoyed under him. A Mr. Moran of the Limerick and Clare Farmers' Club took the trouble, in February 1880, of going through that gentleman's property and of enquiring into each case that came under his notice. He tabulated on the spot information he had reliably obtained. Mr Moran quoted a number of statistics to show, that the tenants on the property in question were charged for their small holdings rents about 250 per cent in excess of the government valuation of forty years previously. One tenant had a holding of 6 acres 2 roods 32 perches statute measure, the valuation being £6, and the yearly rent £13. Another tenant had a holding of 6 acres 0 roods 2 perches. The valuation was £1 15s, and the yearly rent £5. The hardest case of all was where a tenant had one acre. The valuation was only 5s, but the yearly rent was £4.

Twenty-three years before, the owner of that property was agent for it. He was then the kindest man alive, the tenants assured Mr Moran; but when he bought the property, his first act was to increase the rental 70 per cent. An increase of 25 per cent was put on the rents some time before the famine year of 1879; and yet not a single abatement would be made in favour of the distressed tenants. When applied to for an abatement the answer of the landlord and chairman of the County Court was a blank refusal.[1] When instances of a similar character might easily be multiplied, can we wonder at the general revolt that has lately taken place throughout Ireland against the payment of excessive rents?

****

We learn from a statement of Mr Denis Godley, secretary to the Commissioners of the Disestablished Protestant Church in Ireland, that far from repudiating their engagements, the new proprietors of the church lands, created by the operation of the Irish Church Act, to the beginning of 1880, had shown an honourable anxiety to pay their debts. Notwithstanding the severe pressure of previous years, the total sum receivable by the Commissioners in 1879 for land instalments and interest on mortgages was £132,800, while arrears due on the 31st of December that same year were only £450. Mr Denis Godley has certified the forgoing facts in a letter to the *Freeman's Journal*, and dated from the Office, 24 Upper Merrion St. Dublin, January 28th 1880, in his capacity of Secretary. The same gentleman adds, regarding the parishes of Forkhill and Faughart, in the diocese of Armagh, there were then some owners of small plots of land who owed the Commissioners, not instalments of purchase-money nor interest on purchase-money, but 'tithe rent charge' due out of their lands. These tithe rent-charges had proved difficult of recovery, because the land owners declared that they were not liable for them. But these cases had not the least connection with that of peasant proprietors refusing to fulfil their obligations to pay for the land. Such facts are worth a thousand assertions to the contrary, that Irish peasants should want

---

[1] Statement of Mr James Moran of Rathkeale on Saturday March 6th 1880, reported in the *Freeman's Journal* of Monday, March 8th 1880.

the will or the ability to purchase lands, provided reasonable facilities for borrowing money on property mortgages were afforded them by Government.

In 1880, an Irish land committee was formed, chiefly through the instigation of the Conservative Irish Landocracy to prepare a series of Tracts, which have served, for the most part, to misrepresent the past and present conditions of landholding in Ireland. Their office was established at No 31 South Frederick Street, Dublin. Thence emanated a series of anonymous pamphlets in ready succession, and efforts were made to procure for them an extensive circulation. Among these publications may be named 'Notes upon the Government Valuation of Land in Ireland', 'Facts and Figures', 'French opinion on the Irish Crisis', 'Lord Dufferin on the Three Fs', 'Mr Gladstone on the Three Fs'. These were published at sixpence each, and issued by London and Dublin publishing firms.[2]

****

On its third reading in the House of Commons, on the evening of July 29th 1881, Lord Elcho, a bitter opponent of Mr Gladstone and of his ministry, tauntingly declared, 'It could not be denied that if there had been no Land League, the bill would never have been brought in'. If he spoke the truth, this is praise sufficient for the great Irish organisation, and coming likewise from a source sufficiently hostile. The Duke of Marlborough repeated such a statement, in the House of Lords (speech on the night of August 2nd 1881) on the second reading of this Bill, which he pronounced to be the result of that agitation promoted by the Land League.

---

[2]London. William Ridgway, 169 Picadilly. Dubliin Hodges, Figgis & Co. 104 Grafton Street. And other Booksellers.

Home Rule

THE VASTLY GREATER majority of the Irish people – while among these are particularly included Protestants and even Orangemen – were united in opposition to the extinction of their native parliament. However, when they attempted to give public and constitutional expression to their protests, meetings were almost everywhere suppressed by the arbitrary government of the time. Terrorism and deception were alternately and simultaneously employed to silence opposition or remonstrance from without. Corruption and seduction were shamelessly tried within the Houses of Lords and Commons, already filled with placemen, pensioners, and traders in the sale of boroughs. After some adjustments in the British and Irish Parliaments, the Act of a Legislative Union and its articles of a treaty were proclaimed to the Irish nation, on the 1st day of January, 1801.

Robbed of their rights, which the people had neither the will nor the power to surrender, never from that time to the present have the Irish ratified or acquiesced in the measure for an incorporating union. On the contrary, their protests, complaints, and agitations are on record, every year since the commencement of this century, and daily are they growing in intensity and impatience. They well understand, that the Act of Union has not conferred a single direct benefit, while it has inflicted innumerable evils, upon Ireland. Nor has subsequent beneficial legislation been a consequence; while it has even weakened the power and resources of England, by yearly decreasing the prosperity of our impoverished country. It has driven millions of the Irish race into distant countries, to gain that subsistence abroad which has been denied them at home, and with bitter memories of the national injury perpetrated, to be imparted likewise as an inheritance to their posterity. Public opinion, which is only another expression for the public conscience, imperatively demands a restitution in full measure for the gross injustice perpetrated, and the rights which have been subjected to such shameful violation. The power to frame constitutions and laws for their own just government is inherent in all distinct nationalities, and required for all civilized people; while to that consideration, the mind of every enlightened person in the empire – and especially in Ireland – is now directed, with a view to provide the remedy, and to reconstruct on a surer basis the framework of a national government, securing by ample guarantees the equal rights and liberties of each individual under its jurisdiction, without distinction of class, of party, or of creed.

To repair the evils of past legislation, and to construct a system of government for the future, in harmony with the wants and aspirations of an enlightened people, are now the problems to be solved. In the prosecution of such efforts, while other nations may regard our progress with interest and concern, yet on the inhabitants of these Islands devolves the special obligation of exercising thoughtful deliberation, just and prudent discretion, as also practical and rational action.

It is certain, we cannot in Ireland return to the reconstruction of Grattan's Parliament, so largely composed of political patrons, borough-mongers, placemen, and pensioners, not to speak of nominee and exclusively sectarian members. Without any guarantee for the preservation of independence, it contained the elements of dissolution in its unreformed state. Without an enlarged constituency thoroughly representative of all classes, interests, and creeds, that was a Parliament from which Catholics, composing the vast majority of the Irish people, were altogether excluded; and which the other larger section of Protestants, the Dissenters, were not permitted to enter, without taking an oath for subscribing to the Sacramental Test, repugnant alike to their feelings and principles. The governmental system of that time fostered venality and subserviency, as also personal and family ambition, to the subversion of public or national aspirations and interests.

Popular representation has since become more of a reality, and parliamentary reform has greatly quieted – if not wholly dissolved – the spirit of disaffection and distrust, among those persons and classes in Ireland, who formerly despaired of redress for admitted evils and through constitutional methods. It is quite true to state, that Mr. Gladstone's introduction of the Home Rule Bill for Ireland, and the assent to its principle by the vast majority of the British people, effected almost immediately the conversion of some millions of the Irish people and of the Irish race to the opinion, that all their dearest wishes might yet be gratified through moral force without resort to rebellion, or without the expectation, that a rupture of England with some great power might not furnish occasion to welcome the arrival of an invading army on our shores, to excite cooperation in the work of achieving a separate national independence.

It seems altogether unnecessary in this connection to consider the condition of Australia, of the Indian possessions, of Canada, or of South Africa – countries that cannot practically have federative Legislatures and general representation in any European coalition for the enactment of particular or general laws. They are far too widely separated in location and in extent, to have ought but a confederacy of independent States, for convenient intercommunication, and if need requires, these may be aggregated in a common alliance. Indeed the initiative has been already taken for such purposes in Canada and Australia. Moreover, it cannot escape the anticipation of any sagacious statesman or politician, that the time is fast approaching, with a growing and free population, when those countries shall no longer be bound to the mother country in any condition of dependence; for, it must soon be very generally admitted, that they have within themselves all the necessary resources and requirements to create a separate national existence. Even as we learn from several of the best informed among those colonists, such a feeling not only prevails, but it is very generally expressed; nor in the nature of things can there be a valid reason for refusing its gratification, under certain wise conditions and regulations. Only universal benefits and economy can result from the severance of bonds, no longer found to be necessary; while a graceful and an early concession of perfect freedom, to work out their manifest destiny and to exercise their unfettered action, must prove most acceptable to those independent communities, already so far advanced in civilization and intelligence. That friendly and commercial relations be maintained, on a principle of reciprocity between the parent country and her former colonial dependencies, is the most that could be desirable or politic. The British government should thus be released from the very probable complications and difficulties, which foreign, hostile, or colonial protective policy may render very acute, at some future period; while the past historic experiences of European nations and their distant colonies teach us, that the latter, when progressive in wealth and population, must largely drain the resources and energies of the parent countries, and divert their inhabitants, with their enterprise and talents, to new fields for industry and prosperity. The case of Spain – three centuries ago the most powerful of European kingdoms – is a notorious example of the injuries and losses she has undergone, owing to her migratory adventurers, her distant colonization and administrative misgovernment in North and South America.

The present extent of England's possessions, as shown on the map of the world, and their exposure to the ambition and cupidity of other great powers in dangerous proximity with them, are reasons for averting probable future embarrassment and certain loss. Were all peace and contentment within her insular borders, Great Britain should exchange her present real weakness for a condition of moral and material strength she has never yet securely possessed. For many centuries, she was disrupted by rebellions and civil wars; treasons and factions were rife; intolerance and persecution, civil and religious, were fostered; regal and governmental despotism was dominant; and popular representation was proscribed. That this Empire has been preserved, notwithstanding a fortunate escape through many dangerous combinations and wars, is owing partly to her insulated position, her wealth and alliances, and partly to those favourable circumstances, which so fortuitously occurred, at the various junctures in her past history, and which saved her shores from the tramp of invading armies. These results have scarcely been obtained, however, through any superior efforts of statesmanship. Her naval supremacy at sea has hitherto mainly preserved her distant possessions, during the vicissitudes of past great wars; the loss of her American colonies – now known as the United States – being the only notable exception. Yet, the independence of the United States has since proved to be a great commercial gain, as securing the best customers and markets in the world for England: their direct imports from the United Kingdom amounting to £43,878,934, in 1889; while all the Colonies of England united have scarcely dealt directly with the mother country to that amount. Moreover, the United States have exported in values £95,461,475 direct to England, that very same year; nearly twice as much marketable supplies as all her united colonies of the world have exported to the United Kingdoms of Great Britain and Ireland. The latest trade returns most probably shall establish the evidence of a nearly similar relative scale, notwithstanding existing national jealousies and commercial rivalries, with the operation of artificial and ill-adjusted tariffs that still obstruct the natural laws of commerce.

Disembarrassed in foreign relations, for the people of these Islands the strain on home taxes, official, military, and naval armaments should be greatly lightened; the home defences for an insulated confederacy of united and yet independent nations, with a regular army as a nucleus, and with a militia and volunteer force as a reserve on land, could less expensively and yet more efficiently be provided. An adequate naval equipment and a serviceable marine might be maintained, so that no hostile power could hope to invade these shores, in case of an aggressive or a defensive war. Friendly diplomatic and commercial intercourse established with the present colonies – raised to the character of independent states – should most certainly increase their rapid growth and wealth, as also with many direct and indirect advantages to the mother country: moreover, the manufacturing and trade capabilities and products in our home federation of

135

free and united nations should receive still greater extension, with a continuous and progressive development, proportionately as the distant colonies advanced in population and resources; while demand for our native goods should be unceasing, and additional market necessaries and even luxuries for life should be furnished, so that under such conditions, reciprocal benefits must undoubtedly ensue in the exchange of commodities between the parent country and her emancipated colonies.

The vastly increased and constantly growing business affairs of the British Empire, at home and abroad, have long since over-strained the powers of a centralised Parliament to manage with any degree of effective or beneficial legislation. A division of labour, for this public assembly as in every other flourishing private concern, is requisite, in order to secure a saving of time, an exercise of intelligence, perfect organization, method, attention, supervision, and despatch. Nor can general managerial administration be suitably directed to minute details, only practicable for divisional examination and execution. What must we think about the wisdom of a great railway company's directors, who should try to carry on its concerns, in complete ignorance of local requirements, and without having sufficient time to consider their successful bearings or results, with a view towards procuring the satisfaction of patrons or shareholders? What, if the public travelling or traffic should be restricted by an insufficient number of carriages suited to every class and condition, or of goods-wagons wholly inadequate for purposes of increased and increasing traffic, or of vans for the deliveries of parcels and merchandise to the consignees? What, if their stores were too small or choked with goods, which must remain locked up, although a demand be urgent for distribution to the individuals or companies, who have a right to their possession? Yet, in the Imperial Parliament while the most urgent and comprehensive law reforms, and problems of the highest social importance, have still to receive matured consideration and solution from the most enlightened representative men; matters and questions of a minute and subordinate character, which could easily and safely be dealt with in a national legislative assembly, or even in a local municipal council, are allowed to intrude, and often to afford an excuse for neglecting those concerns of greatest import. However absurd the mercantile mismanagement already alluded to may be considered, by every intelligent person; nevertheless, it must be regarded as but slightly irrational and distracting, when compared with the general concerns of a whole Empire, sacrificed to sectional or party differences and in a state of legislative confusion, owing to the fact that we are still obliged to follow precedents and systems that should be regarded as obsolete, or forms and practices only suited for olden-time progression, and totally behind the necessities of advanced order, civilization, and reform. We trust that no political party at the present day shall regard true conservative life as synonymous with the retention or fostering of any – even the least – admitted abuses.

It may be argued that under the past and existing forms of government, the wealth, commerce and manufacturing industries of the Empire have increased, are increasing, and still likely to increase. This is notoriously false, so far as Ireland exceptionally treated is concerned; and as relates to the other three nations, associated and individual enterprise in them has mainly overcome many of the legislative restrictions to which industry and production have been subjected. Ameliorative and imperial legislation has only been a slight factor in achieving such good results; and it may be safely asserted, in a general way, that the energy, industry, and comparative comforts of the people have not hitherto been procured through legal enactments or governmental patronage, but mainly through natural causes, in despite of restricting laws and feudal obstructions, as little beneficial to the privileged few as to the vast majority of the industrial population. Nor can such evils be wholly removed, until intelligently and fairly dealt with by responsible representatives, in a national legislative assembly, bound to consult impartially for the welfare of all their constituents.

Difficulties in the creation of a new and an improved order of things ought never deter a freedom-loving people from attempting their solution, nor oblige them to adhere unwisely to traditional usages, which only tend to obstruct their material prosperity and social comforts. With the ignorant and unenlightened alone are bad precedents and unworkable institutions a fallacious superstition and a blind guide for the future growth and government of this Empire. While thus intellectually enslaved and politically weak, Great Britain and Ireland cannot be socially or morally respected by the other prosperous, powerful, and civilized nations of the world. Too long have those realms submitted to the rule and influence of oligarchical classes, who have restrained royal prerogatives only in their own particular interests; the just aspirations, wants, and rights of the people remaining unheeded, postponed, and unredressed.

Excluding a consideration of distant colonial possessions, the British Empire consists of four very distinctive home nationalities: viz., those of England herself, of Ireland, of Scotland, and of Wales. For each of these nations, there is a separate and a varied history, a diversity of creeds, of language, of laws, and of institutions, a peculiarity of social feeling, of manners, and of customs; geographically distinct, yet are they closely bound together by trade and commercial relations, by ties of mutual sympathy and interest, as also very generally by family and friendly intercourse. Domestic legislation and national representation – for all purposes not extending beyond their limits and jurisdiction – should procure for each country the exact selection of members, and the appointment of officials who could most exercise an intelligent discretion to develop their material resources and to harmonise their religious, political and social interests, in accordance with a just and sound public opinion.

Whether the federation between England or Ireland be duplex, or whether, as seems most probable ultimately, it shall be a multiple confederation between the four distinct nationalities of which Great Britain is composed – not to particularise the Isle of Man,

Guernsey, and Jersey now so prosperous under their own laws and modes of self-government – a general and free constitution should be framed, which must be sovereign and comprehensive in its provisions, prerogatives, and powers. It ought even take into account, the probability of Scotland and Wales very generally demanding a separate national life in this confederacy of States; for the desire is not only natural, but the movement in such a direction is already popular and evidently progressing.

Supreme dominion and sovereignty over the subordinate National governments, should vest in an Imperial government and legislature; but only for matters of international and higher policy, such as the making of treaties or alliances with foreign powers; the declaration of war or of peace; the general regulations of customs, of excise, of tariffs, of commerce, of trade, and of navigation. The army, navy, postal service, the supreme courts of justice, and great public establishments, civil and official, should be under their control, with the power of taxing and the right of voting money from the Imperial revenues still vested in the popularly represented branch of the Imperial Parliament, as also the power of issuing loans for state or local purposes of great public necessity or advantage, on approved securities and at remunerative rates of interest. Such powers presuppose national representatives when constituting the supreme legislature and administration, and in regulated proportion; for, the great English philosopher John Locke was the first to propound the doctrine that taxation without representation should be unjust and unconstitutional; while his most intimate friend, the celebrated Irish jurist and member of Parliament, William Molyneux, held that English parliamentary laws had no force binding in reason over Irish subjects, unless voluntary assent were given to them by Irish representatives. These constitutional maxims and principles were brought by the emigrating and evicted Ulster Presbyterians into the American Colonies; and when the government in England sought to tax them against the will of their people, the cry became universal that 'taxation without representation was tyrannical and a grievance'. It soon led to armed resistance, and ultimately to the Declaration of Independence. Afterwards, the Irish Parliament obtained concessions of freedom, but without sufficient guarantees for its maintenance. Notwithstanding its imperfect composition, however, Ireland materially prospered under its influence and management; while we have much reason since for regret that too soon it had been shamefully sacrificed and abolished, to gratify the reckless policy of an unscrupulous Prime Minister, who plunged the Empire into unnecessary wars, and who created an enormous public debt, to subsidise foreign mercenaries, and to fail in all his European coalitions, leaving England in a state of great alarm and peril at the moment of his death.

Relations existing between the Imperial government and the several National governments should be expressly defined by a written – not a vague traditional or interpretative – constitution, so that all future danger of conflict or misunderstanding may be removed. The hitherto unwritten constitutional principles or maxims – supposed to have regulated parliamentary proceedings – were never clearly apprehended, and they are always liable to be misapplied and misinterpreted. Hence, it should be most necessary, clearly to expound, resolve and extend the Imperial Constitution in relation to all questions of supreme importance. This general Constitution when justly framed should be universally accepted and enforced; while the subordinate Constitutions, also defined in written articles, sections, or clauses, should be guarantees for and in conformity with all national rights, while not conflicting with the supreme jurisdiction.

In such a possible federation, the Crown ought naturally represent the bond of unity; while a Lord Lieutenant, Chief Governor or Commissioner should be appointed with delegated authority and constitutionally limited to act as vicegerent, in each of the capital cities of Ireland, Scotland, and Wales, and to exercise the royal prerogatives, but only within the respective national jurisdiction, for which he had been selected. The Imperial Legislature and government should solely have the right to regulate questions regarding privilege, succession, regency, the royal household, and its suitable maintenance; while to the Lower House, as in the past, must be reserved the imposition of taxes and the grants of money for all items affecting the royal establishments, as for other chief departments relating to the public service. In the great work of re-construction, hereditary legislators should be eliminated from the House of Peers, and elective ones substituted; the spirit of feudalism having introduced and too long continued an irrational institution, quite out of harmony with the enlightenment of our age.

The several National governments should be very perfect in organization and practically unrestricted at least in the legal exercise of a domestic and limited power, to frame or execute all merely national, local and municipal laws or regulations; to organize and control a police system and force, for the due preservation of order and the detection of crime; to grant charters or patents; to levy national taxes or sanction divisional rates, and through representative agents to direct their most economical and efficient disbursement; to erect and regulate courts of justice; to nominate qualified judges or magistrates for the trial of criminal or civil cases, at the superior or inferior tribunals, and within their proper jurisdictions. To establish corporations and trusts, boards and commissions; to design and supervise public works; to promote education; to foster arts and manufactures, trade and commerce; to extend and encourage navigation and ship-building; to develop and increase our fisheries; to construct harbours or improve those already formed: these are some only of the many functions which should devolve on a home legislature and on a responsible administration. A cabinet, with heads of departments duly constituted, must direct the affairs of state, and subject to the ordinary control of parliamentary representatives, the natural guardians of a people's liberties.

While the Imperial government directs and controls the regular and militia forces, Ireland should have her volunteer companies on the footing which prevails in the sister countries, and those citizen soldiers would not be exceptional in loyalty or heroism, if the country needed their active services. The Irish Volunteers of the past century were a formidable force to powerful nations then hostile to England; while they were both firm and moderate in their Declaration of Rights and in their demand for Free Trade. Having secured a better and freer constitution than could then be obtained, the volunteers would be more capable of safe-guarding it, and the moral effect of such an institution must serve to remove mistrust from the minds of fellow-citizens for the permanence of their newly-born liberties, and assure the Empire of an additional element of strength, so long as the federal compact should be irrevocably preserved. The very nature and component elements of embodied and well equipped volunteers in a free country imply patriotism and public spirit, combined with a love of law and order of which they become guardians; while generally recruited from the most intelligent citizens, townsmen, and land-holders, they are conservative of rights and property, in a measure unknown to the soldiers of a regular army.

The several states, having each a distinctive constitutional existence, should jealously protect their own liberties, and prevent any infringement of rights guaranteed to any one of those in the confederated union. Their respective progression should only become a motive for mutual congratulation as tending to the general welfare; while a friendly rivalry in the pursuit of national and individual prosperity could only develop additional energies and resources for the whole Empire. The articles of federation might easily be framed, so that nothing unnecessary or incompatible with national or individual freedom be permitted in the Imperial legislative or governmental powers.

While laying down the fundamental principles on which subordinate legislation must proceed, it ought to prove no difficult task, by a general constitutional and permanent enactment, fully to guarantee and respect the interests and feelings of all classes, parties, and creeds. To promote the happiness and enjoyment of all citizens, without special favours or privileges to individuals or sects, cannot justly offend any reasonable person; while equal rights, and their most ample and assured exercise, are alone worthy the acceptance and maintenance of a free people. Powers of legislation and of administration not reserved to the Imperial government should be allowed respectively for the separate National governments to exercise, within the sphere of their prescribed jurisdiction.

The intricacies of British law are so varied, and oftentimes conflicting, that a council of able jurists might possibly be required to abrogate, amend or adjust several articles or provisions of the statutes while drafting the Imperial and National Constitutions, before these could be finally submitted for legislative consideration, discussion and adoption. However, such proceedings need not greatly delay legislation, nor the preliminary drafting of provisions for a settlement, subject to future amendment or determination, like treaties between the higher powers, often accepted as final in meaning and terms, although not even formally ratified. But, mainly must it rest for the most enlightened and intellectual of statesmen and legislators to reflect on the rescinding or subordination of powers still existing, and to resolve on those enactments that are most useful and calculated to give general satisfaction.

As the best devised schemes for the establishment of human institutions must leave room for improvement, so imperial and national constitutions should be sufficiently provisional and elastic to admit of amendments and alterations, which neither impair their essential stability nor affect the general principles of justice and right on which they are founded. Changes of time, matured experience, and unforeseen circumstances in the life of nations, require powers for administrative amendment, with the concurrence of representatives reflecting just public opinion, and constituting at least two-thirds in the separate Houses of the imperial Parliament, and equally so of the national subordinate Legislature. Such accepted alterations should not

ᴄíʀ ᴀᴡus ᴄeᴀnᴡᴀ.

Branch for Sandymount

A Meeting will be held in the School-house Sandymount on Thursday, **29th November**, to inaugurate a Local Branch of the Gaelic League. The chair will be taken at 8 p.m., by Very Rev. Canon O'Hanlon, P.P.

Many Prominent Gaelic Leaguers will Address the Meeting, and Irish Music and Songs will be rendered.

All Interested are Cordially Invited.

O'Brien & Ards, Printers, 62 Great Britain Street, Dublin.

trench respectively on the legitimate independence and authority of either administration, but be regarded as a compact for mutual advantage and fair reciprocity.

Whether the Legislative Assembly of Ireland assumes the constitution or form of a Parliament, consisting of a distinct Upper and Lower House – as seems most conformable to past Anglo-Irish historical precedent; or whether it be a sort of Convention formed of one chamber, but with distinctive class divisions – as appears more nearly resembling the original native Irish system for deliberation and resolution; it is generally conceded that the number of national representatives for home legislation ought to be more numerous than at present, while their electoral districts in a corresponding ratio ought to be multiplied. The establishment of Home Rule in Ireland, on the basis of equal rights for all creeds and classes, could not fail to allay the sectarian strife and political rancour that have hitherto so poisoned social intercourse. The multiplication of landed proprietors must tend greatly to remove the present unsatisfactory relations between landlords and tenants, while securing the residence of a large number deeply interested in the peace and welfare of the whole community. The desire to effect needed reforms and general interests must nearly altogether supersede polemic or factious differences, as also chiefly engage the attention and concern of all. Indeed, it should soon be found that great divergencies of thought and of action must subside into a rivalry among all parties, to promote the agricultural, manufacturing, mining and commercial resources and interests of this country. The very best, the most public-spirited, the most intelligent, and the most capable of her sons, should most probably be sought for, irrespective of creed, party or class, to serve as representatives or to fill governmental and official positions. Moreover, in an Island largely composed of landed proprietors and of wealthy or prosperous traders, the conservative element must always be required to influence – if not sometimes to control – the legislative or the administrative power, should either tend in any dangerous socialistic or doubtful direction.

We believe, that unless our country were to have a dual representation, in the Imperial and National Parliaments, her acquired home rights and privileges could not be sufficiently protected from distinctive or divergent legal and administrative encroachments, or from mistaken policy, arising from a want of common understanding. Besides, conflicts of jurisdiction might arise, and in many different ways, which could be avoided by friendly conference and mutual explanations. As we have already seen, Anglo-Irish commissioners – regarded in the light of Anglo-Irish representatives – had been summoned in former reigns, to guide or take part in the deliberations and decisions of an English Parliament; while those representatives were persons charged with consulting and administrative powers, in the distinct kingdom of Ireland. To that assembly, they brought the weight of a governmental experience, with a knowledge of general and local requirements, which served to inform and direct the action of the king, of his council, of his lords spiritual and temporal, and of his commons, at the chief centre of dominion. The reasonable regulation of paying Irish representatives for their parliamentary attendance and services was one well considered and very necessary in former times; while, it must always be just to remunerate public servants for their public services. In the case of parliamentary deputies, it is more especially necessary to secure their private interests and personal independence, while in return they give their time and abilities to the promotion of the most important and useful measures. In any case, the relative proportion of Irish representatives in the Imperial parliament, as compared with those of England, Scotland, and Wales, should be maintained, to give adequate expression and weight in deliberations, debate, and resolutions on the wider questions of public policy. Those representatives must be required to maintain friendly co-operation and the balance of power between the Imperial and the Home Governments and Legislatures; to prevent possible misunderstandings or collisions on questions of international law and of constitutional rights; to voice the varied feelings, wishes, and requirements of the national sentiment; and above all, to become the steadfast and zealous guardians of the honour, interests, and welfare of the whole Empire and of each Nation composing its constituent parts.

It may well be supposed, that time, place, and order of proceeding can readily be found for the diverse but harmonious action of the Imperial and National Representatives, without inconveniently encroaching on their ordinary occupations and duties, or without exposing them to over laborious attendances; except perhaps, on occasions of great particular or general emergency. For some years to come, a strain – successively diminishing – might be required on their physical exertions and mental faculties; but, the separation of powers and the divisional working of the distinct Assemblies should necessarily supply a remedy, at no very distant time, for the admitted arrears of legislation, in regard to repeal, to reform, and to creative expedients. Moreover, those departmental functions – vigorously and steadily prosecuted from the commencement – should soon tend to diminish the labours of future sessions.

There are two distinct ways imaginable in the plan of appointing Representatives for the Imperial and National assemblies. One might be to have separate members, with regulated numbers, qualifications, constituencies, and powers, for the respective Legislative Bodies – such a system dividing and diminishing very considerably the labours and responsibilities of individual members composing each class, while giving ample time and opportunity for the conducting of imperial and national business. Another and perhaps the better mode might be to leave the separate National Representatives the power of selecting by ballot from among the members of their respective Houses, that required numerical delegation, who should constitute the Imperial Representatives – such a system must be attended with the advantages and economy, of avoiding intrigue and invidious preferences in the selection; of dispelling personal pretensions and selfish ambition; of dispensing with separate national electoral divisions or elections for two different sets of members; of acquiring the very best talent and influence likely to be secured by secret voting; and of having able and experienced men trained to habits of public business selected from their domestic Legislature, to mould and shape national opinion and sentiment with less clashing of general interests in the settlement of great public questions and policy.

It might be well, in the supposition of such constructive form of dualistic legislation being approved, that different seasons be set apart for the assembling of members, or that alternate times, such as apportioned weeks or months, be devoted to their diverse delegated tasks; while the intervening interruptions should have no effect on progressive business in either Legislature, nor in any of its branches composing the national or imperial Assembly. But, still better might it be, to have the distinct legislative bodies simultaneously in session, and within a given time for opening, proroguing, or dissolving. Even this latter plan could seldom create great practical inconvenience. Those individuals charged with a duplex power of representation, especially when they are delegated or left free to select their sphere of duty and of action, could easily arrange their own order of procedure for the despatch of public business. The presence or absence of a section in either Assembly could hardly be of great importance, in the ordinary current of particular or general law-making; but, whenever questions of state policy or of national interest fluctuated in prominence and importance, public attention must in turn be chiefly directed to the point of attraction and concern that most engages the immediate and prospective welfare of the people. As in all other confederated states, under a general government, the vicissitudes of the time, the local occasion, and the relative importance of matters under deliberation, are sure to direct intelligent popular regards towards the measures and men most deserving of momentary and rational consideration, in the management or settlement of public affairs.

While it might be highly impolitic for any responsible states-man or for any political party, favourable to the general principles of Home Rule, prematurely to produce a detailed statement of plans and procedure, intended for final acceptance by the people of these Islands; there can be no sufficient reasons alleged for withholding communications and theories, honestly conceived and advanced by writers and publicists, with a view to examine or resolve those courses and means, best calculated in their opinion to procure the just promotion and direction of the movement towards its inevitable consummation. No species of petty intrigue or factious combination should be allowed even a chance for designing or directing libellous attacks on the parliamentary members or ministers, charged with the duty and desire to forward a grand scheme for the general welfare of the whole community. Misrepresentation of motives and opposition to reforms are unfortunately familiarised to our experiences, under the working of free and liberal institutions, as under the most absolute and despotic forms of government. So long as private interests, passions and prejudices prevail among leading politicians, the people must be vigilant and careful to guard against those influences, which are the vices of our nature, and which tend so much to effect confusion in their councils and disorganisation in their ranks. Meantime, let their trusted leaders, like able and skilful generals, guard their well-matured and really valuable secrets of plan and of action, from the dangerous cognizance and malevolent designs of an enemy, until the proper moment arrives for a development and force that should secure the rewards of their prudence and patriotism.

On such a comprehensive subject, and one so intricate, when considered in all its bearings, it is not possible to develop in a few paragraphs a train of thought or an array of arguments at all adequate to satisfy the inquiring minds of statesmen and philosophers; but, as the question of Home Rule for Ireland has advanced beyond the stage of debatable politics to that of constructive effort, so has the editor of the succeeding Essay deemed it expedient to offer a few individual reflections and suggestions, which may possibly arrest the attention and study of some, who have devoted more time and understanding to a matter so fraught with such expectancy and importance for all our fellow-countrymen. Being now happily ripe for solution, and yet a question for speculative and theoretical adjustment; it must be desirable to elicit enlightened opinion and reasoning on the principles and practices, which may best serve to build up with solidity in all its constituent parts the fortunes and prosperity of a great Empire. In such a union of affections and of interests, Ireland should have free scope to work out her own and the general welfare; while these desirable objects being secured, to the intelligence, union, energy, and industry of her sons must be due the revival of national prosperity, with the firm preservation of her rights and freedom, throughout all future ages.

6

Star of the Sea

St Mary's Church, Star of the Sea

D URING MANY GENERATIONS, the primitive little Chapel of Irishtown served the inhabitants of the neighbourhood, for the celebration of divine service, and as a place for worship. There are numbers of persons yet living, who recollect how circumscribed were its limits, and how miserably inadequate were its appointments, to satisfy the wishes of those, who were obliged to frequent this small and poor building for devotional purposes.

For a long term of years, the Very Rev. Charles Finn exercised his pastoral charge over a large district confided to his care, and he was greatly beloved and respected, especially by his parishioners, who were most in communication with him. In the very beginning of this century, and when he was parish priest of Irishtown, Father Finn officiated on [the] occasion of the marriage of Ireland's illustrious Liberator, Daniel O'Connell, with a distant cousin, Miss Mary O'Connell, of Tralee. The date is fixed as June 23rd, 1802, in John O'Connell's Life and Speeches of his father. This circumstance, but still more, the well-known fidelity of Father Finn to every duty of religion and of patriotism, greatly attached O'Connell to the worthy pastor. His influence, moreover, was deservedly great among the people, while he is yet remembered with reverence, by all the older parishioners, who were his contemporaries. During his ministry, Father Finn erected St. Mary's Church, Haddington Road, to accommodate the Catholic parishioners residing in that part of the parish, and who were daily becoming more numerous as the city proper began to grow in that direction. Still, he continued to reside in an humble cottage, near the old Chapel of Irishtown. Full of years and of virtues, the Very Rev. Charles Finn departed this life on the 28th of June, 1849, and his successor in the ministry was shortly afterwards appointed. From the Church of St. Michael and St. John, Dublin, the Very Rev. Andrew O'Connell, P.P., was translated to the parish then vacant.

It was long felt, that the growing Catholic population of the district required more ample accommodation than their house for

John Canon O'Hanlon (*Poetical works of Lageniensis*, frontispiece)

worship could afford. The old Chapel of Irishtown, however vener-able to the people, claimed no architectural pretensions whatever, while it was hidden almost among a group of small and half-ruinous dwellings, during the greater part of its continuance. The situation of that Chapel is now marked by the block of handsome brick buildings, lately erected by Mr. Daniel Mearns, and facing Bath Street at one of its frontages, and having Pembroke Street at the other. It was built within a square plot of ground, enclosed by a low wall.

****

Almost immediately after the accession of the Very Rev. Andrew O'Connell to the pastorship of this large and populous district, sensible of the lamentable insufficiency of church accommodation for his parishoners in the district of Irishtown, Ringsend, and Sandymount, with characteristic promptitude, and seconded by the good wishes and aid of all classes, that zealous and estimable priest resolved on providing a more suitable place of worship. Accordingly application was made to the landlord, the Right Honorable Sydney Herbert, for a larger and more eligible site. With generous liberality, this application was most favourably received, and as further improvements were projected on the property, a new road being struck out towards the strand, and deviating from the main road between Dublin and Sandymount, the present site, on which the Star of the Sea Church stands, was selected as most suitable, and it was accordingly allocated for the erection of a handsome new church. At this period it was part of a field under cultivation, and within that townland, on which Irishtown is built.

****

The design for the new church was furnished by Mr. James J. MacCarthy, architect. A chaste and severe style of mediaeval Gothic architecture characterised the structure; while the interior

154

St Mary's Church, Star of the Sea, 1884 (*Irish Builder* 26 (1884) 37)

presented an effective, a harmonious, and a truly grand appearance. The material specially used was Dublin granite, and laid on a foundation of Dublin calp limestone, having a bed of concrete beneath it.

The old lease for Irishtown Chapel was in due course surrendered, and a map of the site then granted was prepared, on which the necessary measurements were defined. Besides its convenient site, the spot is picturesque, overlooking the wide expanse of Dublin Bay, and lying immediately on the shore, thus rendering most appropriate the present title and former dedication of the sacred structure.

The Right Honourable Sydney Herbert granted a new term for 150 years, and at the rent of £10 a-year, which was regarded as merely nominal. This lease bears date the 5th day of April, 1852, and the tenure commenced from the 25th day of March previous, for that plot of ground set apart for the erection of a church, presbytery, and schools.

The first stone of St. Mary's Church, Star of the Sea, was laid with great solemnity on Wednesday the 7th of May, 1851, by the

Most Rev. Daniel Murray, Archbishop of Dublin, and in presence of a large concourse, including bishops, priests, and many of the most influential citizens of Dublin, as from other parts of Ireland. All the requirements of the ritual were duly complied with, while the usual psalms, litany, and prayers were sung or recited by the choir of clergy, in a most impressive manner. The stone itself bore the sign of the cross deeply cut on each of the surfaces, and on the upper side was hollowed out a space for the reception of the gold, silver, and copper coinage of Queen Victoria's reign, with *memorabilia* of the epoch, coincident with the church's erection. A copy of the *Freeman's Journal* of that date was deposited in the cavity, together with a brass plate bearing the following inscription: 'Illustrissimus Dominus, Dominus Archiepiscopus Dubliniensis, posuit lapidem primarium hujusque ecclesiae edificandae Deo Optimo Maximo, sub invocatione Beatae Mariae, Stellae Maris. Die septimo mensis Maii, Anno Christi, MDCCCLI.' The whole deposit was enclosed within the cavity, and the air of which having been exhausted, it was hermetically sealed, and the stone was lowered to its place. Pontifical benediction was afterwards given to the numerous assemblage present.

Through the untiring zeal and exertions of the venerable parish priest, this work was brought practically to a successful completion. Difficulties of an extraordinary nature were surmounted and overcome. During the great storm of 1852, which happened on the 25th and 27th of December, and when the walls had been erected, and when the roofing had just been commenced, both the front and rear gables, with their elaborate Gothic windows, were levelled to the ground. Renewed efforts were made, however, to repair the damage occasioned. After the lapse of a few years from the commencement of the work, this fine church, so tasteful in its architectural details, and so just in all its proportions, was opened for divine service.

Star of the Sea

Irishtown

IN THE MEDIAEVAL times, when the Palesmen were pent within their walled cities and towns throughout Ireland, and when their gates were jealously closed at night against the Irish enemy; yet were to be found groups of shielings and huts in the immediate vicinity, tenanted by a colony of native craftsmen, sutlers and labourers, who ministered to the wants of those burghers engaged in trades or manufactures. Such villages, as distinguished from houses within the walls and inhabited by the English or Anglo-Irish civilians, were generally known in the aggregate by the designation of Irishtown. As no municipal laws or even proprietorial direction restrained such denizens, so were their cabins and lanes usually detached and scattered about in the most varied forms, and at every imaginable diversity of angle, covering waste spaces, and with hardly any gardens attached. Traces of the original artless grouping may be detected in many existing survivals; and as suburbs are only the parasites of cities and towns, those offshoots hardly ever keep proportionate pace with the relative improvements of the latter. Especially was it so in Ireland, where social conditions were strained and antagonistic; race and prejudice conflicting, mutual jealously and mistrust predominating.

Such an Irishtown as we have described has long existed, without the municipal boundaries of Dublin, yet retaining its name on the sea-shore, and near the harbour entrance. For some centuries past, a primitive thatched chapel stood on the site of Mearns' buildings, known as St. Mary's Terrace, and this served as a place of worship for the Roman Catholic inhabitants of the surrounding districts. Even was it resorted to by many of the Dublin people, when no public church was allowed to be erected within the city. During the reign of Queen Anne, the present Protestant Church was erected; and, at that time, the River Dodder did not join the River Liffey, but rather formed a *delta*, before it reached Irishtown, while one of its branches ran out upon the strand a little to the north, and the other emptied into the sea immediately behind

157

the present Star of the Sea Catholic Church. Irishtown was then an island, but connected by a bridge with the city. Towards the close of the last century, the Dodder was diverted by a sharp bend to form the Grand Canal Basin, and since then, it has made its exit directly north to the River Liffey.

There are those living who recollect the small mound-like appearance presented on that site, where the Star of the Sea Church now stands. Both that piece of ground and Leahy Terrace, on the opposite side of the lately-formed road to the strand, were a field, usually cultivated and planted with potatoes, by the former proprietor of Cranfield's Baths. These have since disappeared. That site also formed an embankment of the Dodder, at one of its branches, and the sub-soil is curiously composed of coarse boulder-gravel, layers of fine sea-sand, with quantities of cockle and other shell-fish relics abounding. That spot was then termed Scald Hill. Near it, on the strand, was Waxes' Dargle; because it is said the impecunious shoemakers, who could not afford to take an outside jaunting-car to the romantic glen near Bray, were able to avail of the twopenny jarvey drive from Dublin to Irishtown, on Easter and Whit Monday, there to dance the merry jig or reel, with their wives, daughters or sweethearts, as the case might be. Of course the local connection with the Wicklow Dargle was only nominal, and the scenery remotely fanciful.

Somewhat removed, and a little above the Dodder cut, was Haig's Brewery, occupying the present site of the Lansdowne-road Station on the Dublin, Wicklow and Wexford Railway. There is still a deep trench on the river-side, with indications of arches now closed up under the elevated railway embankment. These show where the stored waters above made their course for escape to the running waters below, while the mashing process went on within the Brewery. Such topographical sketches may be necessary to give the reader at a distance some general idea of the ground over which we are to travel. Besides, most judicious historians are accustomed to describe the general features of a battle-field before relating the incidents of an encounter. As the scenes have since changed very considerably, and as a remarkable contest has to be recorded in the present legend, with an introduction of the narrator – happily a living authority in the neighbourhood – so may all the particulars be still verified by the curious investigator of folk-lore tradition.

One of the best, most honest-minded and most industrious of men is John Kearns of Irishtown, and while engaged with his well-cared horse in drawing sand for some building improvements at the Star of the Sea Church, he put the following query to the superintendent: 'Did you iver hear the name of this place forty years ago?' The uninformed person replied, that he did not. 'Thin it wint by the name of Scald Hill, afore Dean O'Connell the Parish Priest got the site from the Hon. Sydney Herbert, and thin he built the Star. And I'll tell you besides a stranger thing nor that; for it was here that the great Battle of the Cats took place, now a long time ago, and whin Father Corrigan was curate in the Parish, afore it was divided into three, Donnybrook, Haddingdon-road and Irishtown.'

This was an item of information never before conveyed to the superintendent and his men; so John Kearns was eagerly pressed to tell the story, and all present listened with great attention while he proceeded.

'Well thin, one fine summer evenin' towards dusk, when Father Corrigan was comin' home from a sick call to Irishtown along Simonscourt-road – it was a lonely place thin and few houses along the way – he obsarved an exthrordinary number of cats movin' along, and mewin' as if they were grumblin' to one another, and he wondered where they all kem from, bud he saw they were on the way ahead. Whin he came to Scald Hill, he found it all covered widh other cats, and many were still comin' from different quarthers. There they all set up a thremindous howlin' and screechin'. He thought it mighty quare intirely, but he was tired, and wint home to bed. No sooner was he there, than the noise kep' on at such a rate, that niver a wink he could sleep until afther midnight. Thin the ruction seemed to be over, and he fell asleep, and didn't waken until mornin'.'

'Shure enough, ivery one of the Irishtown people hard the racket as well as Father Corrigan; bud early next day, word kem to him that the whole of Scald Hill was covered with the dead bodies of cats. They had a great battle over night, and kilt one another in hapes, nor was any of thim known to lave that place alive. Well, so great was the number, that it took six of Haig's Brewery carts to remove and bury them durin' the day; and the like of that battle was niver known afore nor since, for the cats kem from all parts of Ireland.'

That was a wonderful story, indeed, but one of the hearers inquired how John Kearns was able to prove that the cats came from all parts of Ireland. 'I'll tell you the rason,' he replied, 'one of thim was found wid a brass collar around its nick, and that had the name of a Galway lady graved on it, so you may be shure whin that was the case, others must have come from places quite as far away.'

Whether the inference warranted the conclusion or not may be questioned; but to have placed upon record such a narrative, relating to the earlier part of the present century and surviving to its close, must add one more to the quaint old popular traditions, now fast fading from the recollections and grasp of curious or interested folk-lorists.

Sandymount

THE TRAM-CARS and railroad conduct the citizens of Dublin in short time to the sea-side village of Sandymount, and thither many repair on Sundays and Holydays to enjoy a pleasant ramble over the winding and umbrageous roads, skirted with handsome villas, or to have a delightful stroll over the far extending strand, when the tide is full out, to inhale the balmy ozone of the Irish Channel. The odoriferous water and air exhalations of the Liffey, confined by the long South-sea Wall to a northern course of fully three miles from the Point of Ringsend to Poolbeg Lighthouse, there undergoes a process of purification in the briny waves of ocean. Besides the crowd of grown pedestrians, who are able to advance very leisurely for three or four miles after the ebb tide, without soiling the sole of a shoe, and to retreat in like manner before the returning flow; groups of little children with their nurses are to be seen, exercising their wooden toy shovels, and busily engaged in searching out the numerous tiny mounds of blue sand, certain indications of the cockle bedded beneath, and soon to be unearthed by the least intelligent and smallest of juveniles. A few years back, the fore-shore was lined with bathing boxes, to many of which ponies and donkeys were yoked, and from those boxes the bathers waded far out into any chosen stage of water for a swim or a dabble, as the case might be; while many humble servitors, men and women, earned a comfortable and honest livelihood, owing to attentions and civility always readily afforded to their patrons. In his baby days, the illustrious and inimitable bard of Erin, Tom Moore, was accustomed to take his morning dip in the shallow tide-waves. At that time, a considerable stretch of green fields – now encroached upon by houses – ran between Sandymount and Dublin, and the roads in the suburbs were infested by footpads. One of these had demanded a gentleman's purse, and received in exchange a pistol shot which left him dead on the roadside. Early in the morning, returning from Sandymount to Dublin, as related in his Diary – Tom Moore and his uncle found the dead robber lying beside the road, and he had been shot just under the eye, there being no other mark than the small hole through which the bullet had entered. An old woman who was present, moved to pity, and doubtless admiring the fine features of the dead, cried out, 'It was the blessing of God it didn't hit his eye,' for she imagined it must have concerned the robber, to present the appearance of a pretty corpse after that untoward accident.

Not alone towards the close of the last century, but far later in the present, Sandymount and Irishtown were gay and stirring villages, especially during the Summer and Autumn season. Crowds of people from the provinces were sure to engage in advance and occupy the various lodging-houses near the strand for the benefit of sea-bathing. The working and middle-class people of Dublin, before the Omnibus and Tram-car service ran, had found a number of the Sandymount outside car-drivers lobbing for fares at College Green, and the 'two-penny' drive was a favourite one, when a party of six could be collected at once. If otherwise, the jarvey was sure to wait until his number was completed, and this was not easily obtained on ordinary days of the week, so that the tide was often out before a start could be made. The hot-water baths at Cranfield's establishment were always beset with a number of expectants for a turn on warm days; while their time and patience were often sorely tried, before all the waiters could be accommodated. That building has since gone to ruin, yet not for want of patronage, could the baths have been extended or otherwise suitably provided.

From the foreshore, likewise, the bathing boxes, which had garnished it for centuries, have been removed during the last few years, thus depriving the general public of a healthful and popular resource during the warm days of Summer and Autumn. This is how it happened. The Pembroke Township Commissioners, having procured Parliamentary powers of jurisdiction over the strand, and having in view the construction of Public Baths and a Promenade Pier, resolved on the destruction of the private bathing boxes, and issued a decree for their removal. This very naturally created great indignation and remonstrance among the inhabitants of Irishtown, Ringsend and Sandymount; more especially, among those industrious people, whose prescriptive rights and means of livelihood were thus unjustly sacrificed, and without the slightest compensation having been made or even offered. The former influx of visitors to the sea-side soon ceased; many of the lodging-house keepers, who in former times hardly ever had to complain of having a vacant room, were ofttimes left without the means of paying their own rents, and were only living in hopes of seeing realised the promised improvement, which it was expected must so greatly benefit the immediate neighbourhood and the general public.

Star of the Sea

The next step taken in that direction was the starting of a
Limited Liability Company for the construction of Public Baths
and a Promenade Pier at Merrion. For a site, no place could
be more eligible or present fairer attractions; all the contingent
facilities and surroundings being admirably adapted to erect a
Pier and Promenade by gradual extension, and as funds were
made available, to carry both for at least three miles over the
strand at ebb-tide, while at the return flow, the flooring might rise
over the surrounding waves, and enable visitors to stroll for such a
length, thus to inhale the refreshing ozone with the salt-sea breeze
during the Summer and Autumn seasons. Moreover, on either
side of the Promenade and at suitable distances from the entrance
gate separate cold water basins could have been constructed,
on one side for gentlemen, and on the other for ladies; while
still more remote from the shore, open sea-bathing and bathing
dresses could be provided for men and women, at respective
stations and apart, with all necessary safeguards against accident
or impropriety. Thus might the cold water baths be rendered wide
of range, free for swimming exercise, and invigorating, owing
to the freshness of the sea-water. Where for the accommodation
of young children or timid adults the bathing must necessarily
be confined to the enclosed basins, the concreted or tiled floors
of these baths should be on a level with, or even slightly raised
over the strand-surface; and a simple pumping apparatus twice
in every twenty-four hours should supply fresh salt-water, while
the former used water could be wholly ejected through a sluice,
at those intervals when the tide was fully out, and even the floors
could be swept clean before admitting a new supply.

Such a general plan should commend itself to ordinary
intelligence; but designers and directors are restrained by
no special desire of accommodating the funds provided by
shareholders to secure useful ends; and accordingly, in the case
of erecting those Merrion Baths and the Promenade Pier, want
of forethought has been most absurdly manifested in a radically
wrong design, and even great expense has been incurred to render

163

St Mary's Church, Star of the Sea, 2005

that design still more objectionable in the mode of construction. The Promenade, for which a Band Stand has been provided, is completely stunted in length, and then blocked up at the end with an octagonal concreted basin, divided by a wall into separate compartments for males and females, of very limited dimensions for cold water bathing or swimming purposes. Moreover, as if to spoil the freshness of the water more effectually, a large sum of money has been spent in excavating a bank of blue mud, and in forming a deep pool under the surface of the strand, so that the water within the basins becomes in a great measure stagnant and foul, and the sediment which collects at the bottom can only be removed by artificial means and at considerable outlay. In other details, various defects both of plan and execution might be specified. Those enumerated, however, have tended largely to send persons who have had experience of them in other directions, to enjoy the benefit of open sea-bathing.

Moreover, it seems not to have been at all considered, that more than half the community, owing to age or constitutional infirmity, cannot avail of cold water baths, and no effort has been hitherto made to provide hot water baths for their accommodation and use. Under such circumstances as these, little wonder may be expressed, that small revenue has been returned from the Merrion Public Baths and Promenade Pier; nor does it seem probable that condition shall be reversed, unless better management prevail, and measures be taken for a complete remodelling of the original construction, and for supplying the wants of patrons, who have means and inclination to indulge in the luxury of sea-water bathing. However, all this is irrelevant to the subject which prompted us to introduce the following narrative, and give it a place in this collection.

Whether it be legitimate or not, to engraft on the stem of legend an 'ower true tale' of Irish life; it may at least be amusing, to record a well authenticated incident, which occurred not many years ago, and which afterwards obtained the ephemeral notoriety of a newspaper paragraph. As a matter of course, it survives in the recollection of many, who were participants in or witnesses to the transaction, and who have often wondered why they had not greater shrewdness of perception, than to be deceived by the evidence of their senses, especially when fairly challenged to submit their judgment to the test of ordinary examination. It occurred, moreover, in the midst of an enlightened community adjoining the city of Dublin, and not in the remote glens or wilds of Connemara or among the mountains of Kerry.

Several years have passed since Mickey Kieran was a well-known and popular resident of Sandymount, where he kept a dairy shop and cows, being in rather comfortable circumstances. Time went by, however, and notwithstanding his industry, fortune proved faithless in bestowing her just awards, and a succession of unfavourable years caused numbers of his cattle to be attacked with disease, which carried them off; and much to the regret of all his neighbours, poor Kieran gradually sank beneath his difficulties, and in his old age, surviving family and relations, he became impoverished to such a degree, that after a vain struggle to maintain himself in the village, no other resource remained than refuge in the South Dublin Union workhouse, since to labour he was unable, and to beg he was ashamed. In his better days, Mickey Kieran was cheerful and good-humoured; indeed regarded by all his acquaintances as a very comical man, and as such, very general sympathy was expressed, but little support tendered, when he had taken the resolution of seeking that shelter from the buffets of adversity. No doubt, some of his former friends and familiars paid him occasional visits; but after a while, these became less frequent, and having in a great measure severed connection from the world without, in turn his very existence was almost forgotten, even by his distant relatives, who yet remembered him with esteem and affection.

At this time, it so happened, there were two Michael Kierans entered on the Admission Books of the South Dublin Union – distinct in family, local origin and connections, yet nearly of an age coinciding, and that was one rather advanced in years. In seems more than likely, they were intimates during the times of social intercourse freely allowed there to the aged and infirm.

Some years having elapsed, one of the two Michael Kierans was overtaken by illness, which confined him to the ward, and it resulted finally in his removal thence to the Dead House. It is customary, when family relations are known to survive out of doors, and living at no great distance, to send word of such an occurrence, so that the corpse may be removed by them for wake and interment, not at the expense of the Union. Having a knowledge of Michael Kieran's former connection with Sandymount, and assuming that his friends there should naturally desire to learn the particulars of his death; an official messenger was hastily despatched thither, and when the news was duly announced, it was resolved, as a mark of respect and sympathy, that a coffin should be procured, and arrangements made for a private interment in the family plot of ground registered in the Cemetery at Glasnevin. Accordingly the undertaker discharged his commission by going to the Dead House, and taking dimensions for the coffin that had been ordered. When the remains had been cased therein, a small cortege of friends attended and brought them to Sandymount, where the lid of the coffin was raised, and the corpse was duly laid out for a wake, with the view further to prepare a public funeral.

On such occasions, it is customary for the friends and acquaintances of the deceased to assemble and manifest by their presence and condolences with each other, their remembrance and respect. All were seated in silence or subdued conversation in the death-chamber, and as a matter of course, having their looks directed towards the corpse, their recollections were carried back over score of years, and to the time when Mickey Kieran was alive and well in the village of Sandymount. At length, among others, when he could spare an hour from duty, the Tramcar driver Michael MacManus entered, and approaching the bedside, he gazed with some surprise on the features of the dead. Then instituting a more rigorous examination, a feeling of incredulity began to arise in his mind. After a little deliberation, yet with a somewhat embarrassed air, at length he cried out to others who were present: 'Why, bless me, but yees are waking the wrong man, for as shure as I'm livin', this is not Mickey Kieran's corpse!' Now, indeed, the people assembled came nearer to the dead body, and eagerly scanned the dead features; still as many years elapsed since they had seen him alive, none could clearly recollect any distinctive peculiarity of countenance, that might lead them to entertain a negative doubt, especially as they had official warrant for the identity of the deceased with the living subject. At last it was agreed, that death oftentimes strangely alters the features, and aged indications undoubtedly corresponded with the appearance of the corpse there lying before them. No further serious questions were raised, and attended by a goodly number of his former friends and acquaintances to the

St Mary's Church, Star of the Sea: interior *c*. 1900, showing altar rails
and pulpit erected 1881 in memory of O'Hanlon's predecessor,
Fr Thomas Leahy.

family place of interment, the last rites were discharged towards
the remains of Michael Kieran in Glasnevin.

Little more was thought about those occurrences for another
year, when it chanced that a poor resident of Sandymount, named
Barney Quinn, was obliged to take up his quarters as an inmate
in the South Dublin Union workhouse. Being duly entered on the
Admission Book, and having donned the gray uniform provided,
no sooner had the new-comer crossed the yard, than he started with
affright. Suddenly his old acquaintance Mickey Kieran of Sandymount appeared and advanced to meet him with a familiar smile
of recognition. Recalling all the circumstances of the former wake

and interment at which he had assisted, poor Barney Quinn fancied he saw the ghost of his old acquaintance and friend, while in his distress, and shuddering at the idea of grasping the proffered hand, he stammered out in amazement: 'Why, Mickey Kieran, I thought we buried you this time twelve months in Glasnevin, and all your friends in Sandymount thought the same, and now to see you livin' again and to the fore!' He then related what had happened at the time, to the no small wonder of his friend, who then understood the reason why he had not received a single visit from any one of the Sandymount people, during the whole of the previous twelve months. The cordiality and friendship of former days were resumed, and reminiscences of the past formed the topic of many a conversation between them, so long as they remained fellow inmates of the South Dublin Bastile, as its poor occupants are pleased ironically to designate that large building.

Soon, however, these incidents were made known, and news reached Sandymount, that its former resident Mickey Kieran was still in the land of the living. Then the sagacity and opinion of Michael MacManus were recognised and approved, although formerly rejected and contemned; while the scorners who attended the wake and funeral of a man unknown did not care to have it stated, they had been vicims of an illusion. Even the ridicule attaching to them, and an unwillingness to revive any recollection of their error, caused them to neglect poor Michael Kieran, who did not long survive the attendance of his friends at the funeral of his namesake. Moreover, it must be related, that when his own death actually took place, his remains were not decreed the usual mortuary tokens of respect in his native village, but were brought, according to the ordinary custom of pauper burial, from the workhouse to the grave.

7

Saints and Holy Places

Saints

THE MAN, WHO has always what he wished for, and who never tires of it, or that man who is what he always wished to be, never regretting that he is not something else, must prove a happy exception among his fellow mortals. Yet, the Saints belong to this exceptional class. They are satisfied to bear crosses and sufferings, disappointment and gloom, life's losses and darkness, when such privations bring with them a crown and strength of soul, comfort and consolation, great gain and great light. After pain comes peace, after rain gleams the sunshine, after the storm tranquillity succeeds; and when the pilgrimage of earth draws to a close, the near vision of eternal life brings with it the rapture of anticipated bliss. Few thoughtful persons will be found to deny, that a way, which leads in such direction must be the right path to a true goal. Like all the best lessons of philosophy, the plainest and the most simple are the most useful. When a principle is clear and well understood, it is not so difficult to solve other questions, that seem dependent and consequential. Therefore, little mystery attaches to that peace and security of mind, which surpasses mere human knowledge, because it is rightly reasoned on from its being a supernatural gift. Once the key to its possession is found, it must be an easy task to unlock the treasure. The pious servant of God only estimates well its real worth. Finding himself rich in the property he prizes, no envy is felt when he sees other men anxious to obtain worldly possessions which can never satisfy their wishes, and which are frequently a source of inquietude, or even an actual loss, to their owner.

St Malachy

THE VIRTUES OF the servants of God are worthy of record, not so much for the glory they have shed upon religion, as for the lessons furnished by them to all persons, whether to such as are faithful to the inspiration of Divine Grace, or to sinners. Instances are presented, in all their glorious actions, of the manner in which

Previously unpublished sketch of Dunshaughlin Abbey, Co. Meath, by
John O'Hanlon, July 1855 (Russell Library MS OH 14/5, p. 519)

the former class of persons might profit by examples of perfection, in various degrees, and as exemplified on different occasions. To the latter class, practices of an exalted kind are presented, which must command respect and admiration, however slow sinners may be to avail themselves of the teaching and impulses of nature in her brighter living examples, directed by the operations of Divine Grace. The condition and circumstances of different holy servants of God may be far removed from ours, in many respects; yet, there are always certain particulars in the life of a true Christian, which must apply to all those who aspire to the same exalted character. The like opportunities may not be furnished to all persons for exercising virtue in a similar manner; but the practice of every virtue, at a proper time, and on a suitable occasion, is a duty devolving on all those who aim at perfection. How suggestive of good impulses, in the minds of the most impenitent sinners, are not the maxims and morals of the just! How conducive to a holy emulation, in these possessing the Grace of Almighty God, arc not the living examples of his servants which pass in review before our eyes, or which live in our recollection, whilst the frail tencment of the body moulders in its kindred dust! Let us recollect the acts and virtues of the Saint, whose memory has already passed under our consideration, and we shall find ourselves possessed of a Christian knowledge, which his own moving exhortations, apart from his actions, would never be able to excite in the minds of his hearers. This is the kind of knowledge 'that maketh wise unto salvation', and that bears its fruit, when cast into the proper soil; but which so often becomes unproductive when it falls upon a barren, unfertilizing surface. The virtues of the Saint, whose actions are here recorded, should be as beacon lights to guide us to the port of our rest, to illuminate our darkness, and to dispel the illusions under which we labour. As a pastor of that Church, whose founder is now his reward, we should take warning by his admonitions, receiving instruction from his counsels, and edification from his actions. Above all, we shall discover how the union of prayer and heavenly contemplation may be perfectly compatible with the most earnest exertion and laborious occupation; and hence derive the consolation that, whilst engaged in the active duties and indispensable labours of our state of life, we may be working out, also, the ends of Almighty God, in accomplishing the great work of our own salvation.

St Gerebern

Along the Rhine

ONE OF THE most delightful and interesting excursions it has ever been the good fortune of the writer to enjoy, and on which his recollections yet linger with pleasure, was made by the royal mail coach from the strongly fortified city of Wezel, on the right bank of the Rhine, to the city of Xanten, and thence to the village of Sonsbeck, within the duchy of Cleves, and kingdom of Prussia. Little time need be lost to effect this visit by the traveller, who frequently passes near those localities, when journeying by railroad between Amsterdam and Cologne, or when ascending or descending the noble Rhine, by one of the many steamers, which are daily cleaving its waters, on their upward or downward passage. For the Irish Catholic, this journey cannot fail to have many attractions, and especially if he desire acquaintance with the interior and rural districts in this part of Germany. Passing through Wezel, pleasantly situated on the river, over which a long floating pontoon-bridge conducts the excursionist, he will start along the direct road to Xanten, for about two leagues, through a rich and populous district. For a considerable portion of this way the route lies along an old channel of the Rhine – now deserted by the main current – over a fine terraced road, overhung on one side by magnificent forest trees, and presenting on the other most extensive and varied views of a truly fertile and picturesque country. Long lines of poplar and other tall trees, flanking the roads throughout their whole extent, and ranging over the landscape in different directions, orchards bending under their loads of fruit, and plains covered with crops, relieve the eye in alternating succession, and present most favourable evidences to indicate the material comfort and prosperity of the inhabitants living in this delightful region.

Sonsbeck

A CUSTOM, AT present prevailing in the town and parish of Sonsbeck, requires all the Catholic inhabitants to attend in their best holiday attire on the Sunday, but not that one immediately succeeding the feast of St. Margaret, virgin and martyr, which occurs on the 13th of June. The place of meeting is in and around the ancient little chapel of St. Gerebern, situated on a beautiful eminence immediately outside the town of Sonsbeck. On the occasion of St. Gerebern's principal festival – the octave of the Sunday after St. Margaret's day – all the parochial Masses are there celebrated, and the doors of the parish church are closed. During the octave, a like custom prevails. At other times, when the people wish their *curé* or *vicaires* to celebrate a votive Mass for them, the little chapel of St. Gerebern is often used for this purpose,[1] As the writer had been informed by the pastor, St. Gerebern's existing chapel dates its origin to the very commencement of the thirteenth century. It is probable, an older ecclesiastical structure occupied its present site. Immediately adjoining St. Gerebern's chapel, covered with rose trees and weeping willows, lies the Catholic cemetery of the parish, which is very neatly kept and enclosed. That it is a very ancient burial-place, we may well suppose, and from the numerous tombs and crosses placed over the graves, it seems a favourite burial-place for the Catholic inhabitants of Sonsbeck and of the adjoining country. The Evangelicals, as all the Protestant inhabitants are called, have their separate place of interment, and the Jews' cemetery is distinct from the two former graveyards. The prospect from the top of the hill, on which the little chapel of St. Gerebern is built, embraces a most extended field of vision; and, on the bright warm sunshine day,[2] when the writer beheld it, the vast plains around were covered with varied

[1] During my short visit at Sonsbeck, I had the privilege of celebrating the Holy Sacrifice of the Mass, within the little chapel of St. Gerebern.
[2] The 1st of August, 1863.

vegetable productions, the harvest was already far advanced, and the industrious inhabitants of the surrounding country were busily engaged in the agricultural operations of the season. Immediately below lay the old town of Sonsbeck, displaying its picturesque high-pitched and red-tiled roofs, with the slate-covered spire and roof of the parish church dominating over all the other houses. Small weather vanes lay motionless on the gables of several buildings, and dense woods spread far away towards the distant horizon. The whole scene was surpassingly picturesque and varied. Rural tranquility prevailed over this extensive landscape, so well harmonizing with the character of the inhabitants, as also with the peace and order reigning throughout this beautiful and productive region. Catholics constitute a preponderating majority of the people in this district of Prussia, and along the Rhemish borders. They live in perfect harmony with their dissenting fellow-subjects; all classes and denominations of people then enjoying religious freedom and protection from the government, without distinction of sect or party. The subjects of this absolute monarchy were greatly reconciled to a deprivation of other political rights and privileges, which they hoped to obtain in due course of time.

St Dympna

Through Belgium

A N IRISH CATHOLIC pilgrim to the shrine of St. Dympna, who desires acquaintance with primitive Flemish manners and customs, after having visited the fine cites and routes usually frequented by the herd of Belgian tourists, can easily accomplish his object without any considerable delay or inconvenience, while combining information and amusement with philanthropic feeling or interest, as also with national predilections or religious emotions. Antwerp is never omitted from his *memoranda*, for a resting place in the tourist's itinerary; and, by starting at an early yet suitable hour from this city, the morning train to Turnhout will leave the traveller at Herenthals station. There, a well-appointed *omnibus* is to be found, waiting to receive its contingent of passengers, baggage, and mail packets, destined for the quaint old city of Gheel. Off at a spanking pace start the vigorous roadsters, over the paved highway, bounded on either side with a broad and much frequented path for foot passengers, while extending under long and regular lines of oak and elm trees. No elevation, deserving the name of a hill, can be seen rising over the level plain that lies between the cities of Antwerp and of Gheel. It is true, at certain points along the road, from Herenthals to the latter municipality, a few broken embankments of light sand-hills diversify this scene, on the left hand side; but they soon disappear amidst the dark pine woods, moors, and marshes that spread over this tract of country. This wild and dreary district, known as the *Campine*, extends through portions of the provinces of Antwerp, Limbourg and South Brabant, as also into the kingdom of Holland. All this natural waste is not, however, unproductive and monotonous. Hedgerows along the roadside are neatly trimmed; white cottages, with their red-tiled roofs, gleam under the warm sunshine of summer;[3] fields wave with heavy crops of wheat, oats, rye and other vegetable esculents; patches of verdure contrast with bare yellow sandbanks and heath-covered moorlands; while from morning dawn to dewy eve, the moving human figures of all ages and both sexes, through rich corn fields, proclaim the steady and tireless industry of these *Campinois*. At various intervals, signposts, indices, and figures, mark the direction and distances of neighbouring cities, by *kilometres*. The country immediately around the old city of Gheel is teeming with fertility, and in the harvest time, it is loaded with the finest crops, covering a deep, rich, sandy, loam soil.

On arriving in the chief public square, adjoining the church of St. Amand, the traveller will find excellent accommodation, board and lodging, at the rather antiquated Hôtel de la Campine, which was built in 1644. It receives this name from the plain extending around the city in which it is situated. When leaving this hostelry,

---

[3]These observations were made by the writer during his excursion to and from Gheel, on the 27th and 28th of July, 1863.

the moderate charges to which the tourist will be liable must prove agreeable – especially when contrasted with exactions of more celebrated, but not more comfortable, guide-book hotels, in the larger and more frequented cities. Another quaint-looking but excellent inn, with the sign of a stork in front, may be found on the open place, opposite the left side of St. Dympna's church.

The Demented of Gheel

WHEN DEMENTED PERSONS arrive at Gheel, they are usually conducted to a house, attached to the church of St. Dympna, where an ecclesiastic offers up prayers for them and affords religious consolation. Afterwards, these afflicted persons are quartered among the inhabitants, and they are especially placed with the farming classes around that city. Although the pension for their maintenance is usually very moderate, yet this class of lodgers is eagerly sought for, by cultivators of land, who take particular care of their *protegés*, and who study the peculiar development of their mental aberrations. Hence, it often happens, that by gentleness, by coaxing or by caressing, the most ungovernable persons are rendered docile, in a short time, and these live perfectly contented with their protectors. Occasionally, a visitor to Gheel may observe groups of afflicted persons engaged in earnest conversation or innocent recreation in the streets, while shrill voices echo from the interior of the houses when passing; but, it is not always easy for a casual observer, to distinguish by their demeanour, between the sane and the insane inhabitants of St. Dympna's city. The latter class appears to enjoy unrestrained liberty, in going on messages, or while performing the ordinary avocations of labour. Hardly any farmer is without one or more of those insane persons, who live with him, and on the same footing, as other members of his family. They seldom give way to violence or to excess. They appear satisfied with their food, plain dress, and manner of living, they show no aversion to rural or handicraft labour, and seldom do they desire to leave those families, with whom they have lived for a number of years. The various towns, cities and districts from which they have been sent, usually engage agents to look after their comforts, and report on the treatment experienced from their hosts. Many of the people, in and about Gheel, believe that a blessing falls on themselves and on their families, when they conscientiously discharge Christian duties towards the insane; so that, few causes of complaint arise, on the score of neglecting duty or through personal injury. So far does a healthy public opinion prevail, on this point, that a farmer, who should fail in his obligations towards one of those afflicted persons, would immediately be deprived of his right of guardianship. His character should also suffer to such a degree, in the estimation of all his neighbours, that no greater punishment could be inflicted upon him, than the general contempt and detestation, with which he should afterwards be regarded.

Images and Names

IN THE CHURCH of St. Paul,[4] Dublin, over the side altar of the Blessed Sacrament, there is a large fresco painting.[5] It was designed, at the suggestion of the Very Rev. Monsignor Yore, to represent St. Dympna and St. Francis of Sales, in a kneeling posture, and adoring the Sacred Heart of our Redeemer, who appears above both saints. In the Cathedral Church, Marlborough Street, Dublin, there is also a very beautiful painting of St. Dympna, more

---

[4]In the year 1835, and on the 17th of March, the Feast of St. Patrick, Apostle of Ireland, the first stone of this fine building, facing Arran Quay, was laid, accompanied by the prescribed ceremonies, and in presence of a large multitude of persons. It advanced rapidly to completion, and now forms one of the most elegant ecclesiastical structures within the city of Dublin. The architectural details of St. Paul's are mainly derived from that much admired monument of antiquity, the Ionic temple of Erectheus at Athens. Some variations, however, were deemed necessary to make this church suitable for the requirements of a Christian temple. Both the conception and completion of this work are highly creditable to the architect, Patrick Byrne, Esq. This church is built of chiselled granite, on the exterior: four beautifully designed pillars support the pediment, which is again surmounted by a graceful campanile. The interior has lately undergone a very tasteful decoration. The fresco paintings, behind their magnificent marble altars within the sanctuary, are greatly admired.

[5]Executed by Frederick S. Barff, Esq., of Dublin.

than life size, with several of the other ancient saints of Ireland. It is probable, that many additional memorials of our saint may be found, in various other Irish churches, chapels, and religious institutions.

Not only in and around Gheel are females called after our saint; but, the custom is sufficiently prevalent, throughout the most distant parts of Belgium. This practice shows the great veneration in which St. Dympna is held, amongst many Flemish families. The name is also common in religion; and some of the consecrated virgins of Christ rejoice in the appellation, as they have doubtless often experienced benefits, derived from the patronage of our holy martyr. Hitherto, various causes have operated to prevent a more popular appreciation of St. Dympna's merits and glorious sacrifices, in her native country; yet, it is to be hoped, the future generations of Catholic mothers and daughters, throughout our island, will hear this virgin's glorious name frequently pronounced in their family circles, while due veneration must be paid to the special patroness of Gheel, when her intercession shall be more generally invoked amongst our people.

Invocation

THE VALUE OF this grace of virginity was a pearl above all price, in the estimation of St. Dympna. Hence, we should not deem it surprising, if in order to preserve it untainted, she considered the pouring out her own blood a small sacrifice, compared with the rewards of her glorious victory. Although nurtured amid the roses of royal purple, she esteemed the white lily of virginity, as surpassing all other flowers in grace and loveliness.

Ever venerated and illustrious Dympna! Under the purple robe of royalty, and in the torrent of youthful blood, which flowed from thy wounds, innocence and purity arrayed thy soul with a vesture of dazzling brightness! Would that mortals always knew how to select this lily, which blooms so gracefully along life's unfrequented pathways! Deluded votaries of pleasure may twine garlands of myrtle, culled from luxuriant bowers of sensual enjoyment; but, from the gardens of the empyrean alone, among

181

all other flowers, this emblematic type of holy purity merits grateful acceptance, in sight of the Most High. Chastity adds an additional beauty and ornament to the body; it gives elasticity and vigour to our spiritual nature; it elevates in moral dignity the children of men, and makes them resemble, in a great measure, the very angels in heaven.

Mundrehid, Queen's County

ONE FINE DAY in summer, after a walk up the southern slopes of Slieve Bloom, in company with some friends, we reached the site of Mundrehid's old ruined church, the walls of which were then nearly level with the ground. The name of this place is derived from the River Men or Mena, which runs near it, and Drehid or Drochid, the Irish denomination for 'bridge', which has spanned the stream from times the most remote. The old and lonely cemetery was round it, a few rude headstones studding its surface. The scenery there was truly deserving our admiration. While our friends were resting on the site and, after taking a few observations, we sat down on the low ruined wall. There about the sixth or seventh century, St. Laisren established his dwelling. On the 16th of September his festival is registered in the Irish Calendars. While resting there, we were soon joined by a shepherd, passing by the way, and his name was Ned Feehery. He lived near the place, and being asked for some information regarding it, he communicated very readily the following legend.

Ever since the old church fell into decay, a Druid had been known to haunt the site. Occasionally he had been seen by the older inhabitants. Before the apparition occurs, a tremendous roar is heard, so that the earth quakes all around. Immediately the ground opens, and then a small black man springs up, covered with armour, and wearing a belt, from which a sword hangs. He draws the sword, and flourishes it over his head. He next races three times around the graveyard, and in a short time he disappears from that spot whence he rose, and sinks under the earth's surface. This strange earthly visitant Ned Feehery declared he had himself once distinctly seen, and towards the dusk of evening.

The richest fields of Ossory surrounded the church, which once belonged to a monastery on that spot. Near it Gortavoragh and the Friar's Garden – where the peasantry root for money – were pointed out beside the little River Turtawn, which appears to have bounded the monastery fields. Through these, headless coachmen and headless horses driving about the paddocks have been witnessed by people, during the still hours of night.

Some twenty years later we returned to Mundrehid, but found that the gentleman farmer in possession had not only levelled the large ditches crowned with finely-grown hawthorns, which surrounded the small paddock fields, but even the stones were uprooted from the old foundations in the grave-yard, and the rude head-stones were removed. No trace of a grave now remains, while not a single vestige of the patron's historic home is left. Living memory alone preserves the site. Countless generations of the dead moulder at present under the levelled spot. Thence their bones may by raised by the future antiquary, to attest the position of that disused cemetery. The deed of the Vandal is still reprobated in that neighbourhood; but the peasants relate how his desire to open wide pastures as a range for cattle did not prosper according to the full extent of the spoiler's wishes, as many of them were carried off by disease, while the herds of other farmers were spared such a visitation.

Moghia, near Lismore, Queen's County

ONCE UPON A time, there were two celebrated monasteries in vogue; one of these was at Aghaboe, in the Queen's County, and the other some eight or ten miles distant, at Monahincha, in the County of Tipperary. Now it happened that the monks of one of these monasteries had a grey horse, past its labour in the field. But he was a hardy and a knowledgeable old animal that was yet turned to good account. He had travelled so frequently in his day between Aghaboe and Monahincha, that he knew every inch of the Ballaghmore or great road.

In those times, there were no postal facilities between the religious of the two houses, and yet they were obliged to keep up a daily communication. At last it was thought, that the Garran Bawn – as the old horse was called – might be trained to travel back and forth each day, with saddle-bags slung on either side of his back to balance each other. Soon did the animal learn to jog along leisurely, with the necessaries and messages for the monks of both establishments contained in the saddle-bags, and without even a guide to direct him. Nor would any of the people along the road molest him, as they knew his office was to bear only what was useful for the monks.

However, there were three rascals living in the neighbourhood, called Deegan, Dooly and Dullany, who had not the same respect for the old horse, nor for the requisites he was accustomed to carry. These men entered into a conspiracy to seize the poor animal one day, and to plunder the panniers. Accordingly, they waited for him on the highway, at a place called Moghia, near Lismore, where the Garran Bawn was stopped, and the robbers, emptying out the contents of the saddle-bags, decamped with their plunder. However, after this shabby transaction, they all came to misfortune and sorrow, as the story goes. They even brought a deep disgrace on all those who belonged to their families. A law was passed in both the religious houses, that no person named Deegan, Dooly or Dullany should be ordained a priest; nor was any monk of the name ever afterwards admitted into the Monasteries of Aghaboe or Monahincha.

St Lóchán of Kilmacahill, County of Kilkenny

THE LAST DAY of the year and of the Calendar closes with a saint, almost unknown to the men of our present age and generation. A digression may be permitted, if in proceeding to describe his former place of living, any casual gleam of light may be reflected on his name or time.

St. Patrick's Literary Institute.

THE COMMITTEE OF THE ABOVE LITERARY INSTITUTE
HEREBY INVITE YOU TO ATTEND

A LECTURE

WHICH WILL BE DELIVERED BY THE

Very Rev. John Canon O'Hanlon, P.P.,

IN THE

PAROCHIAL HALL,

CAMBRIDGE ROAD, RINGSEND,

On SUNDAY, FEBRUARY 6th, 1887,

AT 3 O'CLOCK, P.M.

Subject—

"A VISIT TO MONTE CASINO,"

The great Monastery founded by St. Benedict in Italy.

ADMISSION CHARGE—ONE PENNY.

CAHILL, PRINTERS, DUBLIN.

Saints and Holy Places

The Uí-Bairrche were a tribe, giving denomination to that territory, in which formerly they were seated. Their title was derived from Daire Barrach, second son of Cathaoir Mór, King of Leinster, and monarch of Ireland, in the second century. They were seated between the Ui-Drona and the Ui-Muireadhaigh. The habitants wholly possessed the Slievemargy barony, in Queen's County, with some adjoining districts in the County of Carlow. After the English invasion, the Mac Gormans were driven from this territory. Their chief then settled in the barony of Ibrickan towards the west of ancient Thomand, and in the present County of Clare.[6] From an entry of Cill-mac-Cathail having been within the territory of Ui Bairche, it is evident the latter took in some portion of Kilkenny county, bordering on that of Carlow. Cill-mac-Cathail is now known as Kilmacahill or Kilmocahill, a parish in the barony of Gowran, County of Kilkenny.[7] Locally connected with this district was Bealach Gabhrain, i.e. 'the Road of Gabhran,'[8] a pass-way that extended from this last-named place, in the direction of Cashel.[9] Gowran, formerly a borough town, and a parish, is situated in the barony of the same name. It is only a few miles from Kilmacahill, in the county of Kilkenny. Gowran was formerly a place of considerable importance, and at present may be seen there and tolerably well preserved the ruins of a magnificent ancient abbey-church, a part of which has been appropriated for Protestant services. The remainder has some very interesting details, in the early English style.[10] Among these are a finely pointed arch, in black marble, and leading into the chancel. A series of similar arches are supported by circular and octagonal columns. There are some windows

[6]See Dr O'Donovan's "Topographical poems of John O'Dubhagain and Giolla na naomh O'Huidhrin" n. 369. p. xlvii.

[7]See Lewis' "Topographical Dictionary of Ireland," Vol. II p. 179.

[8]Now Gowran, situated in the County of Kilkenny. See Dr O'Donovan's "Annals of the Four Masters" Vol. 1, n. (a), p. 359.

[9]See Colgan's "Trias Thaumaturga." Vita Tertia S. Patricii, Cp. II.x, p. 26.

[10]A round plan and exterior view of Gowran Abbey appear in Grose's "Antiquities of Ireland" Vol. 1. p. 40.

of elegant design, delicately ornamented in quatrefoil, as also several interior chapels. The door-ways and a baptismal font are of black marble, curiously sculptured. There are several ancient monuments within the ruins.[11] An old burial-ground, enclosed with a high wall, surrounds the Church, the walls of which are picturesquely masked with ivy. It is probable a much older – although a less ornate building – occupied that site covered by the present interesting ruins. It is remarkable that Archdall has given us no information relating to this church, while describing other ecclesiastical foundations in the County of Kilkenny.

In reference to this present saint in the Martyrology of Tallagh, we find noted the festival "Lochani", who bears no other distinction at the ii of the January Kalends, which corresponds with December the 31st.[12] This saint was son to Olild, son of Cathald, son of Cobhtac, son to Enna, son of Alid, son to David, son to Fiachrius. This latter was head over the renowned race of Hy-Fiachrach. St. Locan's festival was kept on this day at Kill-mic-Cathail in the region of Barreke.[13] This place is said in all probability to have been Kilmacahill, in the Barony of Moigoish,[14] four miles north of Inny river, in Westmeath County. Afterwards

[11] See Lewis' "Topographical Dictionary of Ireland," Vol. I. pp. 667, 668.

[12] See Rev. Dr Kelly's "Calendar of Irish Saints &c," p. xi.

[13] Colgan's "Acta Sanctorum Hiberniae" III. Februarii. Vita S. Colmani. App. Cap. II. P. 248.

[14] 'Proceeding to the north of the last mentioned territory (Muinter Tadhgain) we meet a long and narrow tract which retains its ancient name to this day, but somewhat corrupted in the anglicised form of Moygoish (pronounced Mag Uais), which territory hath its name from the posterity of Colla Uais, who settled in it after the destruction of Emania in 333. I have no document here to show whether the antient tribe called Hy-Mac-Uais "nepotes filiorum Uasi" became extinct, or remained in power down to the Anglo Norman invasion. Shane O'Dugan places the O'Henoses here in 1372, but I doubt very much that they were of the race of Colla Uais. I wish Mr Curry would look over Ogygia and Mac Firbisse for Ui Mac Uais and O Haonghusa of Meath. This name O'Haonghusa is now anglicised Ennis. They are still in existence, but not so numerous as to be considered a clan. This territory is sometimes called Cill Fallamhain

   rí ua mec Uais Bhreágh, huiligh
   O h-Aonghusa an árd mhuirir. Shane O'Dugan.'

a monastery was founded here for Franciscan friars of the Third Order.[15] In a copy of the Irish Calendar formerly belonging to the Ordnance Survey Office, now deposited in the Royal Irish Academy's Library, Dublin, our saint is said to have been from Kill Manac. It is more than probable that this must have been a mistake. We have already seen that the simple entry of Locan's name is only to be found in the published Tallagh Martyrology; whereas a festival, noted 'Endei Cilli Manach', is found at the same day, a distinct record, in that Calendar.

The Kilmacahill of this present saint lies near Paulstown village, and on the roadside, not far from the rail-way line reaching between Bagenalstown and Gowran stations.[16] A modern Protestant Church, as a tablet inscription on its square front-tower states, was erected in the year 1806. It rises in the centre of a grave-yard, which is in well-tended condition, while the church most probably occupies the site of a more ancient building. The graveyard surface is elevated a few feet over the road entrance and the adjoining fields. There are many modern inscribed and uninscribed headstones over the graves; but no very ancient ones can be discovered. A modern walled enclosure, entered by an iron gate, secures this graveyard from ordinary intrusion. Several fine old ash and elm trees grow near it. Old hawthorn and elder-berry trees are within the enclosure. The Protestant church is a very plain building, not displaying any

See County Westmeath Letters belonging to the Irish Ordnance Survey, Vol. II. p. 217. Mr O'Donovan's letter, dated Newpass, October 31st, 1837. Two well designed maps, representing tribe-names and situation of septs in Westmeath County, and neighbouring counties, will be found traced on pp. 204, 205, in the same volume.

[15] See Rev. Dr Kelly's "Calendar of Irish Saints," p. xl.

[16] In the "Liber Regalis Visitationes", compiled A.D. 1615 by order of James I, the following report occurs in reference to the church of Kilmocahill, in the Deaconate of Idrone. The rectory is said to have been impropriate; the curate was Thaddeus Currin, who appears to have served other churches; the church and chancel were in repair; while there was a communion-book in Irish. It is noticed, likewise, that the churches in this Deanery were *Straminea*, which we take to mean, 'thatched'.

Saints and Holy Places

architectural style. A rich and fertile tract of country spreads around it, and the landscape near and far presents very pleasing views.

A tradition exists among old inhabitants, living in the vicinity, that four bishops are buried in this graveyard; but at what date they died, the writer, on enquiry, could not ascertain. He was only told that their deaths took place 'long, long ago.' A farmhouse, with its surroundings, lies on that side of the road, opposite to the burial ground. There we were assured by an occupant that many human remains had been dug up in a haggard to the rere. Hence, it has been inferred, that the graveyard formerly extended beyond the road, which must have been cut through it; or, perhaps, as in other cases that might be cited, two distinct places of interment might have been attached to those ancient ecclesiastical foundations at Kilmacahill. No knowledge of the present saint, nor any recollection of patron or festival day, seems to have survived in local tradition.

One of the most original and expressive among descriptive poets has caught various features of the rolling seasons, and indulged his imagination with a play of light and shade those changes were capable of exciting. He has even happily conveyed such impressions in pleasing guise, and he has metaphorically introduced the pictured life of man, as represented in the flowering spring, the summer's ardent strength, the declining autumn, and the cold, concluding winter of his age, as closing all dreams of earthly greatness, and ending the world's restless cares. This poet then adds:

Virtue alone survives
Immortal, never failing – friend of man,
His guide to happiness on high. And see!
'Tis come, the glorious morn! The second birth
Of Heaven and earth! Awakening nature hears
The new-creating word, and starts to life,
In every heightened form, from pain and death
For ever free.[17]

[17] See, Thomson's "Seasons". Winter.

189

As in the works reviewed through inanimate nature, the Poet refers every created thing to the great Almighty Father, ending with a Hymn of Praise and Thanksgiving; so when the Christian directs his thoughts and his prayers to those happy and Immortal Spirits, embellished with choicest supernatural gifts, and enriched with virtues, as with eternal rewards in Heaven, to God does he attribute all the glory, while asking the patronage and intercession of his Saints.

It was a beautiful, warm and bright sun-shiney day in the month of July, 1870, when we wandered among the graves of Kilmacahill's rural place for interment. Perfect-calm and silence were only disturbed for a few moments by the rapid transit of a rail-way train. Some industrious labourers were at work in the adjoining fields. During an interval, which engaged the religious ministrations of our early and dear friend, the parish priest,[18] who had been called into that neighbourhood to visit one of his infirm parishioners, abundant time had been afforded to take notes on the spot, as had often before been our custom, when passing near the sites of many hundred old ruins and grave-yards, scattered throughout Ireland. Here we found leisure, not only to make the necessary observations for a purpose that had preoccupied our thoughts and literary labours for many previous years; but, also, had we moments to meditate among the tombs, on those fleeting yet solemn warnings they afford, during such periods of solitude, and especially while the mind is carried back to ages remote, in seeking to trace out the first probable time when fruits of mortality were gathered to the dust, in such remote, almost forgotten situations.

A prayer to the beatified, and a prayer for the departed were appropriate at this place, and on this occasion. We know from the records of our native calendars, that saints' remains had been deposed here at a very early age; and, we found on enquiry, that popular tradition fully corroborated – as in many similar instances – the accounts of old documents. But, alas! How lost to

[18] Rev. Patrick J. Mulhall P.P. of Goresbridge and Paulstown.

fame, and, as an almost necessary result, to claim on a people's reverence, those holy persons, who flourished during epochs long vanished. Their names, in their old places, were no more remembered. Here no temple or religious house of their erection, or with which they had formerly been connected, then stood. Heretofore, the case had been different. No trace of Saints' shrines or relics had been preserved. Save a popular instinct of veneration, which doubly consecrated in the affections of an indestructible Catholic and Celtic race associations with the spot and the occupants of its soil, little or nothing was known regarding past ecclesiastical history. Yet, saints of our isle had been interred beneath that earth, their names merely surviving through some appropriate and felicitous disposition of Divine Providence. Whole generations of ecclesiastics and laics reposed side by side, where canticles of praise and fervent prayer once and often resounded from the primitive church or cell that crowned such a site. Still many of the villagers and peasants individually hoped to rest there, when, fortified by the Sacraments and graces of our holy religion, their last *fiat* of death had been pronounced. And thus it ever happened, for Heavenly rewards await the advent of numerous happy souls, where a religious people, faithful to their higher destiny, and not unmindful regarding their noblest obligations, pass away from earth and its fleeting visions, to the solitude of the tomb. Myriads still arise from trammels of the grave, to be signed as the servants of God, like that multitude standing before His throne, and in sight of the Lamb, as mentioned in the Apocalypse, while clothed with white robes and having garlands in their hands.

Our enumerated saints are known and commemorated by thousands, as we have shown in the course of the preceding pages; but, festivals of many additional ones, whose memories and public invocation had been once preserved, no doubt have passed away from human thought, with the destruction of ancient ecclesiastical records. Their very names have been long since buried in oblivion. Although the virtues and merits of various holy persons

191

have been crowned with distinction among admiring clients; and, owing to the religious heroism of their examples and lives, still are there other sanctified Christians, who lived apparently unknown, and who died unhonoured, among their fellow mortals, yet, whose names are written in the Book of Life. The Irish Saints, in many instances, prayed that multitudes should arise with them from their burial places, where their own remains had been deposited, for the day of the final Resurrection. We cannot hesitate to assert that such prayers will be heard. Therefore, the faithful departed had first reason for desiring to repose in the old grave-yards that have received the relics of their former Saints, and the dust of their deceased ancestors. On the day of General Judgement, may we devoutly hope a vast number, that no man could count, shall be found from 'the Island of Saints', with the elect of all nations and tribes, without ceasing to proclaim 'Benediction and glory, and wisdom and thanksgiving, honour and power, and strength to our God, for ever and ever. Amen.' THE END.

APPENDIX 1

Chronology of the life and work of John O'Hanlon

Abbreviations: DDA = Dublin Diocesan Archive; NLI = National Library of Ireland.

1821

Born 30 April, Stradbally,[1] Queen's County; baptised 2 May[2] (parents Edward Hanlon,[3] Honor Hanlon;[4] sponsors Patt Brien, Eliza Moore). Honor Downey and Edward Hanlon subsequently have the following children:[5] Michael (bap. 29 September 1825);[6] Edward (bap. 15 August

---

[1] 'A native of this village, often has the writer gazed, with feelings of indescribable pleasure on the lovely scenes around…' (*Lives of the Irish saints* I, 332 n. 19). The O'Hanlon home was one of a series of houses now occupied by the Presentation Convent, beside the Church of the Sacred Heart, Stradbally: 'And now, returning after a long period of absence to find my former dwelling and the homes of so many old friends and neighbours changed or incorporated into the present convent with its admirable industrial school and orphanage, this experience fills me with admiration and joy I cannot express' (O'Hanlon's homily at Presentation Convent Golden Jubilee, Stradbally, 2 April 1902: Archives of Presentation Sisters, Smithfield, File C 46/1(a); see below under 1902).

[2] Stradbally Parish Records, Baptismal Registry, p. 6.

[3] A biographical sketch of O'Hanlon (*Irish Monthly* 14 (July 1886) 400) states that 'his grandfather belonged to Armagh'. Edward Hanlon was a tanner by occupation (O'Dooley, 'Rev John Canon O'Hanlon'). Both Edward and his wife ('Nora') are commemorated on a brass name-plate on a pillar in the Star of the Sea Church, Irishtown.

[4] Daughter of Denis Downey of Kildare; see pp. 20–23 above. In the Registry she is twice called by her married name, twice given the surname 'Moore' (see nn 8–9 below), and she bears her maiden name 'Downey' four times. She died 21 January 1887, St Louis (Mac Suibhne, 'Historian', 8).

[5] A sister, Mary, married in Stradbally in 1845 (see n. 27 below), appears not to be listed in the baptismal records. She died 27 September 1875, and is buried in Kilteale (Mac Suibhne, 'Historian', 9).

[6] Died 4 May 1905, Millwood, Missouri (Mac Ionnraic Archive: Terry O'Hanlon material).

Appendix 1

1827);[7] James (bap. 3 September 1829);[8] Eliza[9] (bap. 15 May 1831);
Charles[10] (bap. 10 February 1833); William (bap. 6 August 1835); Ann
(bap. 12 March 1837).[11]
Attends school in Stradbally.[12]

1834

Commences school with Arthur Hutchins at Ballyroan. Lives for two
years[13] in Pass House, Ballyroan, the home of his grand-uncle, John
Lalor.[14]

[7] Subscriber to *The life of Saint Malachy O'Morgair*: 'Mr Edward O'Hanlon,
Millwood, Lincoln County, State of Missouri, U.S. of America' (p. xi). Died 18
May 1895, Sherman, Texas (Mac Ionnraic Archive: Terry O'Hanlon material).

[8] Mother's name in Registry given as 'Honor Moore'; for connections
between Downeys and Moores of Ballymaddock see Mac Suibhne, 'Historian', 8, and extrapolation in Fennelly, *O'Hanlon*, chapter 1. Subscriber to *The
life of Saint Malachy O'Morgair*: 'Mr James O'Hanlon, P.O. Box 1312, St.
Louis, State of Missouri, U.S. of America' (p. xi). Died 1 April 1885, St Louis
(Mac Suibhne, 'Historian', 11).

[9] Mother's name in Registry given as '[*blank*] Moore'.

[10] Stradbally Parish Records, Baptismal Registry, p. 51 reads 'Ch:'. Died 28
November 1904, Millwood, Missouri (Mac Ionnraic Archive: Terry O'Hanlon
material).

[11] O'Hanlon wrote to his nephew Charles, 29 August 1904, thanking him for
measures he had taken 'to provide for my sister Anne' (Mac Ionnraic Archive).

[12] Nine distinct schools are recorded in Stradbally in 1824: *Second report of
the Commissioners of Irish Education Inquiry* 12, Appendix, pp. 766–7; see also
Brenan, *Schools of Kildare and Leighlin*, 113–14, 590–92.

[13] 'Identification of the site of the engagement at the Pass of the Plumes', 279.

[14] See above, p. 31. O'Hanlon's stay may have been curtailed to two years by
the death of John Lalor, 18 April 1836 (among numerous bequests in Lalor's will
is one of £30 to 'John Hanlon' (National Archives of Ireland, *Irish will register*
1836, f. 623)).

Appendix 1

1836

Attends Daniel O'Connell's public meeting on the Great Heath, Maryborough, Thursday 21 January 1836, and is present at a public banquet afterwards at Richard Leadbetter's mill in Stradbally.[15]

1840

Enters St Patrick's College, Carlow, as a seminarian.

1842

Leaves Carlow in May, his studies incomplete, and emigrates to America, via Quebec.[16]

1843

Arrives in St Louis, Missouri, in autumn. Sponsored by Judge Bryan Mullanphy, he enters Ecclesiastical Seminary in St Louis.[17]

1844–5

Contributes anonymous articles to Bishop Peter Richard Kenrick's *Catholic Cabinet and Chronicle of Religious Intelligence*.

1846

Suffering from ague, his health obliges him to leave St Louis in the autumn and to continue studies in St Joseph, over 200 miles west of St Louis.

1847

Returns to St Louis, and is ordained by Bishop Peter Richard Kenrick,[18] 29 May. Celebrates first mass 3 June (p. 80 above). Appointed curate St

[15]This is referred to by O'Hanlon in 'The Land of Leix' (*Poetical works of Lageniensis*, 91). See *Leinster Express* 23 and 30 January 1836.

[16]Emigration was possibly occasioned by the death of O'Hanlon's father. O'Hanlon's nephew, Joseph (son of Charles) recalled in 1967 that 'my grandfather died in Ireland when my father was small' (Mac Ionnraic Archive: Terry O'Hanlon material). Various accounts give New Orleans or New York as O'Hanlon's destination, but Quebec is confirmed by D. J. O'Donoghue (*Poets of Ireland*, 188, and *DNB*). Quebec was the cheapest destination at the time: *The Irish emigrant's guide*, 71–2.

[17]O'Hanlon's occupation at this time is variously given as a fisherman (*Irish Book Lover* 20 (1932) 16–17), or a fireman on a steamer (Concannon, 'Canon John O'Hanlon', 12). His own account of his meeting with Judge Mullanphy is given above, pp. 72–3.

[18]Became first Archbishop of St Louis, July 1847.

195

Edward O'Hanlon, John O'Hanlon's brother

Appendix 1

Patrick's Church, St Louis. Pastor to Irish settlements of Armagh and Downpatrick, 50 miles west of St Louis.

Editor of Catholic newspaper, *The St. Louis News-Letter* (newspaper ceases publication 1848).

1848

Appointed in May to mission in northern Missouri: based in Hannibal.[19]

Purchases 160-acre farm in Millwood, Missouri, on behalf of his brother, Edward, then resident in New Orleans. Edward later moves to Texas (see 1891), leaving another brother is possession of the farm.[20]

1849

J. O'Hanlon, *An abridgement of the history of Ireland, from its final subjection to the present time* (Boston: Patrick Donahoe, 1849).

1850

Returns in September to St Louis: curate in Church of St John the Evangelist.

1851

Appointed Prefect of Studies at Carondelet Seminary, near St Louis, where he teaches English, Logic, Metaphysics, Ethics and Scripture.

Edward O'Hanlon, now settled in Millwood, Missouri, arranges for emigration of their mother and other brothers and sisters – 'the junior portion of my family' – to Missouri. They arrive in St Louis, and O'Hanlon accompanies them to Millwood.[21]

J. O'Hanlon, *The Irish emigrant's guide for the United States* (Boston: Patrick Donahoe, 1851).[22] See 1890.

[19]Home of Samuel Langhorne Clemens (Mark Twain), and setting of *The Adventures of Huckleberry Finn.*
[20]*Life and scenery in Missouri*, 216. Edward moved to Sherman, Texas, and had issue. William, Charles, and Michael settled in Millwood, and had issue.
[21]Ibid., 258.
[22]Preface signed (p. 8) 'St. Louis, Jan. 1851'. O'Hanlon's dedicatory note (13 November 1857) in his presentation copy to the Royal Irish Academy states: 'As this little work was not corrected by the Author when passing through the press, it contains many typographical errors, some of them affecting the grammatical construction and sense.' The preface to O'Hanlon's 1890 edition states that the 1851 edition 'passed through a great number of impressions'. Modern edition: Maguire, *Reverend John O'Hanlon's The Irish emigrant's guide.*

Appendix 1

'The Life of Saint Malachy O'Morgair' published in *Boston Pilot*.[23]
J. O'H., 'A legend of Loughrea' [poem beg.: 'Woe to the land! for a warning is given'], *Dublin University Magazine* 37 (June 1851) 676–7.[24]

1852

Resumes position as curate, Church of St John the Evangelist, St Louis, November.

1853

Attack of bronchitis in spring forces O'Hanlon, on doctor's advice, to leave St Louis for Ireland in August. By 10 December he is in Ireland, when he makes a sketch of old church ruins at Coolbanagher, Queen's County, on that date.[25]

'Life of Saint Patrick' published in *Boston Pilot*, February–April.[26]

1854

His health recovered, he writes from Ballymaddock[27] in January to Paul Cullen, Archbishop of Dublin, seeking an appointment for six months

[23] *The life of Saint Malachy O'Morgair*, vi.

[24] 'About the year 1849, while residing in a distant country, the "Legend of Loughrea," with notes attached, had been sent to a gentleman in Dublin. It would seem that the *Dublin University Magazine* editor got possession of this fragment, and gave it insertion in the xxxvii. vol. at p. 676. It is there acknowledged as bearing a foreign postage mark. At a subsequent period, the lines in question, with notes somewhat different, were offered to and accepted by a successor in the editorial chair. It is only right to observe, however, that neither this gentleman nor the author had been cognizant of the fact relating to the first insertion, when the Legend obtained a second and misplaced introduction to the pages of our national Magazine' (*Legend lays of Ireland*, xxiv).

[25] *The life and works of Saint Aengussius*, 7 n. 1.

[26] *The life of Saint Malachy O'Morgair*, vi. See *Lives of the Irish saints* III, 399–831.

[27] Probably from the home of his brother-in-law, William Cantwell. William had married Mary Hanlon, 16 June 1845 (Stradbally Parish Records, Marriage Registry, p. 22); he had a substantial holding of around 70 acres in Ballymaddock (Griffith, *Queen's County ... Primary Valuation*, 19), and was a subscriber to *Lives of the Irish saints* (volume I, p. 610). In a letter (8 February 1856) to his colleague, Fr P. E. O'Farrelly, O'Hanlon says: 'About the beginning of last month I was obliged to apply for a sum of money to my kind brother-in-law residing in the country, to enable me to meet my current expenses' (DDA Cullen Papers 1856, Secular Clergy).

Charles O'Hanlon (John O'Hanlon's brother), and his daughter Grace

Appendix 1

(see Appendix 2 § 1), still intending to return to St Louis, and enclosing a testimonial from Archbishop Kenrick.[28]

Appointed Assistant Chaplain, South Dublin Union.[29]

1855

Member Ossianic Society; address given: 159 James's St, Dublin.[30]

1856

Member Kilkenny and South-East of Ireland Archaeological Society (later Royal Society of Antiquaries of Ireland), May 1856. Address given: 40 Parkgate St, Dublin.[31]

Reports on Ordnance Survey records of Co. Kilkenny and Queen's County, *Journal of the Kilkenny and South-East of Ireland Archaeological Society* New Series, 1 (1856–7) 153–4, 192–4.

1857

John O'Hanlon, *The life of St. Laurence O'Toole, Archbishop of Dublin, and Delegate Apostolic of the Holy See, for the Kingdom of Ireland* (Dublin: John Mullany, 1857).[32]

[28] 'I take the liberty of presenting to your Grace Rev. J. O'Hanlon of this diocese who revisits his native country in the hope of recovering health. Rev. Mr. O'Hanlon is a most exemplary and amiable person, whom I pray God to restore to us in that vigour of health necessary for the severe duties of our western Mission.' (DDA Cullen Papers 1853, Bishops' Correspondence: Kenrick to Cullen, 20 August 1853.)

[29] 'His health was then utterly shattered as a result of his labours in the ministry in America, and he was unable to undertake any more exacting duties here than those of an assistant-chaplain to one of the public institutions of the city' (Archbishop William J. Walsh, quoted in *Freeman's Journal* 25 July 1910).

[30] *Transactions of the Ossianic Society* II, 214. This is the first address (the house of William Cole, law clerk) given for O'Hanlon in Thom's *Directory* (1855, p. 899). From 1859 O'Hanlon is listed as a member of the Council and of the Committee of Publication of the Society (*Transactions of the Ossianic Society* IV, p. vii).

[31] *Journal of the Kilkenny and South-East of Ireland Archaeological Society* New Series, 1 (1856–7) 71.

[32] Dedicated to Paul Cullen, Archbishop of Dublin. Proceeds donated to 'new church of St. Laurence O'Toole, in the city of Dublin' (Preface, p. vi). Preface signed 'Dublin, 17, James'-street. October 1857'. 'Might I venture to inquire if your Grace has had an opportunity of glancing at the "Life of St. Laurence

200

Appendix 1

Report on statement from Mining Company of Ireland regarding ruins of the ancient church of Glendalough, *Journal of the Kilkenny and South-East of Ireland Archaeological Society* New Series, 1 (1856–7) 246–7.

Reports on Ordnance Survey records of various counties: ibid., 250–54 (King's County), 293–8 (Kildare), 321–4 (Carlow), 392–8 (Wexford), 424–7 (Wicklow).

1858

Assistant Chaplain, St Joseph's Monastery, Clondalkin.[33]

At request of Society of St John the Evangelist, O'Hanlon delivers a lecture – 'The life, labours, and learning of Aengus the Culdee, Irish monk and author of the eighth century' – in Alderman Crotty's Great Rooms, Christ Church Place, 10 September.[34]

Reports on Ordnance Survey records of various counties: *Journal of the Kilkenny and South-East of Ireland Archaeological Society* New Series, 2 (1858–9) 12–15 (Dublin), 42–8 (Meath), 96–105 (Louth).

1859

Curate, Church of Saints Michael and John, 75 Lower Exchange Street, Dublin.[35]

John O'Hanlon, *The life of Saint Malachy O'Morgair, Bishop of Down and Connor, Archbishop of Armagh, patron of these several dioceses, and Delegate Apostolic of the Holy See for the kingdom of Ireland* (Dublin: John O'Daly, 1859).[36]

O'Toole" so as to satisfy yourself that I might be permitted to obtain the indulgence of being allowed to dedicate it to you in a few short and respectful terms. This inscription will not contain all I would wish to say, were I to consult my own feelings on the matter, but I believe quite as much as your Grace could have no objection to see in print' (DDA Cullen Papers 1856, Secular Clergy: O'Hanlon (40 Park Gate Street) to Cullen, 1 December 1856).

[33] *Battersby's Catholic Directory* (1859) 163.

[34] *The life and works of Saint Aengussius*, v. This forms the nucleus for his 1868 publication.

[35] *Battersby's Catholic Directory* (1860) 158. This church was sold to Temple Bar Properties in 1991.

[36] Dedicated to Joseph Dixon, Archbishop of Armagh and Primate of All Ireland. Preface signed: 'St. Michael's and St. John's Parochial Residence, Lower Exchange-street, Dublin, March 1859'.

Grave of Fr John Lanigan, St Canice's Churchyard, Finglas (see 1861)

Appendix 1

'Life of Saint Patrick Apostle of Ireland by the Rev. John O'Hanlon' announced as 'preparing for publication'.[37]

1860

Report on Ordnance Survey records of Co. Westmeath: *Journal of the Kilkenny and South-East of Ireland Archaeological Society* New Series, 3 (1860–61) 193–5.

1861

In conjunction with Eugene O'Curry, O'Hanlon erects a Celtic cross, designed by George Petrie, in St. Canice's churchyard, Finglas, over the grave of Rev. Dr John Lanigan (1758–1828), author of *An ecclesiastical history of Ireland*.[38]

Report on Ordnance Survey records of Co. Longford: *Journal of the Kilkenny and South-East of Ireland Archaeological Society* New Series, 3 (1860–61) 321–3.

Lageniensis, 'Legend lays of Ireland. No. I. – A legend of Killarney' [poem beg. 'O saw you the spectre this moon-paling night'], *Dublin University Magazine* 57 (February 1861) 229–30.

'Legend lays of Ireland. No. II. – A legend of Benevenugh' [poem beg. 'On the dark northern coast, o'er waves of blue'], ibid. (March 1861) 362–4.

'Legend lays of Ireland. No. III. – Legend of Ormonde Castle' [poem beg. 'The cawing rook shall build her nest on Ormonde Castle's pinnacle'], 'No. IV. – Legend of Lough Rea' [poem beg. 'Woe to the land! for a warning is given'], ibid. (April 1861) 501–2.

'Legend lays of Ireland. No. V. – A legend of Cullenagh' [poem beg. 'The Currach meadows ring with hoot'], ibid. (May 1861) 593–604.

'Legend lays of Ireland: No. VI. A legend of Donegal' [poem beg. 'With evening shades descending'], ibid., 58 (August 1861) 217–18.

[37]Prospectus in *The life of Saint Malachy O'Morgair* after p. 222. See 1853 above.

[38]Moran, *Monasticon Hibernicum* II, 83; *Irish Ecclesiastical Record* 3rd Ser., 6 (December 1885) 767. Cf. Fitz-Patrick, *Irish wits and worthies*, 298–304; this includes (p. 303) a humorous account of an encounter between 'a worthy priest' – possibly O'Hanlon – and the vicar of Finglas, when the priest was attempting to locate Lanigan's coffin-plate. See sketch, *Lives of the Irish saints* III, 679, and O'Hanlon's 'Elegy on the grave of Rev. Dr. Lanigan' (*Poetical works of Lageniensis*, 320–22).

Appendix 1

1862

John Gray of the *Freeman's Journal* proposes erection of monument to Daniel O'Connell to be located in Dublin. 'O'Connell Monument Committee' established 13 October, O'Hanlon Honorary Secretary.[39]

Report on Ordnance Survey records of Co. Down: *Journal of the Kilkenny and South-East of Ireland Archaeological Society* New Series, 4 (1862–3)14–36.

Report on 'some discoveries on the site of the Priory of St. John, Dublin': ibid. 4 (1862–3) 148–9.

1863

Travels to Low Countries and Prussia to research lives of Saints Dympna and Gerebern, July–September. Visits Brussels, Douai, Louvain, Cologne.[40]

Officiates at marriage of James Stephens and Jane Hopper, in Saints Michael and John, 11 November.[41]

John O'Hanlon, *The life of St. Dympna, virgin, martyr, and patroness of Gheel; with some notices of St. Gerebern, priest, martyr, and patron of Sonsbeck* (Dublin: James Duffy, 1863).[42]

Reports on Ordnance Survey records of various counties: *Journal of the Kilkenny and South-East of Ireland Archaeological Society* New

---

[39] After a public competition, the work was awarded to John Henry Foley, the London-based Irish sculptor, 4 October 1865. Delays in the production of the sculpture obliged O'Hanlon to write explanatory letters to the press; e.g. *Irish Builder* 9 (1867) 262; 11 (1869) 150. Foley died 27 August 1874, leaving the monument incomplete. In 1878, the task of completing the work was assigned to Foley's principal assistant, Thomas Brock. The monument was unveiled in August 1882 (see below).

[40] *Lives of the Irish saints* I, xlii n. 52, lxxxix n. 239, cxxxix nn. 90–91, cxli n. 117, cxlvi n. 192. VII, 266 n. 10. See pp. 175–82 above.

[41] Ryan, *The Fenian Chief*, 184–5. The best man was John O'Leary. 'Canon O'Hanlon was a Nationalist in the full sense of the word – he believed in the right of his country to sovereign independence, and did not hesitate to say so. He was the priest who officiated at the marriage of James Stephens, and he always referred to the fact with pride' (*United Ireland* 20 May 1905).

[42] See *Lives of the Irish saints* V, 284–374. Preface dated September 1863. Dedicated to Very Rev. Monsignore William Yore, D.D., P.P. St Paul's Church, and V.G. Archdiocese of Dublin. 'Three months have scarcely elapsed since you expressed a desire that a brief *memoir* of our holy Irish virgin and martyr, St. Dympna, should be prepared and published' (p. ix).

Appendix 1

Series, 4 (1863) 238–45 (Antrim), 310–17 (Armagh, Derry, Donegal, and Monaghan).

1864

John O'Hanlon, *Catechism of Irish history from the earliest events to the death of O'Connell* (Dublin: John Mullany, 1864).[43]
Reports on Ordnance Survey records of various counties: *Journal of the Kilkenny and South-East of Ireland Archaeological Society* New Series, 5 (1864–6) 20–27 (Tyrone, Fermanagh, Monaghan and Cavan), 124–31 (Tipperary and Waterford).

1865

John O'Hanlon, *Catechism of Greek grammar* (Dublin: John Mullany, 1865).[44]

1866

John O'Hanlon, *Devotions for Confession and Holy Communion* (Dublin, London, Derby: Thomas Richardson, 1866).[45]
Reports on Ordnance Survey records of various counties, *Journal of the Kilkenny and South-East of Ireland Archaeological Society* New Series, 5 (1864–6) 418–24 (Clare and Limerick), 452–7 (Cork), 486–90 (Kerry).

1867

Reports on Ordnance Survey records of various counties, *Journal of the Kilkenny and South-East of Ireland Archaeological Society* New Series, 6 (1867) 103–9 (Sligo and Roscommon), 212–20 (Mayo, Galway and Leitrim).

[43]O'Hanlon acknowledges (p. vii) the 'pains-taking perusal and critical correction' by Eugene O'Curry of the pre-Christian section of the book.
[44]'Undertaken at the instance of its publisher, in accordance with a suggestion, offered by the compiler, for issuing a complete series of educational works, calculated to facilitate the progress of teachers and pupils, during the incipient stages of scholastic studies' (p. iii).
[45]Dedicated to Very Rev. Monsignore William Meagher, P.P. Rathmines, and V.G. Archdiocese of Dublin. Preface dated October 1866.

Appendix 1

1868

Visits, in the summer, the grave of O'Carolan at Kilronan, Co. Roscommon, occasioning poem ('The buried lady') published in 1877.[46]

'The life and works of Saint Aengussius Hagiographus, or Saint Aengus the Culdee, bishop and abbot at Clonenagh and Dysartenos, Queen's County', *Irish Ecclesiastical Record* 5 (1868) 1–20 (October), 73–81 (November), 97–108 (December).
John O'Hanlon, *The life and works of Saint Aengussius Hagiographus, or Saint Aengus the Culdee, bishop and abbot at Clonenagh and Dysartenos, Queen's County* (Dublin: John F. Fowler, 1868).[47]

1869

Elected Member of Royal Irish Academy.[48]

John O'Hanlon, *The life of St. David, Archbishop of Menevia, chief patron of Wales, and titular patron of Naas Church and Parish in Ireland* (Dublin: John Mullany, 1869).[49]
'Life of St. Laserian, bishop and patron of Leighlin Diocese', *Carlow College Magazine* 1 (1869) 104–7, 180–84, 231–4, 278–81, 328–30, 399–405.

1870

Lageniensis, *Legend lays of Ireland* (Dublin: John Mullany, 1870).[50]

[46]O'Hanlon, *The buried lady*, 23.
[47]See *Lives of the Irish saints* III, 294–318. Originated as a lecture: see 1858 above. Dedicated to Very Rev. Monsignore Patrick F. Moran, D.D., Professor of Irish History in the Catholic University. Dedication dated Feast of Immaculate Conception [8 December] 1868. Moran (later Cardinal Moran, Archbishop of Sydney) was editor of the *Irish Ecclesiastical Record*.
[48]RIA Council Minutes, Vol. 15, p. 366.
[49]Dedicated to Very Rev. James Hughes, P.P. Naas: 'owing, in the first instance, to your suggestion it was begun, and furthermore it should be stated, you have defrayed all the cost of publication' (p. iii).
[50]Dedicated to 'William John Fitzpatrick, Esq., J.P., Kilmacud Manor, Stillorgan'. Preface dated February 1870. Presentation copy to Denis Florence MacCarthy in NLI (Ir 82189 o 24) dated 'Jan. 22nd'. First five legends published separately 1861. Proofs of this work in Russell Library MS OH 42 are dated 1865.

Appendix 1

Lageniensis, *Irish folk lore: traditions and superstitions of the country, with humorous tales* (Glasgow: Cameron and Ferguson, 1870).[51]
'Life of St. Laserian, bishop and patron of Leighlin Diocese', *Carlow College Magazine* 1 (1870) 428–36.
'The missing book of Clonenagh': paper read at Royal Irish Academy, 11 April 1870; published, *Proceedings of the Royal Irish Academy* Ser. 2, 1 (1870–79) 7–12.

1872
Inspects manuscripts in Durham, July.[52]

'On the identification of St Malachy O'Morgair's "Monasterium Ibracense"': paper read at Royal Irish Academy, 26 February 1872; published, *Proceedings of the Royal Irish Academy* Ser. 2, 1 (1870–79) 107–13.
'Notes on some undescribed antiquities in the parishes of Killenny and Kilteale, Queen's County': paper read at Royal Irish Academy, 26 June 1872; published, *Proceedings of the Royal Irish Academy* Ser. 2, 1 (1870–79) 143–54.

1873 – c. 1905

John O'Hanlon *Lives of the Irish saints, with special festivals, and the commemorations of holy persons, compiled from calendars, martyrologies, and various sources, relating to the ancient church history of Ireland* I–X (Dublin: James Duffy; London: Burns, Oates & Co.; New York: Catholic Publishing Society, 1875–1905).[53]

[51] Dedicated to Denis Florence MacCarthy. Preface dated April 1870. Reprint: *Irish folk lore: traditions and superstitions of the country; with humorous tales, by "Lageniensis"* ([Yorkshire]: EP Publishing Ltd., 1973).
[52] *Lives of the Irish saints* I, cxxxi n. 32.
[53] The usual date given for the commencement of this publication is 1875, derived from the signature to the introduction to Volume I: 'Feast of St. Columkille, 1875'. Volume I comprises the thirteen parts already published, with O'Hanlon's comprehensive introduction. Correspondence in Russell Library MS OH 16 (see Appendix 3) shows that Part 1 of the *Lives of the Irish saints* had been published and sent to subscribers in October 1873; and the *Irish Monthly* welcomed its publication in its November number (1 (1873) 302). The dates in the NLI Catalogue for the individual volumes are: 1875 (Vol. I), 1877 (II and III), 1886 (IV), 1890 (V), 1891 (VI), 1892 (VII), 1896 (VIII), 1903 (IX). It appears that Volume X (October 1–21) was published sometime prior to O'Hanlon's death in 1905.

Appendix 1

1874

Visits Abbey ruins at Paisley, Scotland 'in company with Rev. Dr. J. F. S. Gordon, author of the "Scoti-Chronicon" '.[54]

'On the identification of the site of the engagement at the "Pass of the Plumes" (1599)': paper read at Royal Irish Academy, 11 May 1874; published, *Proceedings of the Royal Irish Academy* Ser. 2, 1 (1870–79) 279–88; and published separately (Dublin: Royal Irish Academy 1876).[55]

1877

O'Hanlon becomes member of Society for the Preservation of the Irish Language.[56]

Lageniensis, 'The buried lady: a legend of Kilronan', *Illustrated Monitor* 4/1 (April 1877) 21–5; and separately, *The buried lady: a legend of Kilronan, by Lageniensis* (Dublin: Joseph Dollard, 1877).[57]

John O'Hanlon, *Life of St. Brigid, Virgin, first Abbess of Kildare, special patroness of Kildare diocese, and general patroness of Ireland* (Dublin: Joseph Dollard, 1877).[58]

1880

Appointed Parish Priest of Sandymount, 10 June. Installed as P.P., 15 June, at St Mary's Church, Star of the Sea, Irishtown.[59] Presbytery address: 3 Leahy's Terrace, Irishtown.

---

[54]*Lives of the Irish saints* IX, 380 n. 20.

[55]'Fifty copies only, reprinted by the Academy for the Author' (front cover). Reprinted in Tynan, *Barnaglitty*, 9–24.

[56]Founded 29 December 1876, O'Hanlon chaired one of its early meetings, 27 February 1877 (NLI microfilm P 9173: Minutes, Volume I, p. [7]).

[57]Dedicated to 'Henry Edward Manning, Cardinal Archbishop of Westminster'. Preface dated May 1877.

[58]*Lives of the Irish saints* II, 1–224. No dedication; preface dated Feast of Saint Brigid [1 February] 1877. 'While preparing the following Biography, as a leading feature in his "Lives of the Irish Saints", the author was urged, by many devout clients of St. Brigid, to issue it in a separate form, to satisfy the wants and wishes of numerous kind friends' (p. iii).

[59]DDA McCabe Papers 1880, Secular Clergy: O'Hanlon to McCabe, 12 June 1880.

Appendix 1

19 LEAHY TERRACE,
SANDYMOUNT,
Nov. 10*th*, 1905.

Dear Sir,

Representations have been made to me that an earnest and wide spread desire exists amongst the people of the Parish and a large number of friends outside the Parish, that measures should be taken to provide a suitable Memorial to the memory of the late Very Rev. Canon O,Hanlon, P.P.

Knowing these representations to be well-grounded, and earnestly sympathising with the object in view, I am inviting the Parishioners, and other friends of the late venerated Parish Priest, to attend a Public Meeting to be held in our Parish Church, on Sunday, November 19th, 1905, at 12.45 o'clock—immediately after the termination of the last Mass—to take such measures as may seem advisable to carry out the purpose indicated.

I shall be very thankful to receive, between this and the date of the Meeting, suggestions as to the form the Memorial should take.

There is no monument over the grave in Glasnevin, nor has any provision been made for the erection of such monument.

Earnestly requesting your attendance and co-operation,

I am, dear Sir,

Very faithfully yours,

THOMAS MAGRATH, P.P.

Appendix 1

1881

John O'Hanlon, *The life of Saint Grellan, patron of the O'Kellys, and of the tribes of Hy-Maine* (Dublin and London: James Duffy and sons, 1881).[60]

1882

Death of O'Hanlon's friend, Denis Florence MacCarthy, 7 April. O'Hanlon joins Denis Florence MacCarthy Memorial Committee at meeting in Mansion House, Dublin, 15 April.[61]

Unveiling of O'Connell Monument, Sackville Street, Dublin, 15 August (see 1862 above). O'Hanlon and Edward Dwyer Gray, on behalf of the Committee, present the monument to the Lord Mayor (Charles Dawson) and Corporation of Dublin.[62]

Subscriber to *Irisleabhar na Gaedhilge: The Gaelic Journal.*[63]

1883

[unsigned], 'Irish local legends',[64] *Irish Builder* 25 (1883) 300 (I: Woodstock Castle); 316–17 (II: Mullaghmast).

Lageniensis, 'Old churches of Leix', *Irish Builder* 25 (1883) 339–40; 350–51 (I: Sletty); 370–71 (II: Timahoe); 394 (III: Kilwhelan).

1884

Final meeting of O'Connell Monument Committee, 10 September.

[John O'Hanlon], *History and description of St. Mary's Church, Star of the Sea, Irishtown. Report of the committee appointed to erect the Dean O'Connell Memorial* (Irishtown 1884).[65]

[60]*Lives of the Irish saints* IX, 419–31. No preface. Dedicated 'To the recognised living representative of his distinguished family and name, Cornelius J. Kelly, Count of the Holy Roman Empire, Gallagh Castle, County of Galway' (p. [iii]).

[61]NLI Denis Florence MacCarthy Papers, Accession 1550, Box 5. The memorial involved a bust of MacCarthy by Thomas Farrell RHA, unveiled in City Hall, Dublin, January 1883 (*Irish Builder* 15 (1883) 13); and a new edition of his poems (*Poetical works of Lageniensis*, 326 n.).

[62]*Report of the O'Connell Monument Committee*, lxxii–lxxiii. The monument was still incomplete, the final piece being added May 1883.

[63]*Irisleabhar na Gaedhilge* 1 (1882–3) 400.

[64]This series formed the basis for O'Hanlon's book of 1896.

[65]No author cited, but ascribed to O'Hanlon in the *Irish Builder* 31 (15 October 1889) 253, in an article attributing further improvements in the church to 'the

210

Appendix 1

[unsigned], 'Irish local legends', *Irish Builder* 26 (1884) 143–4 (III: Inisquin or Inchiquin); 162–3 (III continued); 294 (IV: Moghia near Lismore); 329 (V: Aran Islands); 357–8 (VI: Mundrehid).

Lageniensis, 'Old churches of Leix', *Irish Builder* 26 (1884) 6 (IV: Mundrehid); 35 (V: Bocluain); 49–50 (VI: Clonkeen); 62 (VII: Clonenagh); 79 (VII: Clonenagh continued); 103–4 (VIII: Clonenagh continued); 111 (IX: Dysart Enos); 134–5 (X: Dysart Enos continued); 145 (XI: Killabban); 177 (XII: Loughill); 193 (No. XIII: Tascoffin or Tiscoffin); 209 (No. XIV: Tascoffin or Tiscoffin continued); 225 (XV: Clonsost or Clonsast); 262–3 (XVI: Coolbanagher); 272 (XVII: Dysert Bethech); 293 (XVIII: Annatrim); 301 (XIX: Abbeyleix); 348–9 (XX: Kilvahan); 339 (XXI: Killermogh); 350–51 (XXII: Ougheval); 366–7 (XXIII: Kilteal).

1885

O'Hanlon is created a Canon.[66]

Death of Fr John Francis Shearman, author of *Loca Patriciana*, P.P. Moone, Co. Kildare, 6 February; his papers left to O'Hanlon, who, in May, sorts and organises them into 23 bound volumes.[67]

Founds St Patrick's Literary Institute, Cambridge Road, Ringsend.[68]

[unsigned], 'Irish pagan superstitions', *Irish Builder* 27 (1885) 298, 309, 318.

---

artistic taste and sound judgement in such matters possessed by the respected pastor, Canon O'Hanlon'. The book was printed by the *Irish Builder*, and contains, as Appendix III, the text of a sermon preached at the Star of the Sea Church, 6 January 1884, by Most Rev. Patrick John Ryan, Coadjutor Bishop of St Louis, O'Hanlon's lifelong friend from Clonyharp near Thurles, on whom he has a lengthy biographical note in *Life and scenery in Missouri*, 262–72. 'The Most Rev. Bishop Ryan has arrived to-day, and he felt greatly fatigued after his trip which was a night one and uncomfortable; so he lay down to take a little rest, nor had he time until now to devote to preparing his sermon for tomorrow' (DDA McCabe Papers 1884, Secular Clergy: O'Hanlon to McCabe, 5 January 1884). Bishop Ryan was promoted to Archbishop of Philadelphia in June 1884.

[66] See letter of congratulation dated 4 November 1885 in Russell Library Maynooth MS OH 33. Listed as Sub-Diaconal Prebend for Donaghmore (one portion), *Irish Catholic Directory* (1886) 144.

[67] NUI, Maynooth, Russell Library, MSS SH 1–23. A handlist of the Shearman manuscripts, compiled in 1996 by Mary Pat O'Malley, is available in the Russell Library. For Fr Shearman see below p. 279.

[68] Information from Brian Siggins, Ringsend.

Appendix 1

[unsigned], 'The Irish druids', *Irish Builder* 27 (1885) 333.

Lageniensis, 'Old churches of Leix', *Irish Builder* 27 (1885) 7–8 (XXIV: Stradbally); 29 (XXIV: Stradbally continued); 40–43 (XXIV: Stradbally continued); 56 (XXV: Tully or Tullowmoy); 71 (XXVI: Clopooke); 91–2 (XXVII: Kyle or Clonfert Molua); 103 (XXVIII: Kyle or Clonfert Molua continued); 118 (XXIX: Aghaboe); 129 (XXX: Aghaboe continued); 144 (XXXI: Aghaboe continued); 160 (XXXII: Aghaboe continued); 174–5 (XXXIII: Aghaboe continued); 194 (XXXIV: Aghaboe continued); 200 (XXXV: Aghaboe continued); 216 (XXXVI: Aghaboe continued); 229 (XXXVII: Aghmacart); 242–3 (XXXVIII: Killdelig or Kildellig); 260 (XXXIX: Tecolm); 268 (XL: Offerlane); 280 (XLI: Kilcolmanbane); 299 (XLII: Kilcolmanbrack or Cremorgan); 311–12 (XLIII: Borris); 326 (XLIV: Maryborough); 339 (XLV: Maryborough continued).

John O'Hanlon, 'Life and labours of Rev. John Francis Shearman, P.P., Moone', *Irish Ecclesiastical Record* 3rd Ser., 6 (December 1885) 764–78.

1886

O'Hanlon tours Europe, September–November. Travels from Frankfurt to Ratisbon and Vienna.[69] Visits Basilica of St Boniface, Munich;[70] Cologne Cathedral;[71] says mass in St Gall Cathedral (30 September);[72] During visit to Italy,[73] visits Benedictine monastery of Monte Casino, 25–6 October;[74] stays at Hotel Feder (where O'Connell died), Genoa, November.[75]

[unsigned], 'Mythology of the ancient Irish', *Irish Builder* 28 (1886) 11, 30.

Lageniensis, 'Old churches of Leix', *Irish Builder* 28 (1886) 4 (XLVI: Killeny or Killeany); 28 (XLVII: Killeny continued); 43 (XLVIII:

---

[69] *Lives of the Irish saints* VII, 136 n. 45.

[70] Ibid. VI, 139 n. 154.

[71] Ibid. VII, 266 n. 10, X, 434.

[72] Ibid. X, 319 n. 148.

[73] An undated parchment address from 'the members of the Conference, Star of the Sea', welcoming his return from Rome, where he presented a set of *Lives of the Irish saints* to the Pontiff, probably dates from this time (Mac Ionnraic Archive).

[74] *Lives of the Irish saints* VII, 114 n. 64.

[75] See Appendix 3 (MS OH 39/7).

Appendix 1

Curraclone or Corclone); 52 (XLIX: Timogue); 67–8 (L: Straboe); 81 (LI: Moyanna); 101 (LII: Killeshin); 114–17 (LIII: Killeshin continued); 134–5 (LIV: Killeshin continued); 150 (LV: Killeshin continued); 166 (LVI: Rathaspick); 182–3 (LVII: Rathaspick continued); 199 (LVIII: Ballyadams); 209 (LVIX: Ballyadams continued); 225 (LX: Ballintubbert); 238 (LXI: Tankardstown); 250 (LXII: Shrule); 256 (LXIII: Grange or Monksgrange); 283 (LXIV: Ballyroan); 303 (LXV: Cill-Finnich or Killinny); 316 (LXVI: Toulore or Tullore); 326–7 (LXVII: Lea).

1887

[unsigned], 'Irish local legends', *Irish Builder* 29 (1887) 283 (VII: River Delvin Co. Meath); 353 (VIII: Drumsna, Co. Monaghan).

Lageniensis, 'Old churches of Leix', *Irish Builder* 29 (1887) 5 (LXVIII: Lea continued); 20–21 (LXIX: Portarlington); 34–5 (LXX: Portarlington continued); 57 (LXXI: Portarlington continued); 62 (LXXII: Ballyaddan); 90 (LXXIII: Coolkerry); 106 (LXXIV: Dysert-Gallen); 150 (LXXIV [*sic*]: Kilcronan); 164 (LXXV: Erke or Eirke); 190 (LXXVI: Bordwell); 200 (LXXVII: Durrow or Castle-Durrow); 220 (LXXVIII: Rathdowney); 229 (LXXIX: Rathoaran); 246 (LXXX: Skirk or Skeirke); 262 (LXXXI: Donaghmore); 274 (LXXXIII [*sic*]:[76] Rosenallis); 282 (LXXXIV: Castlebrack); 296 (LXXXV: Rearymore or Rerymore); 316–19 (LXXXVI: Kilmanman); 331 (LXXXVII: Ardea or Ardrea); 353 (LXXXVIII: Ballyquillane).

Canon O'Hanlon, 'Ancient Irish Churches', *Dublin Journal* 1/5 (April 1887) 76.[77]

Lageniensis, 'Scenes in Leix. A poem: archaeological and descriptive. No. 1. Stradbally' [poem begins: 'The glowing sunset sinks in distant shadows'], *Dublin Journal* 1/17 (November 1887) 260.

Lageniensis, 'Scenes in Leix. A poem: archaeological and descriptive. No. II. – Brockley Park' [poem begins: 'How calm and peaceful when the moonbeams bathed'], *Dublin Journal* 1/18 (December 1887) 279.

---

[76]Error in 1 June 1887 adjusted here.

[77]This number also prints, p. 80, a letter from O'Hanlon, dated 26 February 1887, complimenting the editor.

Appendix 1

1888

Report of the O'Connell Monument Committee, by Very Rev. John Canon O'Hanlon, P.P., honorary secretary (Dublin: James Duffy and Co., 1888).

[unsigned], 'Irish local legends', *Irish Builder* 30 (1888) 4 (IX: River Lagan, Co. Down); 294 (XI:[78] St. Mullins).

Lageniensis, 'Old churches of Leix', *Irish Builder* 30 (1888) 8 (LXXXIX: Cloydagh or Clody); 14 (XC: Lismore); 54 (XCI: Knockseera); 59 (XCII: Kilmurry); 72 (XCIII: St. John's Parish of Athy); 91 (XCIV: Churchtown or Rheban); 109–10 (XCV: Mountmellick).[79]

[unsigned], 'Historic memorials of Leix', *Irish Builder* 30 (1888) 119.[80]

1889

[unsigned], 'Irish local legends', *Irish Builder* 31 (1889) 1–2 (XII: Tara); 80 (XIII: Lios na Eiblin Oge, Co. Cork).

[unsigned], 'History, statistics, and present condition of the various states comprising the American Union', *Irish Builder* 31 (1889) 20, 36, 49, 71, 86, 110, 122, 133, 144, 161, 173, 189, 196, 213, 219, 231, 247, 256, 268, 291, 309.

[unsigned], 'Irish emigration to the United States', *Irish Builder* 31 (1889) 287.

1890

Foundation stone of Ringsend presbytery laid, 30 November. Ceremony attended by Archbishop Walsh, and by Lord Mayor (E. J. Kennedy) of Dublin.[81]

[78]Legend number X not found.

[79]O'Hanlon's series on the churches of Leix breaks off abruptly at this point (15 April 1888), to be resumed ten years later with a single article on Ballinakill (see 1898 below).

[80]Comparison with *History of the Queen's County* I shows that the series that begins here is the work of John O'Hanlon. It continues regularly through this and subsequent volumes for eight years until breaking off with volume 38 (15 September 1896) 196.

[81]Correspondence on this subject in DDA Walsh Papers 1890, Secular Clergy: O'Hanlon to Walsh, 9, 18, 26, 28 November 1890.

214

Appendix 1

John O'Hanlon, *Life and scenery in Missouri: reminiscences of a missionary priest* (Dublin: James Duffy and Co., 1890).[82]

John O'Hanlon, *The Irish emigrant's guide for the United States, with coloured map and railway connections* First Irish edition, revised, and information brought down to the present year (Dublin: Sealy, Bryers and Walker, 1890). See 1851.

[unsigned], 'History, statistics, and present condition of the various states comprising the American Union', *Irish Builder* 32 (1890) 11, 16, 38, 49, 59, 72, 85, 99, 108, 125, 136, 150, 159, 172, 186, 202, 209, 223, 233, 247, 259.[83]

[unsigned], 'Irish local legends', *Irish Builder* 32 (1890) 98 (XIV: Clogh-mor, Co. Down); 115 (XV: Lough Derg).

'Ancient Irish land tenures', *Irish Ecclesiastical Record* 3rd Ser., 11 (1890) 235–41.

1891

Takes passage on 'Alaska' from Queenstown to New York, 4 October, to attend Golden Jubilee of Archbishop Peter Richard Kenrick in St Louis (30 November).[84] Extensive itinerary during visit includes Quebec,[85] Civil War museum in Chicago,[86] his old parish of Hannibal, Missouri, now grown to a city,[87] and his brother in Texas.[88] Returns for Christmas.

Essay on the antiquity and constitution of parliaments in Ireland. By Henry Joseph Monck Mason, LL.D., and M.R.I.A. A new edition with

---

[82] 'The descriptive and narrative sketches, contained in succeeding pages, for the most part were compiled many years hence, and had been written amidst the scenes, and – towards the close – some time after occurrences, they attempt to delineate. Under the heading "Excursions through Missouri," many of them first appeared in the columns of *The American Celt*, formerly edited by Thomas D'Arcy M'Gee' (p. [v]). *The American Celt* was under M'Gee's ownership and editorship 1850–57.

[83] It must be assumed that this work and that of 1889 are to be attributed to O'Hanlon, as he prepared his second edition of *The Irish emigrant's guide for the United States*.

[84] DDA, Walsh Papers 1891, Secular Clergy: O'Hanlon to Walsh, 19 September 1891.

[85] *Poetical works of Lageniensis*, vii.

[86] *Irish-American history*, 456 n. 109.

[87] See Appendix 3 § 9.

[88] See Appendix 3 § 7.

215

preface, life of the author, and an introduction, by Very Rev. John Canon O'Hanlon (Dublin: James Duffy and Co., 1891).[89]
'Irish parliaments', *Irish Ecclesiastical Record* 3rd Ser., 12 (1891) 116–33, 212–24.

1892

The case of Ireland's being bound by Acts of Parliament in England, stated, by William Molyneux, of Dublin, Esq. A new edition, with preface and life of the author, by Very Rev. John Canon O'Hanlon P.P., M.R.I.A. (Dublin: Sealy, Bryers and Walker, 1892).[90]
'The Catholic Church in the United States', *Irish Ecclesiastical Record* 3rd Ser., 13 (1892) 490–506.

1893

Lageniensis, *The poetical works of Lageniensis* (Dublin: James Duffy & Co., 1893).[91]

1894

Public meeting at Star of the Sea, attended by Archbishop of Dublin and Lord Mayor (Valentine Dillon), to raise funds for completion of parochial residence, Ringsend, 14 October.[92]

1895

O'Hanlon promoted to Diaconal Prebend of Tipper.[93]

'The Catholicity of Thomas Moore', *Irish Ecclesiastical Record* 3rd Ser., 14 (March 1895) 249–58.

[89] Preface dated 17 March 1891. Dedication: 'To the Right Hon. William Ewart Gladstone, M.P., as a slight tribute of admiration for his genius, of respect for his character, and of gratitude for his services to Ireland'.
[90] Preface dated 30 September 1891.
[91] Preface dated September 1893. Dedicated to 'The Right Honourable Isabel, Countess of Aberdeen'. The Countess had visited Sandymount, 22 February 1893: see O'Hanlon's 'Lyric' (*Poetical works of Lageniensis*, 322) composed for the occasion.
[92] *Irish Catholic* 20 October 1894. DDA Walsh Papers, Secular Clergy: O'Hanlon to Walsh, 12 October 1894; further reference to Ringsend debt, O'Hanlon to Walsh, 2 July 1895.
[93] *Irish Catholic Directory* (1896) 100.

Appendix 1

1896

Member of Irish Texts Society.[94]

Lageniensis, *Irish local legends* (Dublin: James Duffy & Co., 1896).[95]
'Alexander Taylor's map of County Kildare', *Journal of the Co. Kildare Archaeological Society* 2 (1896–9) 386.[96]

1897

O'Hanlon celebrates fiftieth anniversary of his ordination (29 May) with reception on Monday 31 May at Sandymount Assembly Rooms.[97] Presented with illuminated address by his parishioners and fellow priests (see Appendix 4).

1898

'Old churches of Leix. No. XCVI. – Ballinakill', *Irish Builder* 40 (1 February 1898) 39–40.

1899

'Philip Flatsbury, a Kildare historian', *Journal of the Co. Kildare Archaeological Society* 3 (1899–1902) 196.[98]

1900

Reult na Mara (Star of the Sea) branch of Conradh na Gaeilge (Gaelic League) founded in Star of the Sea Schools, Sandymount, 29 November. Meeting chaired by O'Hanlon, president of the branch. Branch formally founded on proposal of Pádraig Pearse, seconded by John Gerald McSweeny.[99]

[94]Recruited as member of prospective Society, the first meeting of which did not take place until April 1898. See Pádraigín Riggs, 'The beginnings of the Society', in Ó Riain, *Irish Texts Society*, 2–35: 11.
[95]No dedication. Preface dated December 1896.
[96]A short note.
[97]'After reception and presentation of address, light evening refreshments shall be provided, and several of the ladies and gentlemen present will render songs in excellent style, to enliven our evening conversazione' (DDA Walsh Papers 1897, Secular Clergy: O'Hanlon to Walsh, 17 May 1897). Brief notice in *Irish Catholic* 5 June 1897, p. 5. The Assembly Rooms are now a Gurdwara of the Sikh community.
[98]A short note.
[99]*An Claidheamh Soluis agus Fáinne an Lae* 8 Mí na Nollag 1900.

Appendix 1

The Canon O'Hanlon Memorial National School, Irishtown

'Napolean III and Barry O'Meara's Family', *Journal of the Royal Society of Antiquaries of Ireland* 5th Ser., 10 (1900) 91–2.[100]

1902

Delivers homily at celebration of Golden Jubilee of Presentation Convent in Stradbally, at Church of the Sacred Heart, Stradbally, 2 April.[101]

[100] A short note.
[101] Postponed from 25 February, mass celebrated by Patrick Foley, Bishop of Kildare and Leighlin; see *Irish Catholic* 19 April 1902, and note 1 above. The Church of the Sacred Heart, Stradbally, contains a marble baptismal font with the inscription 'Pray for the donor Very Rev. John Canon O'Hanlon'; beside it is a marble plaque erected in O'Hanlon's memory, and unveiled 22 May 1977.

Appendix 1

Prospectus for *History of the Queen's County* published.[102]

1903

John O'Hanlon, *Irish-American history of the United States* (Dublin, Sealy, Bryers and Walker, 1903).[103]

1904

O'Hanlon suffers partial paralysis.[104] Obliged to use amanuensis for his correspondence.[105]

1905

John O'Hanlon dies, aged 84, at the presbytery, 3 Leahy's Terrace, Irishtown, attended by his grand-niece, Annie Cantwell, Monday 15 May

[102]NLI MS 33460A(50); copy printed in *Leinster Express* 12 April 1902, which also announced the forthcoming publication of 'Stories and poems by John Keegan'. Neither the *History* nor the work on Keegan were to appear during his lifetime.

[103]No dedication: photograph of Theodore Roosevelt as frontispiece. Preface dated 1902. 'For the last week, I have not been in bed before one o'clock – once before three o'clock in the morning – working on the Index of my Irish-American History of U.S.' (Laois County Library, O'Hanlon File: O'Hanlon to Mrs Mary Morrissey, Abbeyleix, 21 December 1901). O'Hanlon presented Archbishop Walsh with the first copy of *Irish-American history*: 'the only one that shall be circulated in Ireland, until the U.S. demand has been supplied. My part in this work was finished more than twelve months ago, but the artists were very slow on this' (DDA Walsh Papers 1903, Secular Clergy: O'Hanlon to Walsh, 20 February 1903). O'Hanlon, reportedly, had been obliged to re-write the book after the original manuscript was destroyed in a fire at Sealy, Bryers and Walker in 1898 (Carey, 'O'Hanlon', 155); local tradition records that he used the teachers in the Star of the Sea Schools to take down his dictation during this rewrite. Reprints: *Irish-American history of the United States by John Canon O'Hanlon; with an introduction by Thomas J. Shahan* (New York: P. Murphy, 1907); *Irish-American history of the United States* (Bristol: Thoemmes, 2003).

[104]'I have been laid up with severe illness … I am somewhat improved in health, but still paralysed, able to move about' (Mac Ionnraic Archive: O'Hanlon to Charles O'Hanlon (nephew), 29 August 1904).

[105]Cf. DDA Walsh Papers 1904 and 1905, Secular Clergy: O'Hanlon to Walsh, 1 August and 14 December 1904, 31 January 1905.

219

Mural tablet in memory of John Canon O'Hanlon, St Mary's, Star of the Sea

Appendix 1

(the anniversary of O'Connell's death).[106] Buried in Glasnevin Cemetery, Wednesday 17 May, after High Mass at Star of the Sea.[107] His will, dated 1 May 1902, leaves 'the residue and remainder of my property and rights of every description ... to His Grace, the Most Rev. William J. Walsh ... for charitable purposes in Ireland at his discretion'.[108]

Public meeting convened by O'Hanlon's successor, Fr Thomas Magrath, Sunday, 19 November, to raise money to erect a memorial to O'Hanlon.[109] A marble mural tablet was installed in Star of the Sea, February 1906;[110] a Celtic cross was erected over O'Hanlon's grave, 11

[106]Records in General Register Office, Dublin. 'The Canon himself soon began to show signs of failing, and in the beginning of the present year had to abandon all duty' (Donnelly, *A short history of some Dublin parishes*, 81). In a letter to his nephew, Francis L. O'Hanlon of Sherman, Texas, 30 March 1900, O'Hanlon refers to 'Annie Cantwell my niece [*sic*] from St. Louis ... She does much type writing for me, for which I regularly pay her, so that she may be stimulated to industry' (Mac Ionnraic Archive, cf. n. 27).

[107]Chief mourners listed in the newspapers were: Charles and Patrick Moore, Ballymaddock, Stradbally; James A. Mulhall, Pass House, Ballyroan; Mrs. Mulhall, 6 Upper Gardiner street; Miss Minnie Dimond; and the following friends: E. J. Morrissey, Abbeyleix; P. T. Lawlor, Athy; E. P. Morrissey, Gerald P. Turner; P. A. Meehan, JP, Chairman, Queen's County Council; Mark Walsh, JP, Chairman Maryborough Town Commissioners; Denis Shaughnessy, Stradbally.

[108]Individual bequests of £25 each were left for masses for his soul; for the poor of the parish of SS Michael and John; for the poor of Sandymount, Irishtown and Ringsend; and to Fr Joseph Grant-Mooney, one of his curates and executors. He left £50 to his housekeeper, Mary Walsh. Correspondence on the subject in DDA Walsh Papers 1901 and 1902, Secular Clergy: O'Hanlon to Walsh, 10 April 1901, 19 January ('the sands of time are now running low in the hour-glass of my life'), 27 February and 7 March 1902; his letter of 10 April 1902 summarized his personal effects as 'the large stock of MSS. Lives of the Irish Saints, Moulds of earlier vols. wood-cuts, &c. &c. and their disposition, with that of over 3000 vols of books'.

[109]The amount received or pledged at the meeting was almost £181, which figure was to be matched by Archbishop Walsh (DDA Walsh Papers 1905, Secular Clergy: Thomas Magrath to Walsh, 20 November 1905).

[110]Tablet contains bust in relief of O'Hanlon, with an inscription in English, and two verses in Irish: 'Glóir Dé, onóir na hÉireann, ba hiad a léigheann na ló: / glóir ó Dhia, onóir ó Éirinn, cóir dúinn féin a n-éileamh dhó. / Naomh-shluagh Fáil, ó 'sé do sgríobh seanchus a ngníomh sa nglanbhuaidh, / aoibhinn leó a theacht na ndáil, an t-athair Seán Ua hAnluain'.

221

March 1907;[111] and the Canon O'Hanlon Memorial School was built beside Star of the Sea in 1909, and opened 1910.[112]

1907

J. Canon O'Hanlon (ed.), *Legends and poems by John Keegan, now first collected... with memoir by D. J. O'Donoghue* (Dublin: Sealy, Bryers and Walker, 1907).[113]

John Canon O'Hanlon and Rev. Edward O'Leary *History of the Queen's County* I (Dublin: Sealy, Bryers and Walker, 1907).[114]

[111] Glasnevin Plot EH $18\frac{1}{2}$ and 19. Age mistakenly given as 85. Inscription in Irish and English, Irish version reads: 'I ndil chuimhne ar an Athair Seághan Ua h-Anluain M.R.I.A. Canónach. Sagart Paróiste Dúmhaigh Mhuirbhtean ó A.D. 1880 go 1905. Do sgríbh sé "Beatha Naomh Éirean" agus mórán eile de leabhraibh seanachais. Fuair sé bás an cúigmhadh lá déag de Bhealtaine 1905 agus é cúig bliadhna agus cheithre fichid. A chairde agus a pharóisteánaigh is iad a chuir suas an leacht so ag taisbeáint méid a mbuartha na dhiaig agus méid a n-urama dá léighean agus do naomhthacht a bheatha. Beanacht Dé le n-a anam. Amen a Thighearna. "Dá bhrígh sin ó airigheas-sa féin trácht ar bhur gcreideamh atá sa Tighearna Íosa agus ar an ngrádh atá agaibh do na naoimh go léir ní stadaim ach ag breith buídhcais mar gheall oraibh" Éph. I. 15.16.'

[112] *Freeman's Journal* 25 July 1910. In his native parish, apart from the font and plaque inside the Church of the Sacred Heart in Stradbally (see n. 101), a roadside commemorative plaque was unveiled, 6 May 2005. Scán O'Dooley ('The Rev. John Canon O'Hanlon') recorded the following in 1955: 'Thanks to the enthusiastic energy of Mr P. J. McGettric and other Gaels of Stradbally, there has been a great revival of interest recently in the life and work of their celebrated townsman. A memorial cup, called the "Canon O'Hanlon Cup" is competed for yearly at the local Feis, by all the Pipe Bands of the country.'

[113] O'Donoghue explains (pp. v–vi) that O'Hanlon, prior to his death, had 'seen through the press the bulk of what constitutes the present volume'.

[114] In his Prefaces to both Volume I (p. viii) and Volume II (p. [iv]), Fr O'Leary explains that his involvement in the publication of the *History* was in response to a death-bed appeal from O'Hanlon. It is probably to this that O'Leary is referring in his postcard to O'Hanlon, 20 August 1904: 'Will have great pleasure in calling soon. Fear you are resting on a broken reed' (Mac Ionnraic Archive). Fr O'Leary had contributed a sketch to *Lives of the Irish saints* (V, 612), and also had illustrated Comerford, *Kildare and Leighlin* III. In an obituary (*Journal of the Co. Kildare Archaeological Society* 4 (1903–5) 502–3), O'Leary stated that O'Hanlon, at his death, had seen four hundred pages of the *History* through the press, the bulk of Volume I. For this, much of the material in 'Historic memorials of Leix' (n. 80 above) was reworked or repeated, and half of the pages – the Parochial History – consisted of a reprint of the 'Old churches of Leix' articles

Appendix 1

1914

John Canon O'Hanlon, Rev. Edward O'Leary, Rev. Matthew Lalor, *History of the Queen's County* II (Dublin: Sealy, Bryers and Walker, 1914).

published years earlier in the *Irish Builder*. Volume II, published seven years later, can scarcely be ascribed to O'Hanlon at all, and credit is due to the editors, and to William Canon Carrigan, who acted as writer and mentor. Reprint: *History of the Queen's County: John Canon O'Hanlon, Edward O'Leary, Matthew Lalor; with an introduction by Edwin Phelan* (Kilkenny: Reprinted under the direction of Leslie Hewitt for the publishers Roberts Books, [1981]).

APPENDIX 2

Miscellaneous letters, and extracts from letters

1. Recovery of Health

Ballymaddock Stradbally P.O.
Queen's Co.
January 16th 1854

Most Rev. and Venerated Lord,[1]

With feelings of the deepest gratitude to the great dispenser of all blessings, I am enabled to state, that since it has been permitted me to return to my native country, I have enjoyed excellent health and increased strength. The present winter, which to me lately leaving a country where it is characterized by intense cold or frequent unhealthy changes, seems one of unequalled mildness, and the precautions I have observed in avoiding exposure, have contributed materially to a recovery, at one period indeed unexpected on my part. Although my very kind and beloved Archbishop left me at liberty to remain until such time as I should feel sufficiently restored to be enabled to return to St. Louis; yet I feel now assured, as I told him I intended, to be able to resume my duties there long before next winter. At present I occasionally officiate in this parish of Maryborough and the neighbouring one of Stradbally for the respected Pastors and their assistants, whom I have the pleasure of numbering amongst my most valued and tried friends, some of the curates moreover having been my old college companions. So delighted have I been with the society of many of the clergymen of this Diocese, and especially of this Deanery, that I would most willingly present the letter to Dr Healy, which his Grace the Archbishop of St. Louis furnished me with on my departure, but that I have learned on the most unquestionable authority, that the Bishop of this Diocese is unable to obtain vacancies for some of his own subjects both ordained, and prepared for the reception of orders. Under the circumstances, I would not think of preferring my request, as I know it would deserve to be rejected. As nothing however could

[1] Paul Cullen, Archbishop of Dublin.

224

House of William Cantwell, Ballymaddock

afford me greater pleasure than a more intimate and general association
with clergymen during the remainder of my stay in Ireland, since I find
from experience that it always contributes much to my health spirits and
happiness, and as the duties of my sacred calling would be in any place
a source of agreeable relaxation to me, I would most earnestly desire
an opportunity of being engaged in some ministerial services for the
term of *six months*, commencing as soon as might be practicable from
the present time. If it would be at all within the power of your Grace
to present me with such an opportunity under your own immediate
jurisdiction, I need not say with what grateful pleasure I would receive
the an[n]ouncement, and how I would endeavour to manifest the
gratitude I should ever feel for this, and the former honor which you
have so kindly and affably extended towards me, by discharging to
the utmost of my humble abilities the trust you might be pleased to
assign me. I feel the more desirous to be attached to the Archdiocese
of Dublin, as I would there find Priests, who were formerly esteemed
College companions, and others whose kindness lately extended to me
commands my most sincere affection and gratitude. I enclose with this

letter the testimonial of the Most Rev Dr Kenrick, which your Grace's respected friend and Secretary Dr Taylor will take charge of for me, thus adding to many other well remembered obligations, which make me in an especial manner deeply indebted to him.

With the most profound respect and gratitude, I have the honor to remain Your Grace's most humble and devoted Servant in Christ

John O'Hanlon.

2. The South Dublin Union, 1855

On Sundays and Holydays my duties, as assigned me by Rev. Mr O'Farrelly are, to say mass at the Female and Male Schools. The former of these schools is about one half mile – perhaps less – from the South Dublin Union Workhouse. On every Sunday, I say my first mass there, and give a suitable instruction to the children – the hour of commencing mass being 7 or $7\frac{1}{2}$ o'clock – according to the season. These duties occupy me for the space perhaps of an hour and a half; when I have to go to the Boys School, by a circuit of fully half a mile, and arrive there by 9 or $9\frac{1}{2}$ o'clock, when mass commences, and I give an instruction as before. It is then a distance of a quarter of a mile at least to my home; where I seldom arrive, until between 11 and 12 o'clock. Since the Tenter's House has been discontinued as the Cholera Hospital of the South Dublin Union, it has been used as an auxiliary workhouse; and the Rev. Mr O'Farrelly has been obliged to say a second mass on Sundays and Holydays for the inmates, in addition to the one at the House ... the duties of Father O'Farrelly and myself have considerably increased, especially during the prevalence of the fearful epidemic of last winter, when at all hours both of day and night we had to visit the Cholera Hospital – often without the opportunity of procuring a car to travel in haste, to a distance of nearly half a mile. For all this exposure of health and necessary additional expenses, the Board would not allow us any remuneration; although additional compensation was allowed the other officers of the house. The very position of a workhouse chaplain involves him in necessary expenses in behalf of the poor, who are often found dying in the infirm wards and hospitals for want of necessary nourishment – a lemon or an orange or some little luxury is required to cool their parched lips – numbers of letters are received and transmitted through the Chaplains, who must defray the postage in many instances, and oftentimes pay double postage, from a habit of sending silver enclosed to friends in the house, under a single postage stamp – the

Appendix 2

Chaplains are often obliged to be the personal visitors of persons living in the most distant parts of the city, or writing to other friends or pastors of the paupers at their request – with a [thousand *deleted*] variety of other matters, which necessarily involve the Rev. Mr O'Farrelly and myself in very considerable expense, during the year.

3. Death of Eugene O'Curry

Dublin, SS Michael & John
August 3rd '62

My dear Fr Shearman,

Only on yesterday morning did I return from London, and on the morning of that day, I was shocked to see a notice of poor Eugene O'Curry's sudden death copied from the *Dublin Evening Mail* into the London *Daily News*. On the evening before, I presented his letter of introduction – probably the last he wrote – to Richard Simms Esq. Manuscript Department, British Museum. His friends there enquired about his health, and were gratified to hear from me that he was now in better health and spirits. Little I dreamed at the time he was a corpse! Such is life!

To-day, I paid a visit of condolence to his bereaved children. His daughter informed me that John E. Pigot and Dr Lyons collected all his letters, papers and MSS, and sealed them up in a press, until letters of administration are taken out, by his only surviving brother, Anthony Curry. As I know all these gentlemen, I will take care your paper is not lost. I could take no breakfast on yesterday, and felt sad and depressed on my journey home. I could scarcely refrain from shedding tears, at both my masses to-day, which I offered for the repose of his soul. I feel the loss of his aid, counsel and society, in an especial manner. Oh! What genuine worth and labour have been lost for Ireland.

Like your own presentiment, his amiable and dear daughter – a beautiful young girl of 19 – told me she had a strong presentiment that night of some great calamity befalling the family, when her father wished his usual kindly "good night," at 11 o'clock on Tuesday evening. When roused [up?] at 4 o'clock on Wednesday morning, her father was a corpse. Neither priest nor doctor arrived in time, although hurrying instant[l]y in breathless haste! Alas! Alas! How truly sad! But he was a good Christian and a true patriot, pure, upright and honest to scrupulosity; and I have the firmest confidence, he was not unprepared to meet the great Judge! His poor darlings, as far as I am aware,

are unprovided for but, his numerous influential friends are about to originate a movement to give substantial sympathy and support to his young family. I feel his loss as much as I would that of a brother, in private doing [so]. His loss to Ireland is irreparable.

Very faithfully yours,

John O'Hanlon

Rev. John F. Shearman C.C.
Dunlavin

4. Apology

Dublin SS Michael & John
Nov. 24th 1879

Most Rev. and dear Lord Archbishop,[2]

In reply to your letter received on this morning, and dictated by evident motives of highest responsibility, prudence, frankness, and even personal friendliness, it gives me all the greater regret, that I should unconsciously, but deservedly, have been the occasion for causing you so much anxiety and annoyance. However, I need hardly assure your Grace, and with perfect candour, I feel truly sorry that certain passages of my letter were fairly exposed to reprehension, and of this I was only fully conscious when I afterwards saw it in print.

To say that I was extremely busy, and that it was most hurriedly written, when sent to Mr Gray, is indeed no proper excuse for indiscreet statement, and which had a chance of being published. I especially regretted, trusting to memory alone, that I could have so confidently pronounced no 'sentence which, fairly interpreted, could be deemed untrue', while immediately afterwards I admitted 'exaggerations' to be [']incident to public speeches in general.' I have no doubt, too, that my feelings got the better of my discretion, when I desired to manifest, in sending my subscription, a sympathy for those arrested and incarcerated, bail being refused, when the ordinary and constitutional mode of summons and plaint should have sufficed to procure their trial.

I am very far from agreeing with their various acts and speeches, nor did I suppose any one but myself could be justly held responsible for what I had written; still, I must admit, the public do not always draw correct conclusions and impressions from words and acts, which may – as in my case – have been very innocently intended. However, I entirely

[2]Edward McCabe, Archbishop of Dublin.

228

concur in the wise admonition of your Grace, that we are living in very exciting times; and now that I have received your paternal and kindly admonition, which I take to be of a private character, I shall promise, also, and with perfect sincerity for the future, never to exceed the rules, which you deem it right for your clergy not to transgress. A sense of duty and of conscience will actuate me in this resolution. Hoping thus to have given the best reparation now in my power to make, for the pain I have unhappily caused you, I subscribe myself, with profound respect, your Grace's most humble servant,

John O'Hanlon

His Grace
The Most Rev. Edward McCabe
Archbishop of Dublin
Kingstown

5. Rome's Decree against the Plan of Campaign

3 Leahy Terrace Irishtown
Sandymount, May 3rd 1888

Most Rev. and dear Archbishop[3]

The extract I enclose and taken from this morning's *Freeman* gave me such a shock, that I felt thoroughly agitated and excited, even during the whole time I had been engaged celebrating the Holy Sacrifice of Mass. After an early breakfast, I hurried into town to see our good friend Canon Daniel, who gave one some consolation, but who has not wholly re-assured me. The city is I find in a high state of excitement, and the question is on every lip, 'Can the news be true?' If it be, I fear it forebodes one of the greatest misfortunes that ever threatened our Irish Church, and I dread that a schism, which might extend to the United States, the Colonies and wherever the Irish Catholics have spread on this habitable globe, might ensue. I most earnestly beseech your Grace, in no eventuality resign the See of Dublin willingly, and pardon frank if over free opinion, you should take no dignity or position in exchange for it. As I apprehend the Canon Law, you could never be deposed without a canonical crime, that no man dare honestly impute to you.

Here we are as sheep without a shepherd, no one as yet to move or direct any action, as I think demanded by the emergency. We are bewildered because you are not at home to guide us. I feel that the bishops of

[3]William J. Walsh, Archbishop of Dublin.

Ireland, who are faithful and true, should assemble and try if possible to allay the sound clerical and popular ferment. I believe, too, each individual in his own humble way should throw off lethargy, and lend his aid to arrest a downward course for the real interests of religion.

Now, I proposed to Canon Daniel to write for the *Freeman* a rather elaborate and yet condensed statement or historical retrospect of the Quarentotti Rescript, sanctioning the Veto on the appointment of our Catholic Bishops, under the vile anti-Catholic and Tory despotism of Spencer Perceval – assassinated by the Irishman Bermingham in the Lobby of the House of Commons – the Earl of Liverpool and Lord Castlereagh &c. &c. He said, 'I don't know whether the Archbishop might approve of it at this time or not'. 'Well then I shall solve the doubt,' said I, 'by writing to him this day.' I intended to treat the matter only as an interesting Chapter of our Irish Ecclesiastical history, to let the Irish public know the facts of that dark and shameful Tory intrigue, and the glorious triumph of our Irish Church, and they can then draw the moral themselves. That was a darker day for Ireland than the present, and it made honest hearts beat heavier. Heaven knows, I pity you from my soul, on account of all the worry you must have had lately; but I know, you are too brave and too firm, to do any thing, that shall either compromise your own high character, or the hopes our Nation forms of you. I anticipate you shall stand forward forever, as a noble figure in the history of Ireland and of the Church; and as the greatest heroes of Christianity and saints had to brave persecution and live down calumny, so shall you gloriously triumph.

Do not write one line to me, if you disapprove of my suggestion; for your time and health must not be wasted with needless trouble. If I can be of the slightest use in any way, I need not say, command my services and they shall be most cheerfully and affectionately rendered. Now more than ever, your most devoted and humble servant,

John Canon O'Hanlon

Most Rev. William J. Walsh DD
Archbishop of Dublin
Irish College
Rome

Appendix 2

6. Wakes

3 Leahy Terrace
Irishtown
Sandymount

April 19th 1890

Most Rev. and dear Archbishop

As invited in your circular, I shall presume to offer a few suggestions, and only on a particular subject – that of Irish *Wakes* especially among the humbler classes of our people. There are grave scandals and abuses connected with them, which I think can only be effectually repressed by a strong pronouncement of your Grace.

Most of our poor people in the city and suburbs belong to the Burial Societies, and on the death of a member belonging to their respective families they draw a sum for burial purposes. I need not state to your Grace, that much if not most of this is spent on intoxicating drink, and generally given to those who are fondest of it. In fact, habitual drunkards are only too ready to crowd the wake-houses and having the pretext of condoling with the surviving members of the family, but the real motive is to get drink. The evil increases, if the surviving head of the family be a toper himself or herself. Then often the visitors sit up all night, with an occasional refreshment of whiskey 'to keep them awake', in the city as in the country.

Could your Grace issue substantially, or with some modifications, the following imperative directions?

1. That on all occasions of a wake or funeral, no intoxicating drinks be allowed in that house. If any refreshment be given at all, that it be simply food, tea or coffee.

2. That the corpse-house be closed against all visitors after – say 9 o'clock P.M. – to a late hour in the morning. The residents of the house or room only to watch the corpse after that hour. In England, the dead room is closed and dark for the night, and no-one watches, when the room can be spared. Our custom to have lighted candles by the corpse requires at least one attendant to remain up all night.

3. That relatives and friends, not belonging to the corpse house, should only as a mark of respect and for charitable or friendly condolence enter the room, and only when the corpse is laid out; then at once kneel down and offer a prayer for the departed, and trying

231

Appendix 2

to console the family by a few kindly words, then go away, even if they promise to return next day, to repeat the *De Profundis*, or some prayer for the dead. This is generally the personal practice of the local clergy; it should be imitated by the laity, and the practice might commend itself as suitable to the mournful solemnity of the occasion.

4. At offices for the dead and for priests or religious, nothing but tea or coffee to be served afterwards. This should have no real use, except to quote it, as a becoming example for the laity to follow. There is also a very proper saving, from the expense of wine and spirituous liquors, in such cases for people of all classes.

5. It is a nefarious custom sometimes practised by low and scheming characters to represent themselves as charitably collecting money for the burial of very poor persons. I recollect a case of this kind at SS Michael's and John's Church; money was collected to wake a poor unfriended person, and all night drunken orgies and even songs kept the priests of the house awake, nor could any thing be done to prevent such practices, unless to remain on sentry all night; for if these characters were put out, they would be sure to return again, and of this, I could even quote an instance. It should be publicly known, that every person dying absolutely destitute is by law entitled to be buried at the expense of the Union.

I shall only call your Grace's attention to another matter. Most of our poor people have only a single room or two for themselves and families. This is often crow[d]ed to inconvenience when the corpse lies, and I need not state, a dead body is in the state of decomposition and sending forth deleterious gases, to make foul air doubly impure. Now could not the sanitary authorities be required to have a law passed, to make it illegal and injurious to the public health – not to speak of that referring to the family in the house itself – to have so many people sitting in the house itself breathing a vitiated air? The police should be obliged at the summons of a clergyman or other sanitary authority, to prevent a danger of this kind. Could not a short Act of Parliament be passed, to close the corpse-houses in Ireland after 9 o'clock, and to effect other useful regulations, and oblige the Police to see it put in force. Yet, I had much rather your Grace's moral and religious influence should effect these reforms.

Excuse me for trespassing so much on your time, and I remain Most Rev. and dear Lord, your obedient servant,

John O'Hanlon

232

Appendix 2

7. Parnell, and the Press

St. Mary's Church, Star of the Sea

Dec. 14th 1890

Most Rev. and dear Lord Archbishop

I am truly glad you are about to take some active steps towards counteracting the cushioning policy of the *Freeman's Journal* and the wire-pulling of the National League. Henceforth Parnell must be a danger in Home Rule politics.

Could not the Archbishops and Bishops draw up another well prepared Address, setting forth the moral and patriotic reasons for discarding him, while at the same time, to conciliate mob opinion and do justice to the fallen, some praise might be bestowed on his past services, with a regret expressed, that a necessity should have been created for a course now unavoidable. This might be read soon from every pulpit and altar in the land by direction of the presiding prelates. It ought to have an immediate effect with the people. Meantime it is absolutely necessary to take measures for the establishment of a Daily Paper in Dublin. It might be called the Home Ruler or have some popular title. While really Catholic in tone and under Catholic control – as are many of the U.S. papers – it need not be exclusively any official organ, but reflect freely and honestly expressed opinions of all our liberal minded countrymen. Could not leading articles be written by the leading minds of the educated and enlightened over their signatures as in the French Journals. It would be a novel feature in Irish journalism.

How poor indeed are the thrashy articles, written for the most part by half-educated young men – poor in study of historic and political literature, and therefore blind guides leading the blind, or writing to order without thought or method to fill up a column. Such are all our present city daily papers and such their class of writers. A new soul should be infused into Irish journalism.

I remain, your Grace's most obedient servant

John O'Hanlon

P.S.
A sapient Parnellite here told me that the autocrat could make terms with the Tories, and get a better Home Rule Bill from them than Gladstone would give!!! So much for the fools that follow his dictation.

Appendix 2

8. Return to America: Archbishop Kenrick's Jubilee

St. Louis, Church of St. John the Evangelist

December 6th 1891

Most Rev. and dear Lord Archbishop,

It was only on this evening I have been enabled to sit down and write to convey to you the special thanks of His Grace the Archbishop of St. Louis, as he directed me, in response to your congratulations on the occasion of his Golden Jubilee. He also handed me your letter for myself marked *Private*. He has received whole piles of felicitations from His Holiness the Pope and the President of the U.S., down to the humblest members of his flock; and indeed I have been wholly astonished at the magnificence and spontaneity of the demonstrations in his honour. But he spoke of you as a Prelate worthy in every way to rule in his native Diocese, and he hopes your life shall long be preserved. I have tried to send you each day of this week, one of the leading City papers; but I can assure you, the meagre reports of our rejoicings here can convey no notion whatever of the reality. Had the Dublin papers such events to describe, some justice might have been done to them; but through the ignorance of the writers, and as believed by many, through the artifices of a few suspected *cranks*, false statements have been spread to the great annoyance of the whole Catholic body, and in the worst possible taste. I must soon see you after my arrival in Dublin, to give you an idea of the Grand Catholicity of this glorious city, which has completely out-grown that which I once knew.

The pent-up feelings of the last fifty years were opened this week in a manner simply indescribable. With a munificence beyond precedent, clergy and laity vied with each other to manifest their reverence for the aged Jubilarian. I had already travelled thousands of miles – from New York to Philadelphia, to Baltimore, to Washington, back again to Boston, to Montreal, to Quebec, to Rimouski, to Toronto in Canada, on to Saginaw City Michigan, to Chicago and to my old missions of Hannibal, New London, St. Paul's, and Milwood, in Missouri – before I arrived in St. Louis, now more than two weeks ago. At once, I went to see the Venerated Prelate in his old house, and before he took his evening walk of three miles; and oh! how pleased he seemed to be that I had come, as without any authority the papers had stated, I was the representative of your Grace and of his native Diocese. At this time, his new residence had been most luxuriously furnished by the Ladies of St. Louis, and his books were being removed to it. He said, I should meet the Vicar General Rev. Philip Brady, Pastor of this Church, who had tendered his house for my residence during my stay in St. Louis, at supper, and what a pleasant evening it was, I shall not soon forget. The Archbishop looked smooth of skin and and [*sic*] clear in complexion, as ever I had known him when young. I then heard of all the grand preparations for the approaching Jubilee. Next day, I started southward 630 miles to see my brother in Texas, spent a few pleasant days with himself and his sons – two of them married – and I returned to St. Louis last Tuesday week, as I wished to see the vast city and several old friends with their families before the distractions of this week had commenced.

Well, on Monday last the spectacle in and around the old Cathedral was truly magnificent. Archbishop Ryan had written and printed what has been published in the papers, but he added much, and in a style of nervous and feeling oratory, that drew tears of emotion from nearly all in the crowded Cathedral. The aged Archbishop bore himself throughout with his usual calm and composure. At two o'clock dinner was served in the Dining Room of the Lindell Hotel, probably the largest in the United States. Only the Prelates and Priests were admitted, with the exception of certain selected Protestant Ministers – especially Episcopalian – who had eulogised the Archbishop in set sermons preached in their respective churches. In the evening was the great popular demonstration, and little Father O'Reilly, whom Most Rev. Dr Croke designated the Governor, and who accompanied Archbishop Ryan to Dublin, brought me to his brother's fine mansion on Pine St., where a whole party of Catholic and Protestant ladies and gentlemen were assembled. On looking out in the street from one end to the other, it seemed a river of fire flowing on continuously for fully three hours. The Pastors in carriages headed the contingents from their respective 52 parishes, and having a guard of honour on horseback on either side decorated with purple silk scarfs. These gentlemen were among the *elite* of St. Louis. Afterwards in eight deep [*sic*] marched the parishioners, each man and boy, in regular military line and step, holding a long pole aloft, and from it swung a parafin-oil lamp, the flame of which could not be extinguished, while rockets flashed up in the sky at frequent intervals, and cheers 'For the Archbishop' were elicited as they passed houses of Catholics and Protestants illuminated and decorated with floating banners and long streamers. In many instances the Volunteer Companies in their splendid uniform marched in the order of Roman and Maltese Crosses, then broke into platoons, and interchanging evolutions created a marked sensation. The Archbishop was sensibly affected, and for the first time in his life yielded himself to the wishes of his friends. All that was very fine; but next morning when the Children's festival took place in the great Music Hall containing seats for 5000, all were in uniform and most elegant dresses, varied according to the Parish Schools. When the fine band of the Christian Brothers' Boys lent its music played in superb time and style to the volume of voices, each boy and girl waved a toy-banner of the U.S. The sight was altogether entrancing, and one once witnessed never to be forgotten.

Hundreds of thousands of dollars were subscribed by the clergy and laity of St. Louis for this grand demonstration. They resolved that there should be no money charge whatever for admission to banquet or halls. Over 5000 families of the City – Catholic and non-Catholic alike – sent word to the Committee, that they should be able to lodge and entertain the Prelates, Priests, and distinguished ladies and gentlemen who came from distant places. The most lavish and elegant hospitalities I ever saw were tendered to the Archbishop, Cardinal, Prelates and Clergy by the fine old Catholic families of the city; while I witnessed several ladies and gentlemen kiss the Archbishop's ring, their eyes moistened with tears. The 'grand old man' dined out every evening this week, to the great delight of host and hostess, nor does he seem to be in the least fatigued.

On tomorrow evening Sunday, the Vicar General and myself dine in the Archbishop's new house, with Archbishop Ryan, who leaves St. Louis with me on Monday. I move to New York, and I expect on this day week to take passage for Ireland, where I hope to arrive before Xmas day. The Archbishop has asked me to write to Rt. Rev. Monsignor Browne DD his thanks for the College address; also to Canon Daniel for that from his native parish; as also to Father Collier for sending the Portrait of his uncle Rev Richard Kenrick formerly PP of St. Nicholas Parish Dublin.

I remain Most Rev. and dear Archbishop your Grace's faithful servant

John O'Hanlon

Most Rev. William J. Walsh DD
Archbishop's Residence, Dublin, Ireland

Appendix 2

9. Daniel O'Connell's anniversary

St. Mary's Star of the Sea
Irishtown
Dublin
April 27th 1897

Most Rev. and dear Archbishop

I wish to convey to you – although not authorised – a desire expressed by all the members of my conference on yesterday evening, that we should not be behindhand with any part of Ireland in honouring the memory of her illustrious Liberator, on the approaching 50th commemoration of his death. I am sure I need not doubt, that the patriotic son of a father – the intimate and trusted friend of the great O'Connell – shall be wanting on the occasion to have a religious service in our Cathedral. Moreover, how greatly should I not desire to see a circular sent to all the Clergy in the Diocese to ask them to have an office for the dead in their respective churches on a suitable day within the week of the 15th of May; and where a High Mass cannot be had, an Evening Office sung by Confraternities presided over by a Priest should I am sure give the greatest possible satisfaction both to priests and people. Moreover, a public letter from your Grace, recalling as you best can do it O'Connell's priceless services to our country and its religion, should just now produce a fine moral effect, by keeping before our so-called leaders a glorious model for them to imitate if they wish to live hereafter in the nation's grateful recollection. I do not think there ought to be a moment's delay, and I would wish to see our early action set the other dioceses of Ireland in motion. It will be a gleam of light, in this darkest hour of our degradation and disgrace in the eyes of the whole world, since Ireland can never be blighted or injured expect [sic] through the ignorance and folly of her own children. I only write these few hurried lines, which I wish you to regard as private and confidential, as I wish to keep my intermeddling propensities from any knowledge of others.

I remain very respectfully your Grace's most obedient and affectionate

John Canon O'Hanlon

His Grace
Most Rev. William J. Walsh DD
Archbishop of Dublin
Archbishop's House
Dublin

Appendix 2

10. School Attendance

St. Mary's Star of the Sea
Irishtown. Dublin

Feb. 7th 1899

Most Rev. William J. Walsh DD
Archbishop of Dublin
Archbishop's House
Dublin

Most Rev. and dear Lord Archbishop

As at our conference on yesterday we had some consideration of the new Urban and County Councils in reference to the enforcement of the Compulsory Education Act, and as you are now holding the highly important position as Commissioner of Education, I have thought it not amiss to observe, that so far as I can judge, the provisions of the Act for the enforcement of attendance will be found very complicated and defective in the administration. Thus, the Inspector as chief executive officer shall only have power to warn parents or guardians of children to have them sent to school and afterwards report their attention to or neglect of the warning to the School Committee, who have still to threaten or order a prosecution, which may cause round about proceedings before a magistrate, which can only result in a fine imposed on the neglectful parents which after all perhaps cannot be enforced. Besides as many of their disobedient children may disregard altogether the orders of their parents and of the board, I do not see how the Act can be wholly effectual without a direction to the police of summary jurisdiction to apprehend and conduct to the school those wild youngsters, who because of the early neglect of their parents have now assumed a mastery over them, and will run away. However, I hope a remedy may be found for such delinquencies and amendments of legislation may prove in the celebrated words of Mr. Gladstone, that the resources of Civilization are not yet exhausted.

Some year in the sixties I spent a vacation of two weeks in London, and exchanged a temporary charge for the Pastor of a church near Woolwich, in Dr. Grant's diocese of Southward, and from whom I received the requisite faculties. I was then rather pained to see the miserably small school and the provision made for popular Catholic education there as compared with what we enjoyed in Ireland under the National Board System. However in the year 1893 I was again in London, and celebrated Mass each morning for the Convent school attached to Maiden Lane

238

Appendix 2

Chapel, and I was quite pleased to see a very fine school well attended by girls and infants, and the Sisters told me much depended on the zeal and energy of a good inspector they had to enforce the attendance.

In 1874 I was in Scotland, and the Pastor of Pollockshaws near Glasgow brought me through his male school composed almost exclusively of the children of Irish parents, and I was delighted with the large attendance and the proficiency of the boys, especially in their knowledge of Scottish history, and from their Catholic History of Scotland they answered all my questions most readily. How I wished the day would ever arrive when Irish History could be taught in like manner in our Irish National Schools. However, I am glad the thin end of the wedge has been introduced, and I have ordered two dozen of Dr. Joyce's admirable Irish History as readers for our advanced boys, and hope soon to test their study and knowledge of the history of their country. The Scotch are far in advance of the English and Irish I believe in the working of primary education; but it is hardly wonderful since they have had a start of about 200 years, when their native Parliament instituted their parochial and burgh schools so well set forth in James Grant's admirable 'History of the Burgh Schools of Scotland' London and Glasgow, William Collins, Sons, and Co. 1876, 8vo.

When last in St. Louis, I learned that it was a rule that the doors should be closed each morning at 9 o'clock, in all the Catholic and Common schools, and no child was admitted after that hour. I learned that the rule enforced a general and punctual attendance.

While I paid a short visit to my former mission of Hanibal – now a city of over 30,000 inhabitants – I found four Catholic schools there, all taught by the Sisters of St. Joseph. One of these was an Infant School; two were for girls; while one was for grown boys. I asked the Pastor, an Irish priest named Fr. McLaughlin, how the latter worked. He told me admirably, and vastly better than if a male teacher were over them; that the Sisters had never to say a harsh word to any of the grown boys, but on the contrary, a chivalrous feeling and respectful demeanour was invariably observed towards the nuns by the Catholic and even by the Protestant boys, many of whom were there.

As a Commissioner of National Education I thought you might like to learn these few jottings, but I do not wish you to spend one moment in reply to this rambling communication. I subscribe myself very respectfully and faithfully your Grace's much obliged and obedient servant

John Canon O'Hanlon

239

Appendix 2

11. John Keegan

St. Mary's Church
Star of the Sea
Irishtown Dublin
September 10th 1901

Dear Mr O'Donoghue,

I feel greatly indebted to you for the interesting series of John Keegan's letters and for the printed Memoir. They must help me materially to eke out an interesting sketch of the writer's life. I hope to go down for a few days before winter sets in to Abbeyleix, and see some of the Campions living there, and learn more about his friend Miss Margaret Campion, and more details of his life, to which the letters and writings I have since seen give me a cue. A young gentleman, Hibernian Bank clerk, a Mr O'Toole and a good amateur photographer, has promised to take photographs for me of the site of the house in which his uncle Maloney and he first taught school, afterwards transferred to Shanahoe Chapel, of Killeaney Castle, of Gortnaclea Castle, of Poor Man's Bridge, and other places alluded to by him. Several are yet living that remember him and loved him in life, but they are old like myself, and therefore no time ought be lost, as my friend Mr Edward Morrissey – whose father's name [is *deleted*] introduced in one of Keegan's sketches in Dolman's Magazine – is most anxious to aid my investigations and drive me out to the scenes once so familiar to poor Keegan. Perhaps I shall muster up courage to see his daughter, whose mother is now for some years dead.

More I may let you know when we meet, and for the present accept my most cordial and grateful thanks for your kindness

David J. O' Donoghue Esq   John Canon O' Hanlon.
41 Kildare St, Dublin

12. History of the Queen's County

12a

St. Mary's Church   Sept 9th 1902
Star of the Sea
Irishtown Dublin

Dear Mr Praeger,

I can scarcely express how grateful I feel for your kind contribution to my 'History of the Queen's County', which must help to give it from the naturalist's point of view a value of peculiar and authentic acceptance. I shall insert it *verbum verbo*, and when the time comes, to be more exact, I shall submit the printer's proofs to you for correction and revision. I am glad to see the plants classed and grouped in their respective localities, which must help to familiarize them more to unscientific readers like myself.

I think I shall be able to submit a pretty complete list of the trees and bushes known in the Queen's County, as an intelligent young country gentleman has promised to furnish me with those having a common name. Afterwards I hope to be able to add their Latin scientific names. In the matter of Zoology too, I hope to have a very complete list of wild quadrupeds, birds, fishes, insects, reptiles, besides the domesticated animals. As these sections of the work are preparing for the press, I shall avail myself of your presence at the National Library to call upon you occasionally for your instruction and direction, on subjects which I believe to be known very specially to yourself.

I send you by this Post, a small volume Poems of Lageniensis, which has many references to the Queen's County, and I ask your considerate regard for its many imperfections, as it is intended to be a slight token of my deep indebtedness to you, remaining, very respectfully and obliged yours faithfully,

John Canon O'Hanlon

Robert Lloyd Praeger B.A. B.E. M.R.I.A.
National Library
Dublin

12b

St. Mary's Church
Star of the Sea
Irishtown Dublin

Sept 18th 1902

My Dear James

I received your kind letter on yesterday evening, and was very sorry to learn that you gave so much of your time and trouble in the vain search to find me in Stradbally and afterwards in Maryborough. I was obliged to leave for Dublin by the early evening train, as I had a good deal of work before me. However, I hope on a future occasion I shall have an opportunity of seeing you in Pass, and still earlier, that you will be in Dublin.

I am busy with 'History of the Queen's County[']', and I have to thank you most gratefully for your zeal and exertions in adding seven subscribers to my list which is filling up to my satisfaction. Jemmy Morrissey of Abbeyleix has promised to draw up for me from memory a very complete list of the wild quadrupeds, birds, fishes and reptiles known in the Queen's County, and I hope he has done something by this time, as the Zoology of the County shall have an early place in the History, and perhaps you would add any *animal* to it he may have forgotten. Professor Praeger of Dublin, a renowned naturalist, has already furnished me with an admirable account of the Botany of the Q.C. which he has scientifically examined, and he has already discovered over 600 species of grass, weeds, wild flowers and plants. Now if you could kindly draw up for me a list of all the trees you know and name them, such as oak, ash &c. and all the bushes and shrubs, such as wild brier, sloe, &c., he has undertaken when submitted to him to give me their scientific Latin names, and to tell me what are *indigenous* or the natural growth of the County and what are *exotics* or introduced, such as the laurel, currant, &c. I hope I am not imposing too great a task, but I am anxious to furnish the most complete inform[ation] I can, on a subject that had never before been treated.

Give my best regards to Annie and to our friends in Abbeyleix, and believe me to remain, my dear James ever faithfully and obliged

John Canon O'Hanlon

Mr James A. Mulhall
Pass House
Maryborough

APPENDIX 3

Manuscripts of John Canon O'Hanlon in the Russell Library, National University of Ireland, Maynooth (in the collections of St Patrick's College, Maynooth)

Following his death in 1905, the books and manuscripts of John Canon O'Hanlon were deposited in the Library, St Patrick's College, Maynooth. All manuscripts contain cuttings, notes, and items of correspondence, loose, tipped in, guarded or mounted. Manuscripts bound unless otherwise stated.

1. Lives of the Irish Saints

Lives of the Irish saints was published in individual numbers, beginning in 1873, and coming to an end shortly before O'Hanlon's death in 1905 with Volume 10 number 106 (see MS OH 14/10). In a memorandum tipped in at MS OH 4, p. 1, O'Hanlon anticipated that he would not live to complete his work:

> It is very certain I shall not survive to complete the "Lives of the Irish Saints;" and I desire to state, that whatever MSS of the work remain unpublished, are merely unfinished and undigested notes to be placed in a better order, many to be elided when previous unnecessary repetitions are found, and all require revision. Other sources for information are far from being exhausted. I regret in the past, that leisure was not afforded me for sufficient research to complete the Lives in a manner quite satisfactory to myself. Several errors and omissions of statement, I have from time to time discovered, and which I shall never find an opportunity for correcting. / John Canon O'Hanlon. Dec. 31st 1899.

A notice of his death in the *Freeman's Journal* reported:

> In the merciful dispensation of Providence, Canon O'Hanlon was spared to accomplish a task which had been the dream of his youth as he roamed through the graveyards of Clonenagh, Dysart Gallen,

Noughavel, Kilabban, Arles, etc., and it is remarkable that the material for the last (December) volume of his 'Lives of the Irish Saints' was prepared for press last Christmas, just before the venerable author became invalided. He himself thought that his illness would not be of long duration, and he had planned some other literary projects, but it was not to be. His monumental work was finished, and, fortunately, he was spared to see through press the penultimate volume of the Acta Sanctorum Hiberniae, the first instalment of which dates as far back as 1857.[1]

In an obituary of O'Hanlon, his friend, Fr Edward O'Leary, gave to understand that the work of completing the *Lives* was in progress: 'Its completion has been taken up by willing hands; and O'Hanlon's "Lives of the Irish Saints" will remain for all time a monument of his persevering energy and scholarly research.'[2] Perhaps it was Fr O'Leary's intention to complete O'Hanlon's work, as he was to do with the *History of the Queen's County*.

In July 1914, nine years after O'Hanlon's death, the publishers James Duffy & Co. replied to a query in the *Irish Book Lover* 5 (1913–14) 202 with the following information:

We are informed that the Material, a collection of notes covering the remaining months, October, November, December, of "Lives of the Irish Saints," is deposited in the Maynooth College Library. The Maynooth College Union, which meets once a year, in June, decided at their meeting in 1912 to subscribe a sum of money towards the completion of the volume, and at their next meeting, to be held this month, we expect to hear of the steps that are to be taken for that purpose. We have the remainder of the previous 103 [*sic*] parts, and are selling them at a low price of 3d. each, and bound volumes slightly soiled at 7s. 6d. Vols. 2 and 8 are now incomplete.[3]

The Maynooth Union project, however, was not proceeded with.[4]

---

[1] *Freeman's Journal* 16 May 1905. The date 1857 refers to *The life of St. Laurence O'Toole*, published in that year.

[2] *Journal of the County Kildare Archaeological Society* 4 (1903–5) 503.

[3] *Irish Book Lover* 5 (1913–14) 221.

[4] '... in 1913 [James] MacCaffrey [of the Maynooth Union] had to report that it was in such a state that no-one could be expected to edit it' (Corish,

Appendix 3

1.1. MSS OH 1–14. Notes and drafts.

MS OH 1: September (Volume II) 9th – 16th. Contains only 'St Lasrian or Laisren, Abbot of Iona in Scotland'.

MS OH 2: September (Volume III) 17th – 26th. Blank

MS OH 3: September (Volume IV) 27th – 30th. Notes on second Sunday of October, Feast of the Dedication of the Churches of Ireland; with note stating that this is to be placed in supplement, with Aphemeral Saints (see OH 13).

MS OH 4: October (Vol II) 14th – 24th. The continuation of the published Lives of the Irish Saints begins here. Beg. October 21, Article 11, St. Munna or Finntan Mac Tulchan, Bishop and Abbot of Clonenagh, Queen's County. Miscellaneous notes and items of correspondence tipped in.

MS OH 5: October (Vol. III) 24th – 31st. Beg. October 24, Life of St. Machar or O'Meagher, Bishop of Cloyne.

MS OH 6: November (Vol. I) 1st – 12th. Beg. November 1, St. Cairpre, perhaps Bishop of Aassaroe now Ballyshannon, County of Donegal, or at Kill-Chairpre, Isiol Faranain.

MS OH 7: November (Vol. I$\frac{1}{2}$) 3rd. Contains pages of O'Hanlon's *The life of Saint Malachy O'Morgair* (1859) mounted, with corrections and additions.

MS OH 8: November (Vol. II) 12th – 18th. Beg. November 12, St. Livinus, Martyr.

MS OH 9: November (Vol. II$\frac{1}{2}$) 14th. Contains pages of O'Hanlon's *The life of St. Laurence O'Toole* (1857), mounted, with corrections and additions. Also, November 6, St. Enora, the Irish wife of the Breton Prince St. Efflamm.

MS OH 10: November (Vol. III) 18th – 30th. Beg. November 18, St. Mombolus.

MS OH 11: December (Vol. I) 1st – 18th. Beg. Article I, December 1, St. Nessan, Patron of Cork.

MS OH 12: December (Vol. II) 18th – 31st. Beg. December 18, St. Hannan, Bishop & Patron of Killaloe (continued). Ends (pp. 572–92) St. Locan, Bishop & Patron of Kilmacahill, County of Kilkenny.

Maynooth College, 286). The Russell Library holds a typescript alphabetical index of the saints in these manuscripts: Eoin McCarney, 'A guide to the unpublished manuscripts of the Very Reverend John Canon O'Hanlon's *Lives of the Irish saints*' (1995–6).

Appendix 3

MS OH 13: 'Lives or Notices of Aphemeral Irish Saints ... to appear after the Month of December has been completed, alphabetically arranged, and before Appendices and General Index.' Beg. Saints Cathaseus, Cathurus, Cathneus, Brothers, and their Sister Cathnea.

MS OH 14/1–4: Four of O'Hanlon's early notebooks, containing notes towards his grand scheme for the Lives of the Irish Saints. MS OH 14/1: 'Lives of the Irish Saints by the Rev. John O'Hanlon / MS. Collections / March 1869.' Miscellaneous notes on saints and places. MS OH 14/2: 'Rev. John O'Hanlon's MS. Collections for Lives of the Irish Saints for the month of October / July 30th 1869.' MS OH 14/3: 'Rev. John O'Hanlon's MS. Collection of Lives of the Irish Saints. For the month of November. / August 19th 1869.' MS OH 14/4: 'Rev. John O'Hanlon's MS. Collection of Lives of the Irish Saints. For the month of December. / August 19th 1869.'

MS OH 14/5: 'The Lives of the Irish Saints / Vol 11 / By Rev. John O'Hanlon.' Drafts of some saints' lives for November and December, noted as being 'transcribed into fol MS'.

MS OH 14/6: 'Alphabetical Index of the Principal Manuscripts, Authors, Works and Editors, consulted and listed in Lives of the Irish Saints. Those rarely and only casually referred to are omitted from the following list.'

MS OH 14/7–8: Two scrapbooks of notes and newspaper cuttings, mainly on ecclesiastical history and architecture. MS OH 14/7: 'Collections for Lives of the Irish Saints By Rev. John O'Hanlon.' Newspaper cuttings, circulars etc. *c.* 1870–90. MS OH 14/8: Stray hagiographical notes, and diocesan succession lists, mounted; some correspondence tipped in.

MS OH 14/9–11: Loose material. Boxed. MS OH 14/9: *Lives of the Irish saints*, galley-proofs and corrected page-proofs for October. MS OH 14/10: *Lives of the Irish saints* Vol. 10/105 (October 16–20) and 10/106 (October 20–21). Last two published numbers of O'Hanlon's work MS OH 14/11: Miscellaneous notes; and cuttings on St Malachy.

MS OH 14/12: Unbound. Folder containing: (a) Notes and jottings, mainly hagiographical, including proofs of *Lives of the Irish saints* Volume II, February 1 and 2 (stamped 28 March 1876 by Dollards). (b) Notes and draft of article on St Columba ('A day at Iona: recollections of Saint Columba'). (c) Miscellaneous printed notices and prospectuses.

Appendix 3

MS OH 14/13: Unbound. Folder containing: (a) Notes and jottings, mainly hagiographical, including notes and drafts on St Columba, and letter to O'Hanlon from [Fr] D. B. Mulcahy, Belfast (21 October 1878). (b) Miscellaneous printed items: prospectuses, invoice for second-hand books (15 June 1895), and loose pages from *Irish Builder* 28 (September, November 1886).

1.2. MSS OH 15–37. Twenty-three bound volumes of correspondence, 1873–90, mainly concerning subscriptions for parts 1–80 of *Lives of the Irish saints*, with some letters concerning printing arrangements.[5]

MS OH 15. January to April 1873.
MS OH 16. May to October 1873.
MS OH 17. October to December 1873.
MS OH 18. January to July 1874.
MS OH 19. August to December 1874.
MS OH 20. January to May 1875.
MS OH 21. June to December 1875.
MS OH 22. January to September 1876.
MS OH 23. September to December 1876.
MS OH 24. January to June 1877.
MS OH 25. July to December 1877.
MS OH 26. January to December 1878.
MS OH 27. January to December 1879.
MS OH 28. January to December 1880.
MS OH 29. January to December 1881.
MS OH 30. January to December 1882.
MS OH 31. January to December 1883.
MS OH 32. January to December 1884.
MS OH 33. January to December 1885.
MS OH 34. January to December 1886.
MS OH 35. January to December 1887.
MS OH 36. January to December 1888; January to December 1889.
MS OH 37. January to December 1890.

1.3. MS OH 38. 318 original wood engravings of illustrations mainly from *Lives of the Irish saints*.

[5] In his binding instructions prefixed to some of the volumes, O'Hanlon refers to these letters as 'business letters'.

Appendix 3

2. Biography of Daniel O'Connell (MS OH 39)

These manuscripts consist of notes and drafts, tipped in or guarded, and cuttings loose or mounted, arranged chronologically, and all pertaining to O'Hanlon's aborted biography of Daniel O'Connell.

In his *Report of the O'Connell Monument Committee* in 1888, O'Hanlon stated:

> It had been projected to issue a compendious and yet a tolerably comprehensive Life of O'Connell, in connexion with the present Report; but, as the completion of that project should involve considerable additional delay, it is now deemed advisable to postpone it, at least for the present. Hitherto, no biography of the illustrious Irishman has appeared, except in an abridged or imperfect form, but in no sufficient manner fully setting forth the extent of his labours, sacrifices, and triumphs, or the noble traits of his character and exalted genius.[6]

O'Hanlon's note prefixed to MS OH 39/7 below elaborates on the circumstances of the abandoned publication, but the proofs in MS OH 39/9, dated March 1898, show that he pursued this project well beyond the life of the O'Connell Monument Committee.

MS OH 39/1: 'Materials for the Life of Daniel O'Connell. by Very Rev. John Canon O'Hanlon. MS. Vol I Chaps I. II. III. A.D. 1775 to 1813.'
MS OH 39/2: Vol. II, 1814–1820.
MS OH 39/3: Vol. III, 1821–1829.
MS OH 39/4: Vol. IV, 1830–1834.
MS OH 39/5: Vol. V, 1835–1842.
MS OH 39/6: Vol. VI, 1843–1847.
MS OH 39/7: Mounted proofs of part of O'Hanlon's *Life of Daniel O'Connell*, with engravings. Explanatory note prefixed by O'Hanlon:

> The following Life of O'Connell had been prepared at the instance of Edmond Dwyer Gray M.P.; but after printing a little over two sheets, it was discontinued as a sequel to the Report of the O'Connell Monument Committee, it being found the surplus funds were inadequate to carry out the project of a large 8vo volume, for which materials had been procured. / John

[6]*Report of the O'Connell Monument Committee*, iii.

Appendix 3

Canon O'Hanlon / The wood-engravings inserted are drawn and engraved by George A. Hanlon, from original photographs specially taken for the work by Laurence, O'Connell St., Dublin. It was intended to have a fine steel-engraved portrait of O'Connell prefixed, and copied from Mulrennan's miniature figure, now in the National Portrait Gallery London. For this the Liberator gave the Artist a sitting. I procured a Genoese photo of the Hotel Feder, when I stopped there in Nov. 1886.

MS OH 39/8: Miscellaneous press cuttings, *c.* 1870, relating to Irish antiquities, mounted on multiple copies of 'Circular of the Sub-Committee appointed to organize the St. Patrick's Day Collection for the O'Connell Monument' (dated 4 March 1864).

MS OH 39/9: Unbound. Folder containing: (a) Notes and drafts for Chapter 4 of O'Hanlon's *Life of Daniel O'Connell.* (b) Galley-proofs (chapters 1–3 and part of chapter 4) and page-proofs (chapters 1–2 and part of chapter 3 (pp. 1–31)) from James Duffy and Co., dated March 1898. (c) Frontispiece and title-page of *Report of the O'Connell Monument Committee* (1888).

MS OH 39/10: Unbound. Folder containing notes and drafts, mounted, for O'Hanlon's *Life of Daniel O'Connell,* chapters 4 (part), 5 and 6, covering years 1799–1807.

3. Miscellaneous

Volumes consisting mainly of mounted newspaper cuttings on historical, political, and literary subjects.

MS OH 40: 'Common-Place Book / Rev. John O'Hanlon March 7th 1862. / Dublin, SS. Michael & John.' Newspaper cuttings, mainly 1860s, with MS annotations by O'Hanlon. Other miscellaneous items include Irish Archaeological and Celtic Society's subscription list for 'unprovided family' of the late John O'Donovan; and autograph envelope of Daniel O'Connell. Towards end of MS are (a) cuttings on death of Denis Florence McCarthy (April 1882).[7] (b) Mounted subscription slips, filled in, for O'Hanlon's *The life of Saint Malachy O'Morgair* (1859).

MS OH 41: Mainly newspaper cuttings, 1870s and 1880s, mounted. Some uncorrected galleys of *Legend lays of Ireland*, guarded.

[7] O'Hanlon dedicated *Irish folk lore* (1870) to this poet (1817–82); see Appendix 1, under the year 1882.

249

Appendix 3

MS OH 42: Newspaper cuttings, 1880s, mounted on pages made from posters concerning Parnell, and Church of St Mary Star of the Sea. Mounted proofs, corrected, of *Legend lays of Ireland* (1870), dated 1865. Publications loose or bound in: (a) *History of the Irish Invincibles: their Brotherhood of Bloodshed* (London n.d.). (b) *The popular guide to the new House of Commons* Pall Mall Gazette Extra no. 21 (19 December 1885). (c) *John Morley: the Irish record of the new Chief Secretary* Pall Mall Gazette Extra no. 23 (6 February 1886). (d) *Irish Monthly Illustrated Journal* ed. T. C. Irwan, Vol. 1 (1 January 1873), loose. (e) Assorted trade catalogues (stained glass, ironwork, grocery). (d) Assorted prospectuses.

MS OH 43: Newspaper cuttings, 1860s and 1870s, mounted on pages made from pp. 30–36 of 'Unpublished Geraldine documents edited by the Rev. James Graves'.[8] Inside front cover: 'Rev. John O'Hanlon's MS. Collections of Lives of the Irish Saints / March 1st 1862.'

MS OH 44: Material relating to Gladstone's Land Act of 1881: (a) Cuttings from *Freeman's Journal*, 1876–81, mounted, unbound. (b) MS draft notes by O'Hanlon (115 pp) on Land Act. In cover with 'Tracts on the Irish Land Question' on spine.

MS OH 45: Newspaper cuttings, mainly verse, mounted.

MS OH 46: Newspaper cuttings, 1870s. Proofs of 'Irish folk-lore mythology by the Rev. John O'Hanlon' bound in for use as mountings.

MS OH 47: O'Hanlon's copy of his *The life of St. David, Archbishop of Menevia* (1869), with pp. [iii]–iv (dedication to Rev. James Hughes) in proof, corrected, tipped in. Loose material: (a) Newspaper cutting. (b) Prospectus (in proof) for *Lives of the Irish saints.*

MS OH 48: [Thaddeus Connellan], *An English Irish dictionary, intended for the use of schools ... 1814*, with some of O'Hanlon's domestic bills (1891 and 1893) loose inside front cover.

MS OH 49: Newspaper cuttings, 1870s, mounted in three columns (with index by O'Hanlon), mainly concerning sermons given in America by Fr Thomas Burke, 1872.

---

[8] *Journal of the Royal Historical and Archaeological Association of Ireland* 4th Series, 4/1 (1876).

APPENDIX 4

ADDRESS TO THE Very Reverend John Canon O'Hanlon P.P. on the occasion of the Golden Jubilee of his priesthood, from the priests and parishioners of St. Mary Star of the Sea.

Very Rev. and Dear Canon O'Hanlon.   Irishtown, May 29th 1897.

On behalf of the priests and people of St. Mary Star of the Sea we offer you this tribute of our joy on the happy attainment of the Golden Jubilee of your Priesthood. To few is allotted the joyful experience of fifty years in the holy service of the Most High. By you this glorious privilege has ever been utilised for the greater glory of God and the Salvation of His people.

We ourselves are mindful of your great zeal as a priest, and your earnestness as a friend of those who have been committed to your pastoral care. Since your advent amongst us, now some seventeen years ago, we have had frequent evidence of your deep anxiety for both the Spiritual and Temporal welfare of your flock; while in beautifying God's House, almost every year of your mission with us has seen permanent improvements and adornments to our Parochial Church of St. Mary Star of the Sea and to the Auxiliary Church of St. Patrick.

But it is not alone in your Sacerdotal life that the excellent qualities of your head and heart are made manifest. Genuine Irishman that you are, the national interests of our long suffering country have ever found in you an advocate who has never spared himself in endeavouring to realise the highest aspirations of our race.

In addition, we must all feel a pride in recording here the position of eminence you occupy amongst Authors as a Hagiologist. The great work which has deservedly earned for you the title of "The Irish Bollandist" will endure as a literary monument, not alone of supreme merit, but of marvellous labour and vast research. While "The Lives of the Irish Saints" mark a triumph in historical publication, your other and many able works, breathing a spirit of truth and of patriotic fervour, are no less a credit to Gifted Irish Authorship.

By us all these potent indications of your dignity as a priest and historian are reviewed with pleasure on this most auspicious occasion, and we feel sure we have the sympathies and good wishes not alone of all Irishmen, but of many residents of other countries, where you are renowned

Appendix 4

as a saintly Minister of Christ and distinguished Scholar, in joyfully according you our most hearty congratulations on your golden Jubilee Day and wishing you a long extension of your pious and holy career with health and happiness.

SIGNED

Joseph Grant Mooney C.C., John Purcell C.C., John C. Healy C.C., J. P. O'Reilly C.C., Jeremiah Howard, J.P., Gerald O'Reilly, T.C., W. McMullen, J. McMullen, Joseph Crinion, G. Doyle L.R.C.S.I., G. R. Peart, Lieut. Col., John Rochford, A. Mac Henry, J. Gerald McSweeny, T. H. Teegan, T. J. Slevin, W. J. Tunney, E. Egan, P. S. Fleming, P. Woods, T. J. Maguire, W. Kennedy, A. J. Nicholson, W. C. Chillingworth, E. J. Larchet, J. Broderick, J. G. Synott L.R.C.S.E., G. Weldrick, T. Mathews, W. Begley, E. O'Sullivan.

APPENDIX 5

Illustrations, Artists and Engravers in *Lives of the Irish saints*

An aspect of *Lives of the Irish saints* that generally passes without comment is the amount of antiquarian sketches it contains. Of significance is O'Hanlon's own involvement in this process, and his engagement with the other artists, and with the engravers employed by him to illustrate his work. Of the 596 drawings listed below, 128 are by him. Like himself, many of the artists were amateurs. The names of others whose work he used – such as William Wakeman, George Du Noyer and George Petrie – are instantly recognisable. Information on most of the engravers – Mrs Caroline Millard, George A. Hanlon, William and Alfred Oldham, Charles and Gregor Grey – will be found in Strickland, *A dictionary of Irish artists*.

Abbreviations: JO'H = John O'Hanlon; dr = drawn (by); engr = engraved by.

Volume I

Frontispiece (St Maelruan's Tree) dr Henry O'Neill, engr George A. Hanlon
4 (Rossory Cemetery) dr William F. Wakeman, engr William Oldham
17 (Clonmore) dr JO'H (February 1873) engraved by Mrs Millard, Dublin
25 (Kildare) engr Mrs Millard from a photograph by Frederick H. Mares
30 (Mungret) dr William F. Wakeman, engr Mrs Millard
35 (Tiscoffin) dr JO'H (March 1873), engr Mrs Millard
40 (Dysart Gallen) dr JO'H (March 1873), engr William Oldham
47 (Doone) engr Oldham from a photograph by T. O'Connor, Limerick
48 (Doone) engr Charles M. Grey from a photograph by T. O'Connor, Limerick
49 (Doone) engr Charles M. Grey from a photograph by T. O'Connor, Limerick
25 (Doone) dr T. O'Connor, engr Mrs Millard
55 (Tamlagh Finlagan) dr Du Noyer, engr Mrs Millard
65 (Kilkeary) dr Maurice Lenihan, engr George A. Hanlon, College Green
69 (Rossinver) dr William F. Wakeman, engr George A. Hanlon
71 (Tallagh) dr JO'H (July 1855), engr Mrs Millard
80 (Killesher) dr William F. Wakeman, engr A. Appleton
82 (Killeen) dr Mr Taylor of Hollypark, dr on wood William F. Wakeman, engr George A. Hanlon

Appendix 5

85 (Drumcliffe) engr Mrs Millard from a photograph by Frederick Mares
98 (Whitechurch) dr JO'H (August 1873), engr Mrs Millard
103 (Cashel) engr A. Appleton from a photograph by Frederick Mares
106 (Cashel) engr Jaquet and Bisson from a photograph by Frederick Mares
128 (Dungiven) dr Du Noyer, engr Mrs Millard
132 (Glendalough) dr Mrs Millard from a photograph by Frederick Mares
149 (Agivy) dr Mr Jordan of Ballymoney, engr George A. Hanlon
160 (Inniskeen) dr William F. Wakeman, engr A. Appleton
173 (Glendalough) engr Gregor Grey from a photograph by Frederick Mares
179 (Clonfert Molua) dr JO'H (May 1872), engr Mrs Millard
187 (Armagh) dr William F. Wakeman, engr A. Appleton
194 (Patrick's Island) dr William F. Wakeman, engr George A. Hanlon
197 (Innisboffin) dr Thomas O'Connor RIC, drawn on wood William F. Wakeman, engr George A. Hanlon
206 (Killeedy) anon. (procured by Aubrey de Vere), dr on wood William F. Wakeman, engr George A. Hanlon
218 (Creevy) dr JO'H (August 1873), engr Gregor Grey
240 (Kilfursa) supplied by Fr Patrick Ryan, dr on wood William F. Wakeman, engr George A. Hanlon
258 (Rosserrilly) dr William F. Wakeman from a photograph by Frederick Mares, engr George A. Hanlon
286 (Monea) dr William F. Wakeman, engr Appleton
294 (Clonmacnoise) engr Bisson and Jacquet, Paris, from a photograph by Frederick Mares
319 (Inismacsaint) dr William F. Wakeman, engr William Oldham, Dublin
331 (Oughaval) dr JO'H (July 1873), engr Gregor Grey, Dublin.
333 (Faughanvale) dr and engr Gregor Grey
340 (Tullamain) dr and engr Gregor Grey
347 (Bremore) dr Martin O'Carroll LRCSI, Dublin, engr George A. Hanlon
348 (All Hallows) dr J. J. McCarthy, engr William Oldham
355 (Timoleague) dr JO'H after John Windele, engr George A. Hanlon
364 (Ard-Oileán) dr William F. Wakeman, engr George A. Hanlon
367 (Fore) dr Du Noyer, engr Mrs Millard
373 (Drumcliffe) engr Gregor Grey from a photograph by Frederick Mares
384 (Ballytarsna) dr Du Noyer, engr Gregor Grey
391 (St Bride's) dr William F. Wakeman after Jeremiah Smith, engr George A. Hanlon
406 (Tullyallen) dr JO'H (May 1874), engr William Oldham
409 (Tamlaght) dr William F. Wakeman, engr A. Appleton
425 (St Canice's) dr William F. Wakeman, engr William and Alfred Oldham, 8 Lower Gloucester Street, Dublin
434 (Lisgoole) dr William F. Wakeman, engr William Oldham
452 (Inver Naile) supplied by Mrs Barrett, Bruckless, engr William Oldham
453 (Kinawley) dr William F. Wakeman, engr George A. Hanlon

Appendix 5

455 (Kilcrony) dr JO'H (September 1873), dr on wood William F. Wakeman, engr George A. Hanlon
460 (Killeshin) dr William F. Wakeman, engr Alfred Appleton
462 (Iniscathy) engr Jacquet and Bisson from a photograph by Frederick H. Mares
470 (Moylogha) dr William F. Wakeman, engr Mrs Millard
496 (Kildare) dr William F. Wakeman, engr William Oldham
510 (Glenealy) dr JO'H (June 1871), engr Gregor Grey
526 (Drumlane) dr William F. Wakeman, engr George A. Hanlon
553 (Ferns) dr Du Noyer, engr Mrs Millard
561 (Kilmacduagh) anon (Ordnance Survey), dr on wood and engr Gregor Grey
583 (Mahee Island) dr JO'H (May 1874), dr on wood William F. Wakeman, engr George A. Hanlon

Volume II

Frontispiece (Clonenagh) Henry O Neill, engr Mrs Millard
10 (Kildare Ruins) engr Mrs Millard from a photograph by Mares, Dublin
27 (Foughart) dr JO'H (May 1874), engr William Oldham
31 (Foughart) dr Du Noyer, engr Gregor Grey, Dublin
64 (Ardagh) dr Du Noyer, engr Gregor Grey, Dublin
81 (Slane) artist not cited, engr Mrs Millard, Dublin
108 (City of Armagh) dr William F. Wakeman from a photograph by Mares, engr George A. Hanlon
129 (Kilbride) dr John O'C. Robinson engr George A. Hanlon
131 (Scattery Island) dr William F. Wakeman, engr George A. Hanlon
144 (Tullagh) dr John O'C. Robinson, dr on wood William F. Wakeman, engr George A. Hanlon
161 (Kilcullen) engr Mrs Millard from lithograph of the architectural design
184 (Grey Abbey) dr JO'H (December 1875), dr on wood William F. Wakeman, engr George A. Hanlon
195 (Killester) dr JO'H (Jan 1876), engr Mrs Millard
209 (Wexford) engr Mrs Millard from a local photograph
249 (Castle Dillon Graveyard) dr John O'C. Robinson, dr on wood William F. Wakeman, engr George A. Hanlon
258 (Derrynahinch) dr JO'H (March 1873) engr Mrs Millard
272 (Temple Mac Duach) dr William F. Wakeman, engr George A. Hanlon
296 (Gallagher's Island) dr JO'H (July 1868), dr on wood William F. Wakeman, engr George A. Hanlon
299 (Church Island) dr JO'H (1868), dr on wood William F. Wakeman, engr George A. Hanlon
327 (Cathedral of St. Mary) dr on wood William F. Wakeman, engr Mrs Millard
335 (Cork, Shandon and Blackpool) dr on wood William F. Wakeman from a photograph by Mares, engr Mrs Millard

372 (Holmpatrick Ruins) dr Du Noyer, engr Mrs Millard
384 (Portloman) dr JO'H (June 1876), engr Mrs Millard
386 (Lough Owel) dr JO'H (June 1876), engr Mrs Millard
400 (Kill of the Grange) engr Gregor Grey from a photograph by Mares
433 (Drumlease Cemetery) dr JO'H (June 1876), dr on wood William F. Wakeman, engr Mrs Millard
436 (Creevlea) dr on wood William F. Wakeman from a photograph by Mares, engr Mrs Millard
452 (Glendalough) engr Mrs Millard from a photograph by Mares
458 (Lavey Graveyard) dr JO'H (June 1876), dr on wood William F. Wakeman, engr Mrs Millard
465 (St Gobnet's Cloghaun) dr Du Noyer, engr Gregor Grey
468 (Ballyvourney) dr John Windele, engr Gregor Grey
480 (Urney Church) dr JO'H (June 1876), dr on wood William F. Wakeman, engr Mrs Millard
504 (Cathedral of Armagh) engr Mrs Millard from a photograph by Mares
522 (Lemanaghan) dr JO'H (June 1876), dr on wood William F. Wakeman, engr Mrs Millard
540 (Glendalough) engr Gregor Grey from a photograph by Mares
545 (Kilbarrack) dr William F. Wakeman, engr George A. Hanlon
564 (Downings) dr JO'H (April 1874), dr on wood William F. Wakeman, engr Mrs Millard
576 (Churchfield) dr JO'H (July 1873), dr on wood William F. Wakeman, engr Mrs Millard
579 (Cloncnagh) dr JO'H (July 1873), engr Messrs. Jacquet et Bisson, Paris
582 (Cromogue) dr JO'H (August 1856), dr on wood William F. Wakeman, engr Mrs Millard
589 (Agha) dr Du Noyer, engr Gregor Grey
596 (Mountrath) from an original working design by architect John S. Butler, Dublin, dr on wood William F. Wakeman, engr Mrs Millard
602 (Trim) artist not cited, dr on wood William F. Wakeman, engr William and Alfred Oldham
606 (Trim) engr Jacquet et Bisson from a photograph by Mares
617 (Derryloran) dr Du Noyer, engr Gregor Grey
642 (Lusk) dr William F. Wakeman, engr Mrs Millard
647 (Armoy) dr on wood William F. Wakeman from a photograph, engr Mrs Millard
650 (Clonmacnoise) dr on wood William F. Wakeman from a photograph by Mares, engr Mrs Millard
656 (Arboe) dr William F. Wakeman, engr Mrs Millard
660 (Killybeggs) dr JO'H (April 1874), dr on wood William F. Wakeman, engr Mrs Millard
664 (Londonderry) dr William F. Wakeman, engr Mrs Millard
682 (Old Leighlin) dr William F. Wakeman, engr Mrs Millard

Appendix 5

691 (Iona) dr William F. Wakeman, engr Mrs Millard
709 (Kinsaly) dr Rev. John Francis Shearman, engr Gregor Grey
725 (Bangor) dr William F. Wakeman, engr Mrs Millard
732 (Slieve Leag) dr JO'H (July 1868) engr Gregor Grey

Volume III

Frontispiece (Priory and Cathedral, Cashel) John O'Hanlon, C.E., (1834), engr William Oldham
48 (St. David's Wales) dr William F. Wakeman, engr George A. Hanlon
52 (Naas) dr William F. Wakeman, engr George A. Hanlon
66 (Clonfert) dr JO'H from autotype, dr on wood William F. Wakeman, engr George A. Hanlon
81 (Blaris) dr Mr Goodwin, dr on wood William F. Wakeman, engr George A. Hanlon
83 (Kilmantan Hill) dr on wood William F. Wakeman from a photograph, engr George A. Hanlon
85 (Lisburn) dr on wood William F. Wakeman from a photograph, engr Mrs Millard
100 (Saggard) dr JO'H (July 1855), dr on wood William F. Wakeman, engr Mrs Millard
106 (Templeogue) dr JO'H (April 1874), dr on wood William F. Wakeman, engr George A. Hanlon
128 (Tubbrid) dr Du Noyer, dr on wood William F. Wakeman, engr George A. Hanlon
131 (Seirkyran) dr JO'H (June 1873), dr on wood William F. Wakeman, engr George A. Hanlon
146 (Knockseera) dr JO'H (Aug 1872), dr on wood William F. Wakeman, engr George A. Hanlon
174 (Aranmore) dr JO'H (June 1877), dr on wood William F. Wakeman, engr George A. Hanlon
180 (Kilmoon) dr JO'H (June 1877), dr on wood William F. Wakeman, engr George A. Hanlon
188 (Antrim) engr Mrs Millard from a photograph by Mares
197 (Killiney) dr William F. Wakeman, engr Mrs Millard
199 (Kilbride) dr JO'H (July/Aug 1873), dr on wood William F. Wakeman, engr George A. Hanlon
207 (Ardmore) dr William F. Wakeman, engr Mrs Millard
219 (Corcomroe) dr William F. Wakeman, engr Mrs Millard
233 (Scattery Island) dr on wood William F. Wakeman from a photograph by Mares, engr George A. Hanlon
258 (Aghaboe) dr JO'H (Summer 1856), dr on wood William F. Wakeman, engr Mrs Millard
268 (Oughterard) dr William F. Wakeman, engr George A. Hanlon

275 (Kiltoole) dr JO'H (March 1878), dr on wood William F. Wakeman, engr Mrs Millard

284 (Clondalkin) dr JO'H (July 1855) dr on wood William F. Wakeman, engr Mrs Millard

300 (Dysart) dr JO'H (July 1873) engr Gregor Grey

332 (Inis Meadhoin) dr JO'H (June 1877), dr on wood William F. Wakeman, engr Mrs Millard

345 (Leigh) dr Mrs Margaret X. White, dr on wood William F. Wakeman, engr Mrs Millard

347 (Leigh) dr JO'H (May 1878), dr on wood William F. Wakeman, engr Mrs Millard

350 (Rock of Cashel) dr on wood William F. Wakeman from a photograph by Mares, engr Mrs Millard

362 (Lindisfarne) dr William F. Wakeman, engr Mrs Millard

369 (Gougane Barra) dr William F. Wakeman, engr Mrs Millard

376 (Ireland's Eye) dr George Petrie, dr on wood William F. Wakeman, engr George A. Hanlon

385 (Innisfallen) dr on wood William F. Wakeman from a photograph by Mares, engr George A. Hanlon

387 (Innisfallen) dr on wood William F. Wakeman from a photograph by Mares, engr George A. Hanlon

397 (Lismore) dr on wood William F. Wakeman from a photograph by Mares, engr Mrs Millard

449 (Boulogne) dr on wood William F. Wakeman from a French photograph, engr Mrs Millard

462 (Dumbarton) dr on wood William F. Wakeman from a photograph, engr George A. Hanlon

466 (St. David's Cathedral) dr on wood William F. Wakeman, engr Mrs Millard

468 (Glastonbury) dr on wood William F. Wakeman from an engraving of Hollar, engr Mrs Millard

491 (Slieve Mish) dr on wood William F. Wakeman from a photograph, engr George A. Hanlon

496 (Boyne) dr William F. Wakeman, engr Mrs Millard

504 (Tours) dr on wood William F. Wakeman from a French photograph, engr Mrs Millard

506 (Marmontier) dr on wood William F. Wakeman from a French engraving, engr Mrs Millard

510 (Mont St. Michel) artists not cited

537 (Vartry River) dr on wood William F. Wakeman from a photograph, engr George A. Hanlon

540 (Skerries Harbour) dr William F. Wakeman, engr Mrs Millard

548 (Saul Church) dr on wood William F. Wakeman from local sketch, engr Mrs Millard

Appendix 5

556 (Tara Hill) dr on wood William F. Wakeman from a photograph, engr Mrs Millard

573 (Donoughmore) dr William F. Wakeman, engr Mrs Millard

581 (Edentinny Fort) dr JO'H (June 1876), dr on wood William F. Wakeman, engr George A. Hanlon

591 (Duleek) dr William F. Wakeman, engr Mrs Millard

597 (Aghagower) dr James C. Fitzgerald-Kenny, dr on wood William F. Wakeman, engr Mrs Millard

603 (Murrisk Abbey) dr and engr Gregor Grey from a photograph by Mares

621 (Boyle Abbey) dr William F. Wakeman, engr Mrs Millard

627 (Abbey Assaroc) dr William F. Wakeman engr Mrs Millard

635 (Grianan of Aileach) dr Mr Joseph P. Addey, dr on wood William F. Wakeman, engr Mrs Millard

637 (Aileach Fort) dr Mr Joseph P. Addey, dr on wood William F. Wakeman, engr Mrs Millard

651 (Dunseverick) dr JO'H (June 1879), dr on wood William F. Wakeman, engr Mrs Millard

656 (Glenarm) dr on wood William F. Wakeman from a photograph, engr Mrs Millard

659 (Coleraine) dr on wood William F. Wakeman from a photograph, engr Mrs Millard

667 (Clogher Church) dr William F. Wakeman, engr Mrs Millard

670 (Altadaven Glen) dr JO'H (June 1878), dr on wood William F. Wakeman, engr Mrs Millard

673 (Donagh) dr JO'H (June 1878), dr on wood William F. Wakeman, engr Mrs Millard

675 (Donaghmoyne) dr William F. Wakeman, engr Mrs Millard

679 (Finglas) dr George Petrie, engr George A. Hanlon

681 (St Patricks Cathedral, Dublin) dr on wood William F. Wakeman from a photograph by Mares, engr Mrs Millard

700 (Ardpatrick) dr William F. Wakeman, engr George A. Hanlon

718 (Drumbo) dr William F. Wakeman, engr Mrs Millard

720 (Louth Abbey) dr JO'H (June 1879), dr on wood William F. Wakeman, engr Mrs Millard

728 (St Patricks Cathedral, Armagh) dr and engr by William Oldham from a photograph

735 (Clonfeacle) dr JO'H (June 1879), dr on wood William F. Wakeman, engr Mrs Millard

753 (Saul Church) dr on wood William F. Wakeman from a photograph by Rev McCann, engr Mrs Millard

763 (Inchagoill) dr William F. Wakeman, engr Mrs Millard

780 (Downpatrick Cathedral) dr on wood William F. Wakeman from an original sketch, engr Mrs Millard

790 (Downpatrick) dr on wood William F. Wakeman from a photograph, engr Mrs Millard

808 (St Patricks College, Maynooth) dr on wood and engr William Oldham from a photograph

810 (St Patricks College, Carlow) dr on wood and engr William Oldham from a photograph

814 (St Patricks Cathedral, New York) dr on wood William F. Wakeman from an illustration, engr William Oldham

819 (St. Louis) dr on wood William F. Wakeman from a photograph, engr Mrs Millard

838 (Kilconnell) dr William F. Wakeman, engr Mrs Millard

847 (Freshford) dr William F. Wakeman, engr Mrs Millard

852 (Killashee) dr George Petrie, dr on wood William F. Wakeman, engr Mrs Millard

863 (Kilmochudrick) dr JO'H (August 1878), dr on wood William F. Wakeman, engr Mrs Millard

898 (Durham) dr William F. Wakeman, engr Mrs Millard

902 (Maybole) dr on wood William F. Wakeman from a photograph, engr Mrs Millard

915 (Killeany) dr JO'H (June 1877), dr on wood William F. Wakeman, engr Mrs Millard

919 (Killeany) dr Howard Helmick, dr on wood William F. Wakeman, engr Mrs Millard

924 (Lough Corrib) dr William F. Wakeman, engr Mrs Millard

933 (Kildallan) dr JO'H, dr on wood William F. Wakeman, engr Mrs Millard

944 (Inniscaltra) dr William F. Wakeman, engr Mrs Millard

956 (Kilmallock) dr William F. Wakeman, engr George A. Hanlon

988 (Aranmore) dr Howard Helmick, dr on wood William F. Wakeman, engr Mrs Millard

994 (Enniskillen) dr William F. Wakeman, engr Mrs Millard

1012 (Struell Wells) dr on wood William F. Wakeman from a photograph, engr Mrs Millard

1031 (Armagh) dr William F. Wakeman, engr Mrs Millard

Volume IV

Frontispiece (Inis Cloghran) dr George Petrie, engr William Oldham

6 (Emania) dr W. J. P. Malcernan, dr on wood William F. Wakeman, engr Mrs Millard

9 (Kilgobbin) dr JO'H, dr on wood William F. Wakeman, engr Mrs Millard

12 (Kilbroney) dr William F. Wakeman, engr Mrs Millard

18 (Roscommon) dr J. C. Fitzgerald-Kenny, dr on wood William F. Wakeman, engr Mrs Millard

26 (Clones) dr William F. Wakeman, engr Mrs Millard

Appendix 5

28 (Clones) dr William F. Wakeman, engr Mrs Millard

32 (Killkine) dr JO'H (July 1873), dr on wood William F. Wakeman, engr Mrs Millard

48 (Clonmacnoise) dr on wood William F. Wakeman from a photograph by John L. Robinson, engr Mrs Millard

61 (Innisfallen) dr on wood William F. Wakeman from a photograph, engr Mrs Millard

68 (Derrynane) dr on wood William F. Wakeman from a photogaph, engr Mrs Millard

78 (Bangor) dr JO'H (June 1857), dr on wood William F. Wakeman, engr Mrs Millard

82 (Lough Conn) dr on wood William F. Wakeman from a photograph, engr Mrs Millard

86 (Kilbeg) dr on wood William F. Wakeman from a sketch, engr Mrs Millard

90 (Kinure) dr JO'H (August 1882), dr on wood William F. Wakeman, engr Mrs Millard

107 (Clonmore) dr JO'H (August 1882), dr on wood William F. Wakeman, engr Mrs Millard

116 (Aghowle) dr JO'H (August 1882), dr on wood William F. Wakeman, engr Mrs Millard

136 (Iniskeen) dr William F. Wakeman, engr Mrs Millard

138 (Lough Mac Nean) dr William F. Wakeman, engr Mrs Millard

143 (Birr) dr on wood William F. Wakeman from a photograph, engr Mrs Millard

147 (Kilcolmanbrack) dr JO'H (1865), dr on wood and engr Gregor Grey

151 (Lorrha) dr JO'H (August 1856), dr on wood William F. Wakeman, engr Mrs Millard

183 (Egilshay) dr on wood William F. Wakeman from a sketch, engr Mrs Millard

194 (Cong) dr on wood William F. Wakeman from a photograph, engr Mrs Millard

195 (Cong) dr William F. Wakeman, engr Mrs Millard

216 (Dublin Bay) dr William F. Wakeman, engr Mrs Millard

236 (Moyne) dr William F. Wakeman, engr Mrs Millard

246 (Inishchlorin) dr William F. Wakeman, engr Mrs Millard

267 (Crook) dr on wood William F. Wakeman from a sketch, engr Mrs Millard

273 (Glendalough) engr Mrs Millard from a photograph by Mares

287 (Killaloe) dr William F. Wakeman, engr Mrs Millard

333 (Limerick) dr on wood William F. Wakeman from a photograph, engr Mrs Millard

352 (Killaloe) dr William F. Wakeman, engr Mrs Millard

375 (Inis-Caltra) dr William F. Wakeman, engr Mrs Millard

407 (Clontarf) dr William F. Wakeman, engr Mrs Millard

412 (Conquer Hill) dr William F. Wakeman, engr Mrs Millard

440 (Mr Collin's Demesne) dr William F. Wakeman, engr Mrs Millard

450 (Swords) dr William F. Wakeman, engr Mrs Millard

453 (Kilmainham) dr William F. Wakeman, engr Mrs Millard
459 (Wexford) dr on wood William F. Wakeman from a photograph, engr Mrs Millard
463 (Ladys Island) dr William F. Wakeman, engr Mrs Millard
482 (Kirk Maughold) dr on wood William F. Wakeman from a photograph, engr Mrs Millard
488 (Croghan) dr JO'H (August 1883), dr on wood William F. Wakeman, engr Mrs Millard
502 (Clonkeehan) dr JO'H (August 1883), dr on wood William F. Wakeman, engr Mrs Millard
513 (Raheny) dr on wood William F. Wakeman from a photogaph, engr Mrs Millard
522 (Monahincha) dr William F. Wakeman, engr Mrs Millard
527 (Roscrea) dr on wood William F. Wakeman from a photograph, engr Mrs Millard
528 (Roscrea) dr William F. Wakeman, engr Mrs Millard
531 (Ennistymon) dr on wood William F. Wakeman from a photograph, engr Mrs Millard
535 (Sceilig Michil) dr JO'H 'from Miss Stokes' admirable work',[1] dr on wood William F. Wakeman, engr Mrs Millard
541 (Kilcullen) dr JO'H (August 1883), dr on wood William F. Wakeman, engr Mrs Millard
555 (Donaghmore) dr Du Noyer, dr on wood William F. Wakeman, engr Mrs Millard
567 (Clonsast) dr JO'H (August 1883), dr on wood William F. Wakeman, engr Mrs Millard

Volume V

Frontispiece (Louvain) dr and engr William Oldham
7 (Killala) dr William F. Wakeman engr Mrs Millard
12 (Turlogh) dr on wood William F. Wakeman from a photograph, engr Mrs Millard
18 (Cork City) dr on wood William F. Wakeman from a photograph, engr Mrs Millard
30 (St. Brieux) dr on wood William F. Wakeman from a French etching, engr Mrs Millard
45 (Wicklow) dr William F. Wakeman engr Mrs Millard
56 (Fennor) dr JO'H (Aug 1883), dr on wood William F. Wakeman, engr Mrs Millard
66 (Ullard) dr William F. Wakeman engr Mrs Millard

[1] *Early Christian architecture in Ireland.*

Appendix 5

72 (Old Connell Graveyard) dr JO'H (Aug 1883), dr on wood William F. Wakeman, engr Mrs Millard

80 (Old Connell Moat) dr JO'H (Aug 1883), dr on wood William F. Wakeman, engr Mrs Millard

93 (Newbridge) dr on wood William F. Wakeman from a photograph, engr Mrs Millard

104 (Barnane Ely) dr William F. Wakeman engr Mrs Millard

109 (Iona) dr William F. Wakeman engr Mrs Millard

116 (Errigal Keerogue) dr JO'H (June 1878), dr on wood William F. Wakeman, engr Mrs Millard

122 (Wood Quay) dr William F. Wakeman engr Mrs Millard

141 (Kilnasantan) dr JO'H (May 1873), dr on wood William F. Wakeman, engr Mrs Millard

161 (Bangor) dr William F. Wakeman engr Mrs Millard

169 (Raghery Island) dr William F. Wakeman engr Mrs Millard

175 (Carlow) dr on wood William F. Wakeman from a photograph, engr Mrs Millard

183 (Rathmichael) dr William F. Wakeman engr Mrs Millard

195 (Shanraghan) dr Du Noyer, dr on wood William F. Wakeman, engr Mrs Millard

212 (Moycreddin) dr JO'H (Aug 1874), dr on wood William F. Wakeman, engr Mrs Millard

216 (River Dodder) dr William F. Wakeman engr Mrs Millard

219 (Derrybrusk) dr William F. Wakeman engr Mrs Millard

227 (Dromiskin) dr JO'H (Aug 1883), dr on wood William F. Wakeman, engr Mrs Millard

233 (Mourne Mountains) dr on wood William F. Wakeman from a photograph, engr Mrs Millard

248 (Rathan) dr Mr J. A. Mitchell, dr on wood William F. Wakeman, engr Mrs Millard

257 (Inis-Pict) dr William F. Wakeman engr Mrs Millard

259 (Rahan) dr Mr J. A. Mitchell, dr on wood William F. Wakeman, engr Mrs Millard

274 (Lismore) dr on wood William F. Wakeman from an engraving, engr Mrs Millard

278 (Kilmalkedar) dr William F. Wakeman engr Mrs Millard

300 (St. Daphne's Station) dr JO'H (June 1876), dr on wood William F. Wakeman, engr Mrs Millard

326 (Gheel) dr on wood William F. Wakeman from an etching, engr Mrs Millard

360 (Tedavnet) dr JO'H (June 1878), dr on wood William F. Wakeman, engr Mrs Millard

374 (Finglas) dr on wood William F. Wakeman from a photograph, engr Mrs Millard

263

Appendix 5

387 (Arrigal Mountain) dr on wood William F. Wakeman from a photograph, engr Mrs Millard

398 (Fenit) dr on wood William F. Wakeman from a photograph, engr Mrs Millard

405 (Ballydavid Head) dr William F. Wakeman engr Mrs Millard

410 (Kilbarrind) dr on wood William F. Wakeman from a photograph, engr Mrs Millard

413 (North Blasket Island) dr Du Noyer, dr on wood William F. Wakeman, engr Mrs Millard

448 (Annaghdown) dr William F. Wakeman engr Mrs Millard

457 (Inisgloria) dr on wood William F. Wakeman from a sketch, engr Mrs Millard

465 (Ardfert) dr on wood William F. Wakeman from a photograph, engr Mrs Millard

474 (Rahan) dr William F. Wakeman engr Mrs Millard

482 (Dulane) dr William F. Wakeman engr Mrs Millard

485 (Tara Hill) dr William F. Wakeman engr Mrs Millard

491 (Devenish Island) dr William F. Wakeman engr Mrs Millard

504 (Clane) dr JO'H (April 1874), dr on wood William F. Wakeman, engr Mrs Millard

511 (Caradoc) dr William F. Wakeman engr Mrs Millard

517 (Kilcolman) dr JO'H (June 1885), dr on wood William F. Wakeman, engr Mrs Millard

524 (Drumcullen) dr JO'H (June 1885), dr on wood William F. Wakeman, engr Mrs Millard

526 (Kilbarron) dr William F. Wakeman engr Mrs Millard

537 (Cork City) dr on wood William F. Wakeman from a photograph, engr Mrs Millard

546 (Inishboheen) dr JO'H (July 1873), dr on wood William F. Wakeman, engr Mrs Millard

552 (Kilcommon) dr JO'H (June 1871), dr on wood William F. Wakeman, engr Mrs Millard

559 (Terryglass) dr JO'H (June 1885), dr on wood William F. Wakeman, engr Mrs Millard

563 (Iona) dr William F. Wakeman engr Mrs Millard

570 (Kilpeacon) dr Du Noyer, dr on wood William F. Wakeman, engr Mrs Millard

573 (Stigonnell) dr William F. Wakeman engr Mrs Millard

580 (Lough Oughter) dr JO'H (June 1876), dr on wood William F. Wakeman, engr Mrs Millard

591 (Killyon) dr JO'H (June 1885), dr on wood William F. Wakeman, engr Mrs Millard

612 (Nurney) dr Rev. Edward O'Leary, dr on wood William F. Wakeman, engr Mrs Millard

Appendix 5

620 (Slane) dr William F. Wakeman engr Mrs Millard

Volume VI

Frontispiece (Iona) dr and engr William Oldham

7 (Lismore Castle) dr on wood William F. Wakeman from a photograph, engr Mrs Millard

24 (Kilclief Castle) dr William F. Wakeman engr Mrs Millard

36 (Luggela) dr William F. Wakeman engr Mrs Millard

46 (Glendalough) dr JO'H (May 1871), dr on wood William F. Wakeman, engr Mrs Millard

49 (Glendalough) dr on wood William F. Wakeman from a photograph by Mares, engr Mrs Millard

65 (Glendalough) dr on wood William F. Wakeman from a sketch, engr Mrs Millard

70 (Glendalough) dr William F. Wakeman engr Mrs Millard

85 (Killadrina) dr JO'H (April 1878), dr on wood William F. Wakeman, engr Mrs Millard

92 (Glendalough) dr William F. Wakeman engr Mrs Millard

99 (Armagh) dr William F. Wakeman engr Mrs Millard

103 (Chambery) dr Martin Haverty, dr on wood William F. Wakeman, engr Mrs Millard

109 (Lemenc) dr on wood William F. Wakeman from a photograph, engr Mrs Millard

117 (Jerusalem) dr William F. Wakeman engr Mrs Millard

127 (Tours) dr on wood William F. Wakeman from a photograph, engr Mrs Millard

150 (Utrecht) dr William F. Wakeman engr Mrs Millard

163 (Rome) dr William F. Wakeman engr Mrs Millard

176 (Choir of Maintz) dr on wood William F. Wakeman from a local photograph, engr Mrs Millard

193 (Munich) dr on wood William F. Wakeman from a photograph, engr Mrs Millard

204 (Cluainfois) dr JO'H (1860), dr on wood William F. Wakeman, engr Mrs Millard

210 (Tuam) dr on wood William F. Wakeman from a photograph by Mares, engr Mrs Millard

216 (Kilcock) dr on wood William F. Wakeman from a photograph, engr Mrs Millard

236 (Dromore) dr on wood William F. Wakeman from an etching, engr Mrs Millard

242 (Kilaspugbrone) dr William F. Wakeman engr Mrs Millard

280 (Gartan) dr Alexander McHenry, dr on wood William F. Wakeman, engr Mrs Millard

Appendix 5

285 (Kilmacrenan) dr Alexander McHenry from sketches of Mrs G. H. Kinehan, dr on wood William F. Wakeman, engr Mrs Millard

293 (Glasnevin) dr William F. Wakeman engr Mrs Millard

297 (Londonderry) dr William F. Wakeman engr Mrs Millard

307 (Durrow) dr on wood William F. Wakeman from a photograph, engr Mrs Millard

314 (Kells) dr William F. Wakeman engr Mrs Millard

318 (Skreen-Columcille) dr William F. Wakeman engr Mrs Millard

333 (Moone) dr JO'H (Feb 1886), dr on wood William F. Wakeman, engr Mrs Millard

348 (Torry Island) dr William F. Wakeman engr Mrs Millard

358 (Culdrumman) dr William F. Wakeman engr Mrs Millard

379 (Iona) dr on wood William F. Wakeman from an approved picture, engr Mrs Millard

385 (Loch Ness) dr William F. Wakeman engr Mrs Millard

408 (Iona Sound) dr William F. Wakeman engr Mrs Millard

430 (Tiree Island) dr William F. Wakeman engr Mrs Millard

433 (Loch Coiruisg) dr William F. Wakeman engr Mrs Millard

445 (Grampian Mountains) dr William F. Wakeman engr Mrs Millard

467 (Inch Colum) dr William F. Wakeman engr Mrs Millard

478 (The Mullagh) dr on wood William F. Wakeman from a photograph by Thomas Predy, engr Mrs Millard

481 (Enagh Hill) dr on wood William F. Wakeman from a photograph, engr Mrs Millard

504 (Killasnet) dr JO'H (June 1876), dr on wood William F. Wakeman, engr Mrs Millard

517 (Londonderry) dr on wood William F. Wakeman from a photograph, engr Mrs Millard

551 (Kells) dr William F. Wakeman engr Mrs Millard

555 (Knock Columcille) dr A. Nicholl, dr on wood William F. Wakeman, engr Mrs Millard

556 (Kilcolum) dr William F. Wakeman engr Mrs Millard

566 (Holywood) dr on wood William F. Wakeman from a photograph, engr Mrs Millard

596 (Downpatrick) dr on wood William F. Wakeman from a photograph, engr Mrs Millard

604 (Iona) dr on wood William F. Wakeman from a drawing, engr Mrs Millard

613 (Rathlihen) dr JO'H (Aug 1888), dr on wood William F. Wakeman, engr Mrs Millard

636 (Mount Melleray) dr on wood William F. Wakeman from a copper-plate engraving by R. Hendrick, engr Mrs Millard

643 (Ceis-Corran) dr William F. Wakeman engr Mrs Millard

652 (Temple Coemghin) dr William F. Wakeman engr Mrs Millard

657 (Clonmacnoise) dr William F. Wakeman engr Mrs Millard

Appendix 5

666 (Castle-Kieran) dr William F. Wakeman engr Mrs Millard
671 (Wexford) dr William F. Wakeman engr Mrs Millard
684 (Lambay Island) dr William F. Wakeman engr Mrs Millard
696 (St. Mullins) dr William F. Wakeman engr Mrs Millard
701 (St. Mullins) dr William F. Wakeman engr Mrs Millard
711 (St. Mullins) dr on wood William F. Wakeman from a photograph, engr Mrs
Millard
721 (Timolin) dr JO'H (Feb 1886), dr on wood William F. Wakeman, engr Mrs
Millard
751 (Kilwhelan) dr JO'H (Aug 1888), dr on wood William F. Wakeman, engr
Mrs Millard
756 (Durrow) dr JO'H (Aug 1888), dr on wood William F. Wakeman, engr Mrs
Millard
762 (Castledermot) dr William F. Wakeman engr Mrs Millard
766 (Kilberry) dr JO'H (July 1888), dr on wood William F. Wakeman, engr Mrs
Millard
775 (Mahee Island) dr J. H. Burgess, dr on wood William F. Wakeman, engr Mrs
Millard
782 (Gaile) dr Du Noyer, dr on wood William F. Wakeman, engr Mrs Millard
788 (Killeigh) dr JO'H (Aug 1888), dr on wood William F. Wakeman, engr Mrs
Millard
800 (Tehelly) dr JO'H (Aug 1888), dr on wood William F. Wakeman, engr Mrs
Millard
812 (Ardnurcher) dr JO'H (Aug 1888), dr on wood William F. Wakeman, engr
Mrs Millard
828 (Salzburg) dr on wood William F. Wakeman from a local photograph, engr
Mrs Millard

Volume VII

Frontispiece (Trinity College) dr and engr George A. Hanlon
10 (Christchurch Cathedral) dr on wood William F. Wakeman from a photograph
by William Lawrence, engr Mrs Millard
30 (Kirkwall) dr on wood William F. Wakeman from a drawing, engr Mrs Millard
40 (Isle of Man) dr on wood William F. Wakeman from an illustration, engr Mrs
Millard
48 (Louth) dr William F. Wakeman engr Mrs Millard
60 (Edinburgh Castle) dr William F. Wakeman engr Mrs Millard
64 (Tumna) dr William F. Wakeman engr Mrs Millard
87 (Slieve Gullion) dr William F. Wakeman engr Mrs Millard
100 (Tallagh) dr William F. Wakeman engr Mrs Millard
108 (Tallaght) dr on wood William F. Wakeman from a drawing, engr Mrs
Millard

267

Appendix 5

114 (Monte Cassino) dr on wood William F. Wakeman from a copperplate engraving, engr Mrs Millard

136 (Wurtzburg) dr on wood William F. Wakeman from a photograph, engr Mrs Millard

138 (Wurtzburg) dr on wood William F. Wakeman from a photograph, engr Mrs Millard

148 (Dublin) dr on wood William F. Wakeman from a photograph, engr Mrs Millard

164 (Killeshin) dr JO'H (Sept 1889), dr on wood William F. Wakeman, engr Mrs Millard

173 (Dunamase) dr William F. Wakeman engr Mrs Millard

179 (Kinsale) dr William F. Wakeman engr Mrs Millard

188 (Clonmany) dr on wood William F. Wakeman from a photograph by William Lawrence, engr Mrs Millard

194 (Strasburgh) dr on wood William F. Wakeman from an engraving, engr Mrs Millard

212 (Quimper-Corentin) dr on wood William F. Wakeman from an engraving, engr Mrs Millard

235 (Aghade) dr JO'H (Sept 1889), dr on wood William F. Wakeman, engr Mrs Millard

248 (Moville) dr on wood William F. Wakeman from a photograph, engr Mrs Millard

250 (Ardbraccan) dr on wood William F. Wakeman from a photograph, engr Mrs Millard

257 (Antwerp) dr William F. Wakeman engr Mrs Millard

266 (Cologne) dr on wood William F. Wakeman from an engraving, engr Mrs Millard

272 (Taney) dr William F. Wakeman engr Mrs Millard

277 (Timoleague) dr John Windele, dr on wood William F. Wakeman, engr Mrs Millard

296 (Inis-Cumscraigh) dr William F. Wakeman engr Mrs Millard

317 (Ardmore) dr William F. Wakeman engr Mrs Millard

324 (Ardmore) dr on wood William F. Wakeman from a photograph, engr Mrs Millard

341 (Ardmore) dr on wood William F. Wakeman from a photograph, engr Mrs Millard

347 (Ardmore) dr John Windele, dr on wood William F. Wakeman, engr Mrs Millard

357 (Lough Derg) dr William F. Wakeman engr Mrs Millard

362 (Kilcronan) dr JO'H (July 1888), dr on wood William F. Wakeman, engr Mrs Millard

383 (Mungret) dr William F. Wakeman engr Mrs Millard

388 (Toumoulin) dr JO'H (June 1877), dr on wood William F. Wakeman, engr Mrs Millard

Appendix 5

393 (Kilcrittan) dr JO'H (Aug 1888), dr on wood William F. Wakeman, engr Mrs Millard
398 (Moville) dr William F. Wakeman engr Mrs Millard
401 (Ferns) dr William F. Wakeman engr Mrs Millard
430 (St. Doulough's Church) dr William F. Wakeman engr Mrs Millard
494 (Tully) dr William F. Wakeman engr Mrs Millard
498 (Iniscealtra) dr William F. Wakeman engr Mrs Millard
513 (Kilnamanagh) dr Du Noyer, dr on wood William F. Wakeman, engr Mrs Millard
516 (Santry) dr William F. Wakeman engr Mrs Millard

Volume VIII

Frontispiece (Lough Ree) dr and engr Alfred Oldham
5 (Inisboffin) dr on wood William F. Wakeman from a photograph, engr Mrs Millard
10 (Inisboffin) dr on wood William F. Wakeman from a photograph by J. T. Hoban, engr Mrs Millard
12 (Lough Ree) dr on wood William F. Wakeman from a photograph by J.T. Hoban, engr Mrs Millard
25 (Nurney) dr JO'H (Oct 1889), dr on wood William F. Wakeman, engr Mrs Millard
33 (Ardtrea) dr on wood William F. Wakeman from a photograph, engr Mrs Millard
37 (Clontarf) dr William F. Wakeman engr Mrs Millard
48 (Farney) dr JO'H (June 1878), dr on wood William F. Wakeman, engr Mrs Millard
51 (Slieve Bloom) dr JO'H (Oct 1890), dr on wood William F. Wakeman, engr Mrs Millard
57 (Kyle) dr JO'H (Oct 1890), dr on wood William F. Wakeman, engr Mrs Millard
67 (Kyle) dr JO'H (Oct 1890), dr on wood William F. Wakeman, engr Mrs Millard
88 (Rheims) dr on wood William F. Wakeman from an engraving, engr Mrs Millard
94 (Strangford Lough) dr W. Gray, dr on wood William F. Wakeman, engr Mrs Millard
100 (Clondalkin) dr William F. Wakeman engr Mrs Millard
106 (Melrose Abbey) dr on wood William F. Wakeman from an engraving, engr Mrs Millard
128 (Achonry) dr William F. Wakeman engr Mrs Millard
134 (Cavan) dr on wood William F. Wakeman from a photograph, engr Mrs Millard

269

Appendix 5

144 (Dunblane) dr on wood William F. Wakeman from an engraving, engr Mrs Millard

154 (Boyle) dr William F. Wakeman engr Mrs Millard

165 (Holy Well of St. Attracta) dr William F. Wakeman engr Mrs Millard

175 (Killala) dr William F. Wakeman engr Mrs Millard

180 (Ennismurry) dr William F. Wakeman engr Mrs Millard

186 (Armagh) dr on wood William F. Wakeman from a photograph, engr Mrs Millard

198 (Kilfenora) dr on wood William F. Wakeman from a photograph, engr Mrs Millard

200 (Kilfenora) dr on wood William F. Wakeman from a photograph, engr Mrs Millard

222 (Monaghan) dr on wood William F. Wakeman from an engraving, engr Mrs Millard

241 (Tory Island) dr William F. Wakeman engr Mrs Millard

249 (Kilbeggan) dr JO'H (Aug 1888), dr on wood William F. Wakeman, engr Mrs Millard

258 (Inniskeen) dr on wood William F. Wakeman from a photograph, engr Mrs Millard

266 (Rathnew) dr William F. Wakeman engr Mrs Millard

269 (Iona) dr Miss Mary McHardy, dr on wood William F. Wakeman, engr Mrs Millard

289 (Bobbio) from the work of Miss Margaret Stokes,[2] dr on wood William F. Wakeman, engr Mrs Millard

298 (Kilroosk) dr JO'H (June 1879), dr on wood William F. Wakeman, engr Mrs Millard

329 (Coolbanagher) dr JO'H (December 1853), dr on wood William F. Wakeman, engr Mrs Millard

337 (Ardstraw) dr JO'H (June 1879), dr on wood William F. Wakeman, engr Mrs Millard

375 (St. Michan's Church) dr on wood William F. Wakeman from a lithograph, engr Mrs Millard

406 (Killaloe) dr William F. Wakeman engr Mrs Millard

412 (Armagh) dr on wood William F. Wakeman from a photograph, engr Mrs Millard

417 (Bangor) dr William F. Wakeman engr Mrs Millard

506 (Portumna) dr on wood William F. Wakeman from a photograph, engr Mrs Millard

509 (Bobbio) from the work of Miss Margaret Stokes,[3] dr on wood William F. Wakeman, engr Mrs Millard

[2] *Six months in the Apennines.*
[3] Ibid.

Appendix 5

Volume IX

Frontispiece (Franciscan Convent Donegal) dr and engr Gregor Grey
5 (Marseille) dr on wood and engr Gregor Grey from an engraving
6 (Nimes) dr and engr Gregor Grey
23 (Edinburgh) dr on wood and engr Gregor Grey from an etching
32 (Laraghbrine) dr JO'H (July 1873), dr on wood and engr Gregor Grey
45 (Toul) dr on wood and engr Gregor Grey from copper-plate engraving
59 (Nancy) dr on wood and engr Gregor Grey from an engraving
68 (Templecarron) dr on wood and engr Gregor Grey from an illustration
74 (Kells) dr on wood and engr Gregor Grey from a photograph by T. C Erwin
81 (Salzburg) dr on wood and engr Gregor Grey from a local photograph
92 (Lindisfarne) dr on wood and engr Gregor Grey from an illustration
104 (Innisfallen) dr on wood and engr Gregor Grey from a photograph
113 (Copeland) dr on wood and engr Gregor Grey
137 (St. Gall's Church) dr on wood and engr Gregor Grey from a local photograph
170 (Lusk) dr on wood and engr Gregor Grey from a photograph
187 (Roscrea) dr JO'H (May 1870), dr on wood and engr Gregor Grey
190 (Roscrea) dr on wood and engr Gregor Grey from a photograph
195 (Disenbodenburg) dr on wood and engr Gregor Grey from an engraving
213 (Inis-Aingen) dr William F. Wakeman engr Mrs Millard
222 (Inis-Aingen) dr on wood and engr Gregor Grey from a photograph
225 (Athlone) dr on wood and engr Gregor Grey
231 (Clonmacnoise) dr on wood and engr Gregor Grey from a photograph
243 (Killahear) dr on wood and engr Gregor Grey from a photograph by Philip Mulligan
251 (Kiltegan) dr JO'H (Aug 1882), dr on wood and engr Gregor Grey
258 (Moville Abbey) dr Mr Burgess, dr on wood and engr Gregor Grey
288 (Emly) dr on wood and engr Gregor Grey from a sketch
297 (Emly) dr on wood and engr Gregor Grey from a photograph
303 (Devenish) dr on wood and engr Gregor Grey from an engraving
319 (Ennereilly) dr JO'H (July 1897), dr on wood and engr Gregor Grey
326 (Killenny) dr JO'H (July 1873), dr on wood and engr Gregor Grey
333 (Athassel Abbey) dr on wood and engr Gregor Grey from an illustration
343 (King Cormac's Chapel) dr on wood and engr Gregor Grey from a photograph
347 (St. Cormac's Chapel) dr on wood and engr Gregor Grey from an engraving
366 (Cashel) dr and engr Gregor Grey
370 (Cashel) dr on wood and engr Gregor Grey from a photograph
379 (Paisley) dr on wood and engr Gregor Grey from an illustration
390 (Treves) dr on wood and engr Gregor Grey from an engraving
399 (Cloncurry) dr JO'H (July 1873), dr on wood and engr Gregor Grey
404 (Arbroath) dr on wood and engr Gregor Grey from an engraving

Appendix 5

414 (Monadrohid) dr JO'H (Aug 1872), dr on wood and engr Gregor Grey
428 (Kilclooney) dr on wood and engr Gregor Grey from a photograph
444 (Coolock) dr and engr Gregor Grey
463 (Friburg) dr on wood and engr Gregor Grey from an engraving
469 (Enach Lough) dr on wood and engr Gregor Grey from a photograph
475 (Lough Kee) dr on wood and engr Gregor Grey from an engraving
481 (Raphoe) dr on wood and engr Gregor Grey from a photograph
497 (Raphoe) dr on wood and engr Gregor Grey from a photogravure
498 (Raphoe) dr on wood and engr Gregor Grey from a photograph
508 (Derry) dr on wood and engr Gregor Grey from a photograph
526 (Bovevagh) dr Du Noyer, engr Gregor Grey
530 (Letterkenny) dr on wood and engr Gregor Grey from an engraving
544 (Molough) dr Du Noyer, dr on wood and engr Gregor Grey
568 (Cork) dr on wood and engr Gregor Grey from an illustration
582 (Cork) dr and engr Gregor Grey
584 (Cork) dr on wood and engr Gregor Grey from a photograph
590 (Amiens) dr on wood and engr Gregor Grey from an illustration
600 (Lynally) dr JO'H (Aug 1888), dr on wood and engr Gregor Grey
615 (Howth) dr J. M. Kavanagh RHA, dr on wood and engr Gregor Grey
622 (Cruach Mac Dara) dr George Petrie, dr on wood and engr Gregor Grey
635 (Teampull Tecolm) dr JO'H (June 1897), dr on wood and engr Gregor Grey
642 (Kilbreedy) dr JO'II (June 1897), dr on wood and engr Gregor Grey

Volume X

Frontispiece (Franciscan Convent, Dublin) dr and engr Gregor Grey
8 (Rahan) dr George Petrie, dr on wood and engr Gregor Grey
13 (Inchidorry) dr on wood and engr Gregor Grey from a photograph
19 (River Boyne) dr on wood and engr Gregor Grey from an illustration
22 (Fore Abbey) dr on wood and engr Gregor Grey from a sketch
38 (Clonkeen) dr on wood and engr Gregor Grey from a photograph by Mary
   Austin Morrissey
45 (Kilbixy) dr JO'H (April 1900), dr on wood and engr Gregor Grey
53 (Trim) dr William F. Wakeman, engr Gregor Grey
59 (Armagh) dr on wood and engr Gregor Grey from a photograph
64 (Rattoo) dr William F. Wakeman, engr Gregor Grey
88 (Glendalough) dr and engr Gregor Grey
99 (Brecknock) dr on wood and engr Gregor Grey from an illustration
104 (Cornwall) dr on wood and engr Gregor Grey from a photograph
119 (Old Aberdeen) dr on wood and engr Gregor Grey from an illustration
130 (Inchigeela Lakes) dr on wood and engr Gregor Grey from a photograph[4]

[4]Reproduced from original wood engraving in Seymour, *A Maynooth book of days* Month of April.

Appendix 5

139 (Ballyshannon) dr on wood and engr Gregor Grey from a photograph
142 (Usneach) dr JO'H (April 1900), dr on wood and engr Gregor Grey
148 (Kilkenny) dr on wood and engr Gregor Grey from a photograph
157 (Kilkenny) dr on wood and engr Gregor Grey from a photograph
160 (Kilkenny) dr on wood and engr Gregor Grey from a photograph
163 (Kilkenny) dr on wood and engr Gregor Grey from a photograph
178 (Paris) dr on wood and engr Gregor Grey from an engraving
190 (Sletty) dr JO'H (May 1889), dr on wood and engr Gregor Grey
194 (Clopook) dr JO'H (June 1901), dr on wood and engr Gregor Grey
202 (Glasnevin) dr and engr Gregor Grey
206 (St. Movie Graveyard) dr JO'H (June 1901), dr on wood and engr Gregor
   Grey
215 (Derry) dr on wood and engr Gregor Grey from a photograph
222 (Vienna) dr and engr Gregor Grey
237 (Dunblane) dr and engr Gregor Grey
251 (Wurtzberg) dr on wood and engr Gregor Grey from an engraving
263 (Quimper-Corentin) dr on wood and engr Gregor Grey from a plate
284 (Luxeuil) dr on wood and engr Gregor Grey from a copper plate
288 (Zurich) dr on wood and engr Gregor Grey from an engraving
292 (Brigantium) dr on wood and engr Gregor Grey
303 (Constance) dr on wood and engr Gregor Grey
318 (Cathedral of St Gall) dr on wood and engr Gregor Grey from a local
   photograph
333 (Cathedral of Mayence) dr on wood and engr Gregor Grey from a local
   photogaph
345 (Lynn) dr JO'H (1901), dr on wood and engr Gregor Grey
354 (Ardennes) dr and engr Gregor Grey
369 (Kilcolmanbane) dr JO'H (July 1891), dr and engr Gregor Grey
379 (Durrow) dr on wood and engr Gregor Grey from a photograph
394 (Cologne) dr on wood and engr Gregor Grey from an engraving
411 (Cologne) dr on wood and engr Gregor Grey from a local photograph
426 (Cologne) dr on wood and engr Gregor Grey from a photograph
430 (Cologne) dr on wood and engr Gregor Grey from a photograph
447 (Blackrock) dr on wood and engr Gregor Grey from an engraving

273

NOTES

EARLY DAYS

Maternal Grandfather: Denis Downey

Extract from Fitz-Patrick, *"The Sham Squire;"* 321–3. Fitz-Patrick
remarks: 'we are indebted to the Rev. John O'Hanlon ... for the
following traditional reminiscence of his grandfather's connexion with
the rebellion in Kildare.' (O'Hanlon dedicated *Legend lays of Ireland* to
Fitz-Patrick; see Appendix 1, 1861 and 1870.)

In a letter to Richard Robert Madden (author of *The United Irishmen,
their lives and times*, and of *The life and times of Robert Emmet*, etc.),
25 May 1858, O'Hanlon sketched out the information that was later to
appear in the *Sham Squire*; among additional details given in the letter
are the fact that the relative who recruited Denis Downey to the United
Irishmen was Downey's brother, and that 'the death of her father left
[O'Hanlon's mother] an orphan at the early age of a year and a half'
(Trinity College Dublin MS 873/275).

In his *Catechism of Irish history*, 494, O'Hanlon summarizes the event
in question:

> General Dundas had issued a proclamation in Kildare county,
> which induced many of the rebels to lay down their arms and return
> home. This example influenced others to sue for pardon, which
> was accorded by the military authorities. But a diabolical treatment
> was experienced by the insurgents near the town of Kildare.
> Being invited to attend at the Gibbet Rath on the Curragh, for the
> purpose of delivering up their arms and obtaining protection, these
> insurgents were fired upon by the soldiers and some hundreds
> killed – not, however, until they had been deprived of arms and
> were perfectly defenceless. This heartless and deliberate massacre
> occurred on the 29th of May.

A detailed account of this event is Farrelly and Moore, *Massacre at
Gibbet Rath 1798*.

Stradbally

Extract from 'The Baboon's Rescue: Legend of Woodstock Castle, County of Kildare', *Irish local legends*, 10–12. O'Hanlon adds:

> To gratify her own literary taste, and as we think, chiefly for private circulation among her friends, Mrs. St. John printed a ballad poem, intitled 'Ellauna', Dublin, 1815, and divided into four cantos. It is now many years past, and in our school-boy days, when we were gratified with the perusal of that little octavo book, which was all the more interesting to us, because Ellauna happened to be the heroine, and a chieftainess of the great dynast family belonging to the O'Mores of Dunamase, and who formerly ruled over all the Leix territory.

The work referred to is *Ellauna: a legend of the thirteenth century; in four cantos, with notes.*

Ballyroan

Irish local legends, 104–18, where it occurs under the title 'Humours and Humorists: Legend of Ballyroan, Queen's County', with Goldsmith's lines on the village schoolmaster from the *Deserted village* prefixed.

Charley Duffy Charles Duffy is recorded in 1834 as keeping a hedge school at Ballyroan, where he taught reading, writing and arithmetic, and was attended by 51 males and 32 females (*Second report of the Commissioners of Public Instruction* Diocese of Leighlin, 26b).

Jemmy Doxey The story of Sam [*sic*] Doxey is told in Barrington, *Personal sketches* III, 83–90. *Moll Harding* – who 'kept the natest inn at Ballyroan' – is mentioned ibid. I, 163.

Rev. Nicholas Harding 1806–54: see McEvoy, *Carlow College*, 151.

The Seanchaí

Irish local legends, 74–82, where it occurs under the title 'The Witch Transformed: Legend of Cullenagh, Queen's County'. Prefixed to it are excerpts from poems by Mrs. Ellen Fitz-Simon (née O'Connell) and Robert Southey. O'Hanlon quotes testimony from this *seanchaí* regarding the American War of Independence in *Irish-American history*, 227 n. 47, 231 n. 64.

Father Perkinson of Ballyroan Probably Patrick Parkinson, who died P.P. Raheen, 1851 (McEvoy, *Carlow College*, 237).

Patt Lalor of Tinakill etc. Well-known Liberals of the Queen's County during O'Hanlon's youth. He refers to them in his notes to 'The Land of Leix' (*Poetical works of Lageniensis*, 30, 65).

probably in the adjoining graveyard . . . Keegan, as O'Hanlon would subsequently discover, is buried in Glasnevin.

Fr Mathew visits Carlow College

Extract from Maguire, *Father Mathew*, 150–52. Fr Theobald Mathew visited Carlow College, where O'Hanlon was studying, on Sunday and Monday 25 and 26 October 1840, and administered the pledge to the seminarians in Carlow Cathedral. Maguire remarks: 'A respectable clergyman, who was then one of the students of the college, has furnished the author with an interesting sketch of Father Mathew's mission to Carlow, from which is taken the account of what happened on the following days'.

A bigotted view of the visit is given in the *Carlow Sentinel* 31 October 1840. For Fr Mathew's reputed miraculous powers see Kerrigan, *Father Mathew*, 132–52.

In *Life and scenery in Missouri*, 224, O'Hanlon gives an account of Fr Mathew's visit to St Louis, exactly ten years later, October 1850, during which he identifies himself as the 'respectable clergyman' in Maguire's book:

> As many years before, when I had been a student in the Ecclesiastical College of Carlow, and when it had been visited by the Apostle of Temperance, with several of the collegians I had also taken the pledge. I was able also to present a silver medal, I had then with the others received from him, as a token of introduction to the very revered personage, that had now come to labour in a distant land. The account of his Carlow mission I have already written and it has been embodied in the Tenth Chapter of that excellent biography of Father Matthew [*sic*], by John Francis Maguire, M.P., who requested me to prepare a statement of my reminiscences of that incident in the Temperance Apostle's career.

AMERICA

Preparations

O'Hanlon, *The Irish emigrant's guide*, 25–6.

Cautionary words

O'Hanlon, *The Irish emigrant's guide*, 38–40.

Notes

Public works

O'Hanlon, *The Irish emigrant's guide*, 82–5.

Citizenship

O'Hanlon, *The Irish emigrant's guide*, 162–9.

Arrival

O'Hanlon, *Life and scenery in Missouri*, 1–5.

St Louis

O'Hanlon, *Life and scenery in Missouri*, 11–13.

Western Missouri

O'Hanlon, *Life and scenery in Missouri*, 127–38.

Ordination

O'Hanlon, *Life and scenery in Missouri*, 138–40.

Famine-ships

O'Hanlon, *Life and scenery in Missouri*, 140–42.

A priest's life

O'Hanlon, *Life and scenery in Missouri*, 143–7.

Departure

O'Hanlon, *Life and scenery in Missouri*, 291–2.

FOLKLORE AND TRADITION

Irish Marriage Customs

Irish folk-lore, 234–6, without a prefixed verse by Charles Gavan Duffy.

Popular Notions Concerning Good and Ill Luck

Irish folk-lore, 285–9, without prefixed lines by Samuel Lover and Thomas Furlong.

Irish Fortune-Tellers and Predictions

Irish folk-lore, 308–12, without prefixed lines by Byron, James Orr and John D'Alton.

The concluding verse of James Orr's poem is:

Gif Chanticleer's ta'en frae the roost whare he craw't,
Or horse, kye, or sheep, frae the pasture-fiel' ca't,
My head I'll bestow ye, if I dinna show ye
The leuks in a glass, o' the loun that's in faut:
Or else, if ye cleek up, an' toss my delft teacup,
If danger or death's near, the gruns plain will shaw't;
By cuttin' o' cartes, folk, an' no' by black arts, folk,
O' past, present, future, I'll read ye a claut.

The Solitary Fairies

Irish folk-lore, 237–41, without prefixed verses by J. L. Forrest and Thomas Moore.

Divinations, Enchantments, Astrology, and Nostrums

Extract from *Irish folk-lore*, 242–52, without prefixed verses by Mrs Hemans and John Henry Newman.
   the Kildare woman's lines (see *Irish folk-lore*, 192):

Good morrow, Full Moon:
Good morrow to thee!
Tell, erc this time to-morrow,
Who my true love will be –
The colour of his hair,
The clothes he will wear,
And the day he'll be married to me.

After Clontarf

Extract from *Irish local legends*, 33–8, entitled 'Contests of the Clans: Legend of Mullaghmast, County of Kildare'.
   Gortnaclea on the banks of the River Nore Gortnaclea is located on the banks of the River Gully, a tributary of the Nore.

FIVE POEMS

The Land of Leix

Extract from 'The Land of Leix': Fourth Canto, stt VI–X (*Poetical works of Lageniensis*, 60–64).
   These verses, heavily annotated by O'Hanlon, refer to the Ballykilcavan (near Stradbally) evictions of 1828, when forty-two families were evicted by Sir Edward Walsh Johnson and his agent John Robinson Price.

Notes

The final stanza here, as explained by O'Hanlon, is an allusion to Peter Burrowes Kelly.

In his note to *hedge-rows opposite adorned art* O'Hanlon tells us: 'One of the writer's earliest memories brings back the recollection of several unroofed and wrecked homesteads, with their former neat garden and hedge-row enclosures, of which not a vestige now remains' (*Poetical works of Lageniensis*, 61 n.).

To the memory of Fr Joseph M. Paquin

The poetical works of Lageniensis, 324. Fr Paquin was superior of the Ecclesiastical Seminary in St Louis during the early months of O'Hanlon's attendance there, until shortly before his death, in Texas, 9 August 1844. O'Hanlon wrote of him in chapters 3 and 15 of *Life and scenery in Missouri* (see p. 72 above).

There is a balm in the air of old Ireland

The poetical works of Lageniensis, 303–5. The subtitle to the poem states that it was 'written after returning from the United States in 1853'.

John Shearman of the Hill

NUI, Maynooth, Russell Library MS SH 20, signed by O'Hanlon: 'With the author's compliments for coming birth-day. J. O'H.' Hitherto unpublished. John Francis Shearman (see Appendix 1, 1885) served as curate in the united parishes of Baldoyle, Howth and Kinsealy, 1862–83. Born in Kilkenny in 1830, he was a noted antiquarian, who, through his friendship with O'Hanlon, had, early in his career, made the acquaintance of O'Curry and O'Donovan. He supplied a sketch for *Lives* II, 709. A frequent contributor to antiquarian journals, his great work, *Loca Patriciana*, was published in 1879. Of his time in Howth, O'Hanlon wrote (*Irish Ecclesiastical Record* 3rd Ser., 6 (December 1885) 769–70):

> No sooner had Father Shearman found his home on the Hill of Howth, than he began to form the acquaintance of its residents, and to extend his beneficent influences among them; so that he was esteemed and respected, from the lord of the soil, the Earl of Howth, to the humblest fisherman of the primitive Celtic or Fingallian town, so remarkably braving the northern blasts, and perched high over its spacious harbour.

On Death

The poetical works of Lageniensis, 328.

Notes

'HOME RULER AS I AM'

The Land Question

Letter to Edmund Dwyer Gray, *Freeman's Journal* 22 November 1879. The letter refers to the arrest, 19 November 1879, of three Land Leaguers: Michael Davitt and James B. Killen – both arrested in Dublin – and James Daly of the *Connaught Telegraph*, arrested in Castlebar. The three were arrested for speeches delivered at a meeting at Gurteen, Co. Sligo, 2 November, and were imprisoned in Sligo Jail, pending trial. A public meeting was called for the Rotunda on the date of O'Hanlon's letter. For writing the letter O'Hanlon incurred the displeasure of Archbishop McCabe: see Appendix 2 § 4.

the present Earl of Beaconsfield Benjamin Disraeli, British Prime Minister, 1868 and 1874–80.

Notes on Land Tenure

Excerpted from a series of such items drafted by O'Hanlon and preserved in NUI, Maynooth, Russell Library MS OH 44.

Home Rule

Excerpt from O'Hanlon's introduction to his edition (1891) of *Essay on the antiquity and constitution of parliaments in Ireland. By Henry Joseph Monck Mason*, 126–52.

STAR OF THE SEA

In June 1880, O'Hanlon was appointed parish priest of Sandymount, at St Mary's Church, Star of the Sea, Irishtown. When he took over, Irishtown and Sandymount were still very much villages. Despite O'Hanlon's reservations about the manner in which the boundary was drawn, Ringsend, together with Beggar's Bush Barracks, was annexed from Haddington Road to Star of the Sea in 1881.[1] To O'Hanlon's satisfaction, more of Haddington Road was annexed in 1894.[2] Following his death in 1905, Ringsend became a parish in its own right: St Patrick's Parish.

[1] DDA McCabe Papers 1881, Secular Clergy: O'Hanlon to McCabe, 5, 7 and 15 May (with McCabe's draft reply).

[2] DDA Walsh Papers 1894, Secular Clergy: O'Hanlon to Walsh, 23 and 29 June.

Leahy's Terrace, and St Mary's Church, Star of the Sea, *c.* 1900,
showing Canon O'Hanlon's front garden, and (inset) the opening for the
steps down to the shore.

He remained at Star of the Sea up to his death in 1905, thus earn-
ing an unanticipated immortality through his inclusion in the account
of the events of Thursday, 16 June 1904, in the Nausicaa section of
Ulysses. An imagined evening celebration of Benediction in Star of the
Sea ('that simple fane beside the waves') by O'Hanlon and one of his
curates, Fr Bernard Conroy,[3] during a men's temperance retreat given by

[3] Fr Conroy only barely made it into *Ulysses*, having been translated from
Wicklow parish following the death of John Purcell, 18 July 1903; cf. DDA
Walsh Papers 1903, Secular Clergy: O'Hanlon to Walsh, 22 July 1903, requesting him to appoint a new curate. Memorial tablet, and stained glass windows
depicting SS Kevin and Brigid, erected in memory of Fr Purcell in Star of the
Sea. O'Hanlon's Benediction is reprised in the Circe episode, where he elevates
and exposes a marble cuckoo-clock.

Notes

Fr John Hughes SJ, is counterpointed by Joyce with more earthly elevations and expositions on the rocks along Sandymount shore. At the time, the sea-shore came to the foot of Leahy's Terrace, as O'Hanlon himself remarked (p. 155 above): 'the spot is picturesque, overlooking the wide expanse of Dublin Bay, and lying immediately on the shore'.[4]

The object of the Benediction in the novel appears to be the ceremonial declaration of Bloom as a cuckold. (Whether or not, in reality, O'Hanlon's health would have allowed him to celebrate Benediction at this date is a moot point: see Appendix 1 under 1904 and 1905.) Earlier that day, Stephen had observed two women from the Liberties coming to Sandymount strand for the day: 'They came down the steps from Leahy's terrace prudently'. They had, therefore, passed close to O'Hanlon's presbytery at 3 Leahy's Terrace, across the road from Star of the Sea.

A more tenuous connection to O'Hanlon in *Ulysses* occurs later, in the Eumaeus episode, when Bloom, in the company of Stephen, anticipates a sailor's (and his own) return to his wife:

> Mr Bloom could easily picture his advent on this scene – the home-coming to the mariner's roadside shieling after having diddled Davy Jones – a rainy night with a blind moon. Across the world for a wife. Quite a number of stories there were on that particular Alice Ben Bolt topic, Enoch Arden and Rip van Winkle and does anybody hereabouts remember Caoc O'Leary, a favourite and most trying declamation piece, by the way, of poor John Casey and a bit of perfect poetry in its own small way?

The reference to the reciter of the poem, which Bloom misquotes,[5] as 'poor John Casey' can be taken as a Bloom/Joyce allusion, through word association, to the author John Keegan. Keegan (1816–1849) was and is often confused with the Fenian poet John Keegan Casey (1846–1870). O'Hanlon's edition of the works of John Keegan, including his most famous poem 'Caoch the Piper', was published posthumously in 1907, though the poem need not necessarily have been mediated to Joyce through O'Hanlon's book, as it enjoyed frequent anthologising in such works as *Gill's Irish reciter* (O'Kelly, *Féithe Fódla*, 115–17).

[4]This area was subsequently reclaimed, and is now occupied by Beach Road, and by Seán Moore Park.
[5]The original lines read: 'Does anybody hereabouts / remember Caoch the Piper?'

Notes

St Mary's Church, Star of the Sea

History and description of St. Mary's Church, Star of the Sea, Irishtown, 5–9.

Irishtown

Irish local legends, 100–104, occurring under the title 'The Battle of the Cats. Legend of Irishtown, County of Dublin', with lines by Thomas Parnell prefixed.

Sandymount

Irish local legends, 57–64, occurring under the title 'Mistaken Identity: Legend of Sandymount, County of Dublin', with lines by Quintus Horatius Flaccus prefixed.

SAINTS AND HOLY PLACES

Saints

Opening section to O'Hanlon's unpublished life of St Nessan, Patron of Cork: Russell Library MS OH 11, pp. 17–18 (cf. *Lives of the Irish saints* III, 832–3).

St Malachy

The life of Saint Malachy O'Morgair, 221–2.

St Gerebern

Along the Rhine: *The life of St. Dympna*, 137–9 (*Lives of the Irish saints* V, 367). Sonsbeck: *The life of St. Dympna*, 146–8 (*Lives of the Irish saints* V, 370–71).

St Dympna

Through Belgium: *The life of St. Dympna*, 156–8 (*Lives of the Irish saints* V, 321 and 324 n. 19). The Demented of Gheel: *The life of St. Dympna*, 178–80 (*Lives of the Irish saints* V, 356). Images and Names: *The life of St. Dympna*, 226–8 (*Lives of the Irish saints* V, 364–5). Invocation: *The life of St. Dympna*, 231–2 (*Lives of the Irish saints* V, 366).

Mundrehid, Queen's County

Irish local legends, 29–30, occurring under the title: 'The Black Man's Apparition: Legend of Mundrehid, Queen's County'.

Notes

Moghia, near Lismore, Queen's County

Irish local legends, 22–3, occurring under the title: 'The Garran Bawn. Legend of Moghia, near Lismore, Queen's County'.

St Lóchán of Kilmacahill, County of Kilkenny

This previously unpublished life, 31 December, was intended to complete O'Hanlon's *Lives of the Irish saints,* and to bring his huge project to a close. It is included here for that reason. Our text incorporates O'Hanlon's corrections, marked by him in red ink, on Russell Library MS OH 12, pp. 572–92. An earlier draft of this item is to be found in the final twenty-one pages (unpaginated) of MS OH 14/4. (Ceall Meic Cathail was reputed to be a foundation of St Finbarr: Ó Riain, *Beatha Bharra,* 60.87, and note pp. 240–41.)

Rev. Patrick J. Mulhall An uncle of James Mulhall of Pass House, and a subscriber to *Lives of the Irish saints* (I, 619).

APPENDIX 2

1. Recovery of Health

O'Hanlon to Archbishop Paul Cullen, 16 January 1854: DDA Cullen Papers 1854, Secular Clergy. Ballymaddock was the home of O'Hanlon's brother-in-law, William Cantwell (see Appendix 1, n. 27); his grandmother's relations, the Moores, lived next door.

2. The South Dublin Union, 1855

Excerpt from O'Hanlon (159 James' St.) to Cullen, 21 December 1855: DDA Cullen Papers 1855, Secular Clergy. This letter occurs in the context of a dispute concerning remuneration between O'Hanlon and the Chaplain, Fr P. E. O'Farrelly.

3. Death of Eugene O'Curry

NUI, Maynooth, Russell Library MS SH 20. O'Hanlon to Fr John Francis Shearman. Eugene O'Curry, one of the great Gaelic scholars of the nineteenth century, died in his sixty-eighth year, 30 July 1862.

John E. Pigot (1822–71), MRIA, was a barrister, collector of music, and sometime Young Irelander. Dr Robert S. D. Lyons (1826–86), MRIA, was Professor of Medicine at the Catholic University. The paper of Shearman's referred to is probably his 'On some inscribed stones at Killeen Cormac near Dunlavin'.

Notes

4. Apology

O'Hanlon to Archbishop Edward McCabe, 24 November 1879, having being rebuked by McCabe for his letter to the *Freeman's Journal* given pp. 126–8 above: DDA McCabe Papers 1879, Secular Clergy.

5. Rome's Decree against the Plan of Campaign

DDA Walsh Papers 1888, Secular Clergy. The context for this letter is the Vatican's condemnation, in April 1888, of the Plan of Campaign and of Boycotting. The passage from the *Freeman's Journal*, referred to by O'Hanlon, spoke of the possibility of Archbishop Walsh tendering his resignation on conscientious grounds, and of being created a cardinal instead. See Larkin, *The Roman Catholic Church and the Plan of Campaign*, 201–15; and Morrissey, *William J. Walsh*, 109–20.

In 1814 a Rescript was issued in Rome by Monsignor Quarantotti approving the English veto over ecclesiastical appointments in Ireland.

Canon Daniel James Canon Daniel, P.P., Church of St. Nicholas, Francis Street.

6. Wakes

DDA Walsh Papers 1890, Secular Clergy. O'Hanlon's views on alcohol may have been elicited in anticipation of the centenary celebrations of Fr Mathew, which were held in Dublin and Cork in October 1890.

7. Parnell, and the Press

DDA Walsh Papers 1890, Secular Clergy. Two months later, O'Hanlon told Walsh: 'The manner in which Parnell is now playing the part of a mendacious and vulgar demagogue is painful, and he and his backers seem to think the Irish are a nation of fools to be fed such garbage' (DDA Walsh Papers 1891, Secular Clergy: O'Hanlon to Walsh, 23 February 1891).

8. Return to America: Archbishop Kenrick's Jubilee

DDA Walsh Papers 1891, Secular Clergy. See Appendix 1, under the year 1891.

9. Daniel O'Connell's anniversary

DDA Walsh Papers 1897, Secular Clergy.

this darkest hour of our degradation and disgrace O'Hanlon was writing in the aftermath of the nationalist split, and in the context of the apparent abandonment of hopes for Home Rule.

His initiative was not as original as it might appear: Cardinal Logue had issued a pastoral letter, 23 April, outlining plans for a commemoration in St Patrick's Cathedral, Armagh, inspired by celebrations previously announced for the Irish College, Rome; see *Freeman's Journal* 16 and 26 April 1897. The Cardinal's plans were to be imitated throughout the country.

For the association of Archbishop Walsh's father – Ralph Walsh – with O'Connell, see Morrissey, *William J. Walsh*, 3–4.

10. School Attendance

DDA Walsh Papers 1899, Secular Clergy. The Irish Education Act of 1892 had made school attendance compulsory, a provision spoken against, at the time, by Archbishop Walsh.

11. John Keegan

University College Dublin, Department of Archives, MS LA 15/1294. This letter shows that O'Hanlon was aware that Keegan's daughter was still alive, and that the responsibility for the statement, in the subsequent work, that she died in 1896, must be O'Donoghue's alone; see Delaney, *John Keegan*, 6.

12. History of the Queen's County

12a: Letter tipped in after front endpaper of Robert Lloyd Praeger's copy of *The poetical works of Lageniensis*. Praeger donated his copy (NLI Ir 82189 o 25) to the National Library of Ireland, 10 January 1906.

12b: Letter to James Mulhall in Laois County Library, O'Hanlon File. The contributions of both Praeger and Mulhall are acknowledged by O'Hanlon in his preface to *History of the Queen's County* I, iii.

APPENDIX 4

This is the text of an illuminated address, the property of Cáit Bean Mhic Ionnraic.

BIBLIOGRAPHY

Books by John O'Hanlon (*al.* Lageniensis)[1]

An abridgement of the history of Ireland, from its final subjection to the present time (Boston: Patrick Donahoe, 1849)

The buried lady: a legend of Kilronan, by Lageniensis (Dublin: Joseph Dollard, 1877)

The case of Ireland's being bound by Acts of Parliament in England stated, by William Molyneux, of Dublin, Esq. A new edition, with preface and life of the author, by Very Rev. John Canon O'Hanlon P.P., M.R.I.A. (Dublin: Sealy, Bryers and Walker, 1892)

Catechism of Greek grammar (Dublin: John Mullany, 1865)

Catechism of Irish history: from the earliest events to the death of O'Connell (Dublin: John Mullany, 1864)

Devotions for Confession and Holy Communion (Dublin, London, Derby: Thomas Richardson, 1866)

Essay on the antiquity and constitution of parliaments in Ireland. By Henry Joseph Monck Mason, LL.D., and M.R.I.A. A new edition with preface, life of the author, and an introduction, by Very Rev. John Canon O'Hanlon (Dublin: James Duffy and Co., 1891)

History and description of St. Mary's Church, Star of the Sea, Irishtown. Report of the committee appointed to erect the Dean O'Connell Memorial (Irishtown 1884)

(with Rev. Edward O'Leary) *History of the Queen's County* I (Dublin: Sealy, Bryers and Walker, 1907)

(with Rev. Edward O'Leary and Rev. Matthew Lalor), *History of the Queen's County* II (Dublin: Sealy, Bryers and Walker, 1914)

Irish-American history of the United States. (Dublin, Sealy, Bryers and Walker, 1903)

The Irish emigrant's guide for the United States (Boston: Patrick Donahoe, 1851)

The Irish emigrant's guide for the United States, with coloured map and railway connections First Irish edition, revised, and information brought down to the present year (Dublin: Sealy, Bryers and Walker, 1890)

[1]For articles see Appendix 1.

287

Bibliography

Irish folk lore: traditions and superstitions of the country, with humorous tales (Glasgow: Cameron and Ferguson, 1870)

Irish local legends (Dublin: James Duffy & Co., 1896)

Legend lays of Ireland (Dublin: John Mullany 1870)

Legends and poems by John Keegan, now first collected … with memoir by D. J. O'Donoghue (Dublin: Sealy, Bryers and Walker, 1907)

Life and scenery in Missouri: reminiscences of a missionary priest (Dublin, James Duffy and Co., 1890)

The life and works of Saint Aengussius Hagiographus, or Saint Aengus the Culdee, bishop and abbot at Clonenagh and Dysartenos, Queen's County (Dublin: John F. Fowler, 1868)

Life of St. Brigid, Virgin, first Abbess of Kildare, special patroness of Kildare diocese, and general patroness of Ireland (Dublin: Joseph Dollard, 1877)

The life of St. David, Archbishop of Menevia, chief patron of Wales, and titular patron of Naas Church and Parish in Ireland (Dublin: John Mullany, 1869)

The life of St. Dympna, virgin, martyr, and patroness of Gheel; with some notices of St. Gerebern, priest, martyr, and patron of Sonsbeck (Dublin: James Duffy, 1863)

The life of Saint Grellan, patron of the O'Kellys, and of the tribes of Hy-Maine (Dublin and London: James Duffy and sons, 1881)

The life of St. Laurence O'Toole, Archbishop of Dublin, and Delegate Apostolic of the Holy See, for the Kingdom of Ireland (Dublin: John Mullany, 1857)

The life of Saint Malachy O'Morgair, Bishop of Down and Connor, Archbishop of Armagh, patron of these several dioceses, and Delegate Apostolic of the Holy See for the kingdom of Ireland (Dublin: John O'Daly, 1859)

Lives of the Irish saints: with special festivals, and the commemorations of holy persons, compiled from calendars, martyrologies, and various sources, relating to the ancient church history of Ireland / by John O'Hanlon I–X (Dublin: James Duffy; London: Burns , Oates & Co.; New York: Catholic Publishing Society, 1875–1905)

The poetical works of Lageniensis (Dublin: James Duffy & Co., 1893)

On the identification of the site of the engagement at the Pass of the Plumes (1599) (Dublin: Royal Irish Academy 1876)

Report of the O'Connell Monument Committee, by Very Rev. John Canon O'Hanlon, P.P., honorary secretary (Dublin: James Duffy and Co., 1888)

Bibliography

Works referred to, excluding those by John O'Hanlon

[ANONYMOUS], 'Biogram', *Irish Monthly* 14 (July 1886) 400

———, [obituary] *Journal of the Royal Society of Antiquaries of Ireland* 36 (1906) 99–100

———, 'Lest we forget', *Irish Book Lover* 13 (1921) 79–80

———, 'Canon O'Hanlon', *Irish Book Lover* 20 (1932) 16–17

BARRINGTON, Jonah, *Personal sketches of his own time* I–III (2nd ed., London 1830 and 1832)

BREATNACH, Diarmuid agus Máire Ní Mhurchú, *1882–1982: Beathaisnéis a trí* (Dublin 1992)

BRENAN, Martin, *Schools of Kildare and Leighlin A.D. 1775–1835* (Dublin 1935)

CAREY, F. P., 'O'Hanlon of "the Irish Saints"' *Irish Ecclesiastical Record* 5th Ser, 84 (1955) 145–63

COLLINS, Kevin, *Catholic churchmen and the Celtic Revival in Ireland, 1848–1916* (Dublin 2002)

COLM [Colm Ó Lochlainn], 'John O Daly, Irish scholar and bookseller', *Irish Book Lover* 26 (1939) 135

COMERFORD, M., *Collections relating to the Dioceses of Kildare and Leighlin* I–III (Dublin [1883–6])

CONCANNON, Helena, 'Canon John O'Hanlon (1821–1905): his early days in St. Louis', *Irish Ecclesiastical Record* 5th Ser, 69 (1947) 11–19

CORISH, Patrick J., *Maynooth College 1795–1995* (Dublin 1995)

DELANEY, Tony, *John Keegan: selected works* (Galmoy 1997)

DONNELLY, N., *A short history of some Dublin parishes* (Dublin 1905) 79–81

FARRELLY, Brendan, and Michael Moore, *Massacre at Gibbet Rath 1798* ([Dublin] 1998)

FENNELLY, Teddy, *John Canon O'Hanlon: the man and his legacy* (Portlaoise 2005)

FITZ-PATRICK, William J., *Irish wits and worthies; including Dr. Lanigan, his life and times, with glimpses of stirring scenes since 1770* (Dublin 1873)

———, *"The Sham Squire;" and the informers of 1798. With a view of their contemporaries. To which are added, in the form of an appendix, jottings about Ireland seventy years ago* (3rd ed., Dublin and London 1866)

Bibliography

GRIFFITH, Richard, *Queen's County. Barony of Stradbally ... Primary Valuation* (Dublin 1850)

KERRIGAN, Colm, *Father Mathew and the Irish temperance movement 1838–1849* (Cork 1992)

LANE, Pádraig G., and William Nolan (ed.), *Laois history and society: interdisciplinary essays on the history of an Irish county* (Dublin 1999)

LARKIN, Emmet, *The Roman Catholic Church and the Plan of Campaign in Ireland 1886–1888* (Cork 1978)

MCCARTNEY, Donal, 'Canon O'Hanlon: historian of the Queen's County', in Lane and Nolan, *Laois history and society*, 585–600

MCEVOY, John, *Carlow College 1793–1993: the ordained students and the teaching staff of St. Patrick's College, Carlow* (Carlow 1993)

MAC SUIBHNE, Peadar, *Carlovia* I–III (Carlow 1976–7)

———, 'Historian of the Irish saints', in idem, *Carlovia* III, 4–11 [incorporating a contribution from Pádraig Mac Ionnraic]

MAGUIRE, Edward J., *Reverend John O'Hanlon's The Irish emigrant's guide for the United States. A critical edition with introduction and commentary* (New York 1976)

MAGUIRE, John Francis, *Father Mathew: a biography* (London 1863)

MORAN, Patrick F., (ed.), *Monasticon Hibernicum ... by Mervyn Archdall* I–II (Dublin 1873 and 1876)

MORRISSEY, Thomas J., *William J. Walsh, Archbishop of Dublin, 1841–1921: no uncertain voice* (Dublin 2000)

O'DONOGHUE, David J., *The poets of Ireland* (London 1892)

——— [D. J. O'D.], 'O'Hanlon, John (1821–1905)', *Dictionary of National Biography* 2nd supplement 1910–11, 41–2

O'DOOLEY, Johanna, 'Rev. John Canon O'Hanlon', *Leinster Express* 11 and 18 May, and 8 June 1974

O'DOOLEY, Seán, 'The Rev. Canon O'Hanlon', *Leinster Express* 5 November 1955

———, 'The Rev. John Canon O'Hanlon', *Leinster Express* 12 November 1955

Ó GIOLLÁIN, Diarmuid, *Locating Irish folklore: tradition, modernity, identity* (Cork 2000)

O'KELLY, J. J., *Féithe Fódla: Gill's Irish reciter* (3rd ed., Dublin 1911)

O'LEARY, E., 'Obituary. The Very Rev. John Canon O'Hanlon', *Journal of the Co. Kildare Archaeological Society* 4 (1903–5) 502–3

Ó RIAIN, Pádraig (ed.), *Beatha Bharra: Saint Finbarr of Cork: the complete life* ITS 57 (London 1994)

Bibliography

————, *Irish Texts Society: the first hundred years. Essays to mark the centenary of the Irish Texts Society* ITS Subsidiary Series 9 (London 1998)

PHELAN, Edwin, Introduction to *History of the Queen's County: John Canon O'Hanlon, Edward O'Leary, Matthew Lalor* Reprint (Kilkenny [1981])

ROE, Owen, *Reliques of John K. Casey ("Leo") with a biographical and critical introduction* (Dublin 1878)

RYAN, Desmond, *The Fenian Chief: a biography of James Stephens* (Dublin and Sydney 1967)

SAINT JOHN, Mary, *Ellauna: a legend of the thirteenth century in four cantos, with notes* (Dublin 1815)

Second report of the Commissioners of Irish Education Inquiry Volume 12 (British Parliamentary Papers 1826–7)

Second report of the Commissioners of Public Instruction, Ireland Volume 34 (British Parliamentary Papers 1835)

SEYMOUR, Valerie, *A Maynooth book of days* (St Patrick's College Maynooth 1996)

SHANNON-MANGAN, Ellen, *James Clarence Mangan: a biography* (Dublin 1996)

SHEARMAN, John Francis, 'On some inscribed stones at Killeen Cormac near Dunlavin' *Proceedings of the Royal Irish Academy* 1/9 (1864–6) 253–60

————, *Loca Patriciana: an identification of localities, chiefly in Leinster, visited by Saint Patrick and his assistant missionaries; and of some contemporary kings and chieftans* (Dublin 1879)

Society for the Preservation of the Irish Language report for 1905 (Dublin 1906)

STOKES, Margaret, *Early Christian architecture in Ireland* (London 1878)

————, *Six months in the Apennines; or, a pilgrimage in search of vestiges of the Irish saints in Italy* (London and New York 1892)

STRICKLAND, Walter George, *A dictionary of Irish artists* (Dublin and London 1913)

Transactions of the Ossianic Society for the year 1854 II (Dublin 1855)

Transactions of the Ossianic Society for the year 1856 IV (Dublin 1859)

TYNAN, P. J., *Barnaglitty or 'The Pass of the Plumes'* (Vicarstown 1997)